Changing States

Memoirs:
Fragments from a Life
Fragments that Remain
Ephemeron
Grab that Moment
Run with It
Beside the Sea
Between the Mountains and the Sea

Fiction:
Convergence — Aspects of the Change
A Floating World

Non-fiction:
Cinematography Underwater
Aikido - Basic and Intermediate Studies
Aikido - Beyond Questions often asked
Attributes a writer needs
Dreams of Mars - 130 years of stories about Mars

As editor:
Journey of a Lifetime
The Central Zone

Co-editor:
Remembering Sensei

Changing States

Yambu

All rights reserved. No part of this publication may be reproduced by any means including photocopying or other information storage and retrieval systems without written consent of the publisher and author except for small portions which may be quoted for the purpose of reviewing the work as a whole. The right of John Litchen to be identified as the author of this work has been asserted by him in accordance with the Copyright, Design and Patents Act 1988.

ISBN: 978-0-6488801-7-2
©John Litchen, 2023.

Published by *Yambu*
3 Firestone Court Robina, Qld. 4226.
jlitchen@bigpond.net.au

Paasch Eyland Isla de Pascua Ile de Paque Easter Island Rapa Nui (©1997), first appeared in Bruce Gillespie's Metaphysical Review #26/27 Spring 1997.
The worst days of my life, our last two weeks, first appeared in Bruce Gillespie's SF Commentary #107, November 2021. (©2021)

Dedication:
Siempre para Moniquita

*Aunque recién se murió,
ella queda en mi corazón
y continuamente me inspira harto.*

Part One

Moments remembered

1991 — 1994

An important decade

The 1990s was an important decade for us, because changes happened during this decade that affected us for a good part of the rest of our lives. Nothing major, apart from selling our property in Williamstown and moving to Robina on the Gold Coast of Queensland, but small things that over time accumulate and do affect you, such as realizing you are getting older, when the death of another parent occurs, illnesses and injuries, children growing up and problems associated with that. It's impossible to remember everything, nor would I or anyone else be interested in that, but some things do stand out and it is these fragments I relate here.

You do what you know

The moment I started back at work after returning from our overseas trip, I realized that I was no longer felt any desire to continue being in the dry cleaning industry. I had spent a lifetime in that industry and it was time for a change.

As noted in an earlier memoir, *(Ephemeron)* I worked in this industry part time while I still attended school (as a teenager) and after a short stint working in Darwin in agriculture and rice growing, I returned to work in the drycleaning industry from the age of eighteen onwards. In fact, as children, we lived in between the drycleaning shop and the factory where it was done, until I was seven years old and our family moved to Benbow Street Yarraville where we finally lived in a proper home, and not something between a shop and a factory. Basically, all my life I had been in and around a drycleaning business. Phillip too. And the girls, Zara and Christine, although they were never expected to work in the industry, they did do stints as shop assistants and sorters in the family drycleaning business at Williamstown. But it was Phillip and I who spent our lives working as drycleaners.

The thing is, you do what you know, and Phillip and I knew drycleaning and all its aspects because we grew up in this business, which gave us a different perspective from those who came in as adults looking for work. It was inevitable that we would work as dry cleaners for most of our adult lives. Dad had started the business in 1928 and eventually we bought the business (and property where it was housed) from him to continue it in our names. From the 1970s on it was our joint business and we worked for ourselves, and not for Dad as we did before.

Williamstown Dry Cleaners was one of the many generational businesses in Williamstown where children of the original founders took over in some way or another, the businesses created by their parents. Mostly we knew each other as we had all gone to school locally which made for a close-knit friendly community within the city, which was itself a tight community where almost everyone knew everyone because of its history and isolation from mainstream Melbourne. This started changing from the 1990s onwards as new housing on old industrial estates brought an influx of new people into the city. Williamstown had been discovered and would never be the same again. It seemed that it was full of people nobody knew anymore. The town had changed from a quite backwater to a cosmopolitan suburb, almost overnight.

I'm not implying this was bad in any way, it was simply different and would take adjusting to. It was about this same time I could say I had spent 40 years working in the dry cleaning industry, even though I had played music and done other things simultaneously. 40 years was lifetime, and I wanted a change. I was sick of the smell of drycleaning fluid (*in our case at Williamstown, White Spirit*), of being indoors all day, of the sound of the machines operating, and basically every other aspect of life as a dry cleaner, but Phillip was happy with where he was and really didn't want to change. After much discussion we agreed to sell the property which housed the business. He was planning to lease it back and continue as before. He also agreed to buy my half of the business if we could sell the property.

Unfortunately, the time wasn't right to be selling business properties in the middle of Williamstown and our attempt at an auction failed to find any real purchasers. There was one desultory bid from a local property owner which was nowhere near the reserve, and it was knocked back. The lesson we learned from that was to be patient and wait for a better time.

To say I was disappointed would be an understatement. Phillip encouraged me to take the long break Monica and I had been planning, that was a trip to Chile where she could reunite with her family after twenty years of living in Australia. He said he and Chris would run the business and it would give him a chance to see how well he could manage on his own. When Monica and I come back in six months he would take a trip with Chris. He also said he would pay rent for my half share of the business while I was away and that would give me an income which would assist while we were travelling.

It was a good plan and I readily accepted it.

In the meantime, Mum had gone with Zara on a trip to Germany.

— Changing States —

Mum with Zara in the old part of Backnang.

Zara took her there as a 77th birthday present since her birthday was in August. They spent two months, the European summer, in Germany staying with Fred's mother and catching up with the German relatives on Fred's side of the family. It was on this trip that Mum noticed she was having trouble sometimes balancing, and she had difficulty with one eye, having lost vision in the lower part which made walking up or down steps problematic. But she was enjoying herself and that was the main thing. It had been a long time since she and Dad had been there together, and it was good to catch up even though Dad was no longer with us. She sent postcards to each of us during her trip away, and Theo (Fred's oldest and best friend) took photos of her with Zara, as well as one with her writing a postcard that Christine swears was to me. She claims she can see the heading *Dear John* in the enlarged photo she has on her wall.

I remember receiving a postcard, although I have no idea where it might be now. I'll never know if that was the one in the photo, although I like to think it is.

Mum and Zara returned home in August, just before Monica, Brian and I left on our trip to Chile in September 1990). *

* (See ***Between the Mountains and the Sea.***)

Zara with Mum in Backnang, Germany.
Mum with Fred's Mum, (Zara's mother in law,) and her sister Annie,
(Tante Annie) sitting in the back yard of their house in Lippoldsweiler.

Like we'd never been away...

Settling back into work the week after I'd come back, it seemed as if I'd never been away. Nothing had changed. What we did each day was the same. The customers we'd talk to in the shop were the same people we always talked to. The things we talked about were the same.

The six months we'd spent traveling through the USA, Mexico and in Chile faded rapidly into a background of lost memories, becoming dreamlike. It was as if it had happened a long time ago, or in a universe parallel to this one. Thinking about it conjured up images of old faded photographs that had come to light after years of being locked away. It no longer seemed real —and this was only after a week back at work. I couldn't imagine how I would feel in another year or two; didn't even want to think about that. I just had to endure it. I would get used to it, I told myself. Act normal, talk to the customers as if everything was still the same which after all it was. I was the one who had changed, not them.

Finding an Aikido dojo

Almost the first thing I did when we got home and had settled back into a regular routine was to search for somewhere to continue with the Aikido training we'd commenced in Chile. Both Brian and I had enjoyed it immensely and wanted to keep up the training. It came as a surprise to discover there were a lot of different groups practicing what they called Aikido in Melbourne. There was the style taught at *Iwama* by Saito Sensei, there was a group practicing *Yoshinkan* Aikido, which was I thought very similar to what O'Sensei, the founder of Aikido had been doing pre-(2nd World)-War, but that was too rigid and stylized for us.

There were a couple of groups doing something that only vaguely resembled Aikido and was more like wrestling and Judo combined.

I even went to the Melbourne University's Footscray Institute of Technology where I'd seen a notice that a *Tomiki* Aikido demonstration was to take place. This would involve competitions as well as traditional Aikido practice and I thought it might be interesting. I liked it, but it was nothing like the kind of Aikido we had been practicing in Chile.

Finally, a couple of weeks later towards the end of April, I saw a notice about *Aiki-Kai* Australia giving a demonstration in the foyer of the State Bank of Victoria, as part of a Japanese Cultural week. There was to be flower arranging, a tea ceremony, traditional dances, karate, Judo and Aikido demonstrations.

Brian and I went in to see it and realized immediately this was the Aikido we had studied in Santiago with Jorge Rojo Sensei. Rojo Sensei's teacher had been Tamura Shihan who had been a live-in student (*uchideshi*) with O'Sensei in Japan, and the Shihan responsible for teaching in Australia was Sugano Shihan, also an uchideshi of O'Sensei at the same time as Tamura Shihan.

Of course, the Aikido each one taught to their various students was slightly different because each was an individual who lived a different life and this is reflected in their understanding and teaching of Aikido, but basically, as far as underlying principles were concerned, it was the same. Tamura Shihan had been sent to France, while Sugano Shihan had been sent to Australia, just as others of their contemporary uchideshi had been sent to America, Canada and so on.

I was happy to have found an organization that taught the same Aikido that we had commenced learning. I spoke to the person in charge of the demonstration, and he encouraged us to join, which we did.

We commenced our training at Clifton Hill dojo, because that, apart from being the main dojo in Melbourne, was the nearest one to where we lived at Williamstown. The training we had already done didn't count as far as numbers of classes towards our first gradings, but that didn't matter. We had a slight advantage over other beginners who started at the same time because we'd already been doing it for three months. We trained three nights a week to begin with.

The only thing of note was that Brian wasn't so rapt with the training as he had been in Chile. He said it was because everyone here was old.

In Chile, the guys we trained with were in their early to late 20s whereas here in Melbourne, apart from a few beginners, everyone else was in their late 30s and 40s with many having practiced for at least 20 years.

It was a different atmosphere, a different feeling, which didn't bother me because I was already 51, slightly older than some of them but basically in the same generation.

"It's not the same as in Chile," Brian said emphatically after we'd been training for a few months. "Why is everyone so old? Where are the young guys?"

He wanted to train with people his own age, or at the least with guys in their 20s, and not people in their 40s. Even though he hung in there for the first couple of grading tests, he eventually dropped out, leaving me to continue training on my own, which I quite enjoyed.

And this is a problem worldwide for Aikido; it doesn't attract young people because it doesn't have competitions and no short term benefits in training. Long term personal gains are far too obscure to attract the young any more.

When they turn up to watch a class or a demonstration, they usually see older people rolling around, moving not very fast, and falling with softness. (They have no idea of how long it takes to learn how to be soft.) They rarely see something spectacular like a hip throw or someone smashing onto the floor with a resounding breakfall. They are more attracted to competitive jujitsu or cage fighting, wrestling, boxing, or similar fighting arts that attract audiences and where winners gain prizes, money or some such thing. They look at an Aikido class or demonstration and you never see them again after that.

That was in 1990 - 91, and it was already a problem. It's even worse now, 30 years later in 2022.

It was easy to see why Brian had lost interest, not that he wanted to win prizes or money, but he missed the hard more practical training we had been doing in Chile along with the camaraderie of the enthusiastic young guys we'd met there.

Two Kittens

Brian had pestered us about getting a pet dog, which we were not keen on at all, but he missed coyote, the dog that had hung around the cottage we stayed at in San Jose de Maipo in Chile. It had really taken a liking to Brian in particular. As a compromise, I suggested we could get him a kitten for his birthday, and we could do that at the Animal Welfare centre which had recently been advertising about how many cats, kittens, dogs, and puppies they had available for 'adoption'. I didn't mind cats; they were a lot easier to look after than dogs which always required a lot of attention. And you didn't have to take them for walks and pick up their shit. If he wanted a pet, it would have to be a cat or a kitten. That was it. No other option.

He mumbled a bit dispiritedly but eventually decided we would go and have a look at the cats and kittens at the Animal Welfare Centre which had been advertising in the local paper that they had numerous cats, kittens and dogs ready for adoption.

It was a Sunday when we went there, and the weather was bleak. Dark clouds scudded across the sky threatening to pelt us with a downpour at any moment. A cold wind rattled the tops of the trees that were bare and whipped the gum trees and other evergreens into a lashing frenzy. It was the beginning of the winter months in Melbourne and normally the first few weeks in June are pleasant with frosty nights and mornings but with lovely sunny days, even if there wasn't any warmth in the sun. When we got to the animal centre it was crowded, which was unexpected. Parents and children were all over the place and when we went into the area where they had the cats and kittens, there were two kittens left in a cage, one a light ginger, ordinary looking kitten which came forward and meowed at anyone who came close to the cage. The other little thing was almost invisible. Black with some coloured markings on one side of its face and above the paws on the front legs huddled right at the back of the cage.

There were several adults and one young girl looking at a few adult cats in an enclosure walled off from the rest of the room. The girl was holding another darker ginger kitten. I'd seen her selecting that kitten from the cage as we walked into the room. A couple of other kids with a parent had wandered in after us and were also looking around.

"If you want a kitten, you'd better grab one of those two that are left, or they'll all be gone."

"I like that other one," Brian said, referring to the one the girl just ahead of us held, but he reached forward and picked up the lighter ginger kitten and held it close to his chest.

While he was cuddling the kitten and listening to it purr, I reached into the cage to pet the dark one huddled at the back. It raised its head and licked my finger, then slowly stood up and stepped onto my arm. It walked up my arm and sat on my shoulder and rubbed its head against my ear. It too started purring. It had a tortoise shell marking on one side of its face with some lighter colour between its front legs, but the rest of it was black with a couple of faint brown streaks across the back. A beautiful little thing. I held it up to have a closer look and the way it looked at me would melt anyone's heart.

I could see Brian was undecided. "You'd better make up your mind," I said, because these two are the only ones left." The other girl had disappeared with the darker ginger kitten.

He looked at the tortoise shell kitten I was holding, and then at the one he had.

"I don't know," he said.

"I like this one," I said.

"I don't know… I think I prefer this ginger one."

"Good. Then we'll take both. This one for me and that one for you."

Monica was waiting for us at the reception where you sorted the paperwork regarding the animals being adopted and paid a $50 fee for each one, and she was surprised to see us with two kittens instead of one.

"They're from the same litter," I said. "It would be good for them to have each other to grow up with."

She looked at me with an expression I couldn't fathom.

"I didn't choose this one. It picked me. It walked up my arm and sat of my shoulder. What was I supposed to do?"

Outside, the weather had deteriorated. It was freezing and spitting rain. We had the kittens in a box given to us at the reception and this we placed on the back seat next to where Brian sat. Instead of driving straight home, we went in search of a pet shop that might be open because we didn't have anything at home to feed them.

We went through several suburbs, but all the shops were shut. In the end, we found ourselves in St Kilda which being more touristy had many shops open, including a small supermarket where we found bags of dry cat food as well as a few tins of stuff for kittens. We also bought a litter tray and a couple of bags of whatever it was you filled a litter tray with.

Back home, and out of the shitty weather, the two kittens immediately curled up on the floor in front of the heater in the kitchen which was left on to keep the place warm. They purred contentedly with warm air blowing over them.

Sunny

— *Changing States* —

Shady
How could I have resisted a face like that?
Especially when she climbed up my arm and sat on my shoulder.

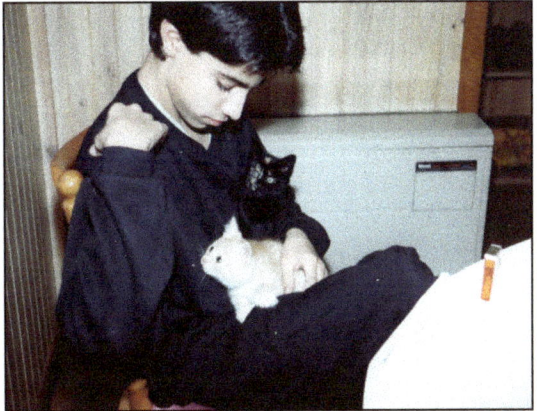

Brian with Sunny in the kitchen.
With both kittens.
Shady and me...

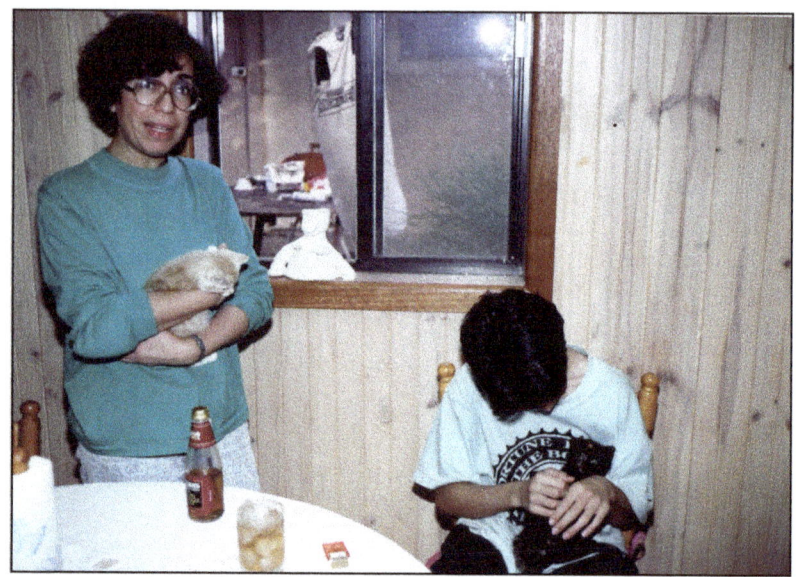

It didn't take long for them to take over the house. They would hide behind the window curtains, under the bedspread in Brian's room, with the tiniest part of their face showing as they watched us come and go. Their favourite spot was always in front of the heater in the kitchen dining area. There was a glass door leading to the courtyard and when the weather improved after a couple of days and we got a bit of wintry sun, I took both kittens outside into the courtyard. I stood by the door and waited for them to start exploring, but neither of them moved. They sat as close as they possibly could, leaning against my legs. So, I walked across the courtyard to the other side. They both followed me. When the ginger tabby we called Sunny started to look at the plants in the garden bed, I walked back to glass door. The little tortoise shell, Shady, followed me staying as close as possible. I left Sunny to his explorations in the garden bed and walked further into the back yard to see if Shady would follow, and she did. We walked around the greater part of the yard together before heading back to the courtyard where Sunny was sitting on the stone barrier to the garden bed. He immediately joined us, and we went back inside where they once again curled up in front of the heater.

At night, watching TV Shady would sit on my lap, whereas Sunny, was content to sit on the floor or on the chair beside one of us. Brian would pick him up and cuddle him, but he often seemed indifferent. If I sat down anywhere, at any time, Shady would always jump up and sit on my lap.

— Changing States —

Sunny soon gained enough confidence to climb trees and was always climbing the trees in the yard. Shady being a bit smaller and female never seemed to be much of a climber, at least in the back yard.

— Changing States —

— John Litchen —

It seemed no time at all before they had doubled in size.
Sunny was easy to photograph, Shady being mostly black was much harder. Together, one was either over exposed or the other was too dark

The next day I opened the glass door and they followed me outside, but this time they both went off in different directions to explore the garden and the backyard. I stayed where they could see me, knowing that they would feel safe while I was around. By the third day they were happy to go out into the yard which was now familiar to them without me having to be there. I stayed inside enjoying a cup of coffee while they wandered about in the yard. When they wanted to come in, they sat by the glass door until I noticed them and opened the door. The same when they wanted to go outside. They would sit by the door and meow to grab my attention. I would come over and open the door so they could go outside.

Shady quickly learnt a better way to attract my attention. She started to tap and scratch on the glass door. Hearing this odd noise, I came to investigate and the moment I appeared, she meowed, as if to say open the door please. Sunny never figured that out. He would sit there until someone noticed him. She would do the same when she wanted to come back inside, if someone was in the kitchen dining area. She'd tap and scratch the glass door. If there was no one inside, she would wait until she saw or heard someone in there, then tap on the glass. Whether she figured this out by herself, or she saw a visitor knocking on the door which resulted in one of us coming and opening the door, I have no way of knowing. But she watched everything. She followed me around in particular and watched everything I did. She was smart enough to quickly work out what actions would cause the result she wanted.

One example of her intelligence was the day we installed a cat-flap on the door of the office. To get there we went through the lounge room into the old grocery shop, and over to the ex-bottle shop that I had turned into a library and music studio, and through to the back room where a wooden door opened into the courtyard.

Once the flap was installed and working properly, I took Shady and put her in front of it. Brian had Sunny with him. And was standing next to us. I pushed the flap open and allowed it to swing shut. I did this a couple of times while she watched attentively. I then placed her right in front with her head almost touching the flap. I gave her a nudge, so she was partly through with the flap up and resting on her head. She resisted a moment but could see into the room, so she walked on through. I then opened the door and went inside. She was watching me. Closing the door. I picked her up and placed in front of the flap so she could see it worked both ways. I pushed her through, and she didn't resist but walked straight through out into the courtyard. She then actually walked through it both ways a couple of times, and having satisfied herself as to

Shady loved sitting and sleeping on the old wooden table in the courtyard. While Sunny would be running up tree trunks and climbing onto the roof.

how it worked, she sat beside me while Brian placed Sunny in front of the flap.

When Brian tried to push him through so he could see and feel how it worked, he resisted, digging his front paws into the mat by the door. It took half a dozen attempts before we could get him through the flap and into the room. Eventually he got it, especially after seeing Shady go through it once more. He finally got up enough courage to follow. After that he was fine. Both of them would come and go through the flap into the office and then walk around through the other rooms to get to the kitchen and dining area. But Shady didn't like the long walk through the big rooms, so she simply came and sat by the glass door and tapped on it for me to open it and let her in or out.

They grew rapidly, and within a few weeks had doubled in size looking more like young cats than baby kittens. They loved a particular dry food which we gave them. This we kept in a packet on the third shelf in the pantry. The pantry had doors which you pulled shut and they clicked into place and were held by a small magnet near the top. When it was time to feed them, they both followed us and saw where the dry food was kept. One morning as I entered the kitchen I heard a scrabbling noise in the pantry. I thought there was probably a mouse in there. We sometimes got mice with our building being very old, although we hadn't seen any since we'd brought the cats home. As I stepped towards the pantry I heard a thump and Shady walked out and meowed. Pushing the door open wider, I saw that she had chewed a hole in the bottom of the cardboard box of dried cat food and had been eating what had spilled out when she heard me come in and jumped down. I gathered what had spilled out and put it in her bowl. I also decided to move the cat food to another cupboard higher up above the fridge. She watched me as I put it up there.

Two days later, I came down early in the morning to see Shady sitting on top of the fridge which jutted out beyond the cupboard above it. She was trying to open the door by hooking her front right paw underneath it and pulling it towards her. She was trying to get at the dried cat food. But the problem she couldn't solve was that the door opened outwards, and by pulling it towards her she was being pushed off the fridge before she could open the door more than a couple of centimetres.

She couldn't get at the food, but she was smart enough to know where it was and to attempt to get it.

Four years later, when we moved to Robina in Queensland, we had sliding doors leading outside and she saw how we opened them. She had no problem hooking her front paw against the edge of the door and sliding it open enough to let herself out, or in if she was outside. What I could never get her to do was close the door after she went through.

Sunny never did figure that out. He always sat and waited until one of us noticed him by the door and would let him in or out.

A devastating illness

What knocked us for a spin a few months after we returned from our trip to Chile was Mum got sick, and almost immediately ended up in Hospital (The Alfred Hospital in Commercial Road, just off St Kilda Road.) She'd seemed fine after we came back and was quite normal at Brian's fifteenth birthday at the beginning of June. We had the fire going in the big round fireplace in the studio and the usual cakes and coffees and everyone had a good time.

Monica and Zara contemplating which cakes to cut up for afternoon tea. Brian had already blown out the candles. Mum is relaxed in the armchair.

Above: Fred and his son David relaxing in the background in the studio while Brian prepares to blow out the candles on his cake.
Mum turns to speak to me while the others are helping themselves to the cakes and the tea and coffee.
These few photos with Mum in them turned out to be the last ones ever taken of her...

Mum with Paul, my youngest brother, and his wife Lynne.

Mum, like most people of her generation, didn't tell us how she was feeling, she simply went about her daily activities as if everything was normal. She was in the family home by herself now that Paul and Lynne had their own place in Spotswood. To make sure she was okay, Zara often dropped in to see her and to have a cup of tea, or Monica would do the same if she was going up to Highpoint West for shopping. She would have to drive past our old street and would always call in to see how Mum was. As it happened this day towards the end of July (1991) both Zara and Monica were going to collect Mum to take her shopping with them.

When they got there, they walked in calling out to let Mum know they were there. With Mum on her own after Dad had died a few years earlier we all had a key to the front door so we could go in at any time in case of an emergency. They found her in the front bedroom sick in bed with a high fever and sweating profusely. They were both stunned, because a day or two earlier she had seemed perfectly fine. What was worse was she had been unable to get out of bed to go the toilet and had made a mess. They cleaned her and remade the bed, and Zara called her doctor (Doctor Peers) who had also been Mum's doctor as well as Monica's, and she came up to see Mum. She took blood samples and sent them off for analysis and put her on an antibiotic for the fever.

The next day, with Mum not looking any better, Dr. Peers rang and told Zara that Mum had a severe Streptococcus infection in her blood that was raging through her body. She needed to be sent to hospital for treatment. It was the 25th of July 1991. That was accomplished while I was at work the next day and I only found out when I got home in the evening. The moment I walked in the door Monica told me what had happened. We rushed over to the Alfred Hospital where she had been taken. Zara was there, quite upset. The doctors explained that the infection in Mum's blood was so serious it had compromised one of her heart's mitral valves, partially destroying it, and that they needed to do an immediate heart mitral valve replacement. They were in the process of prepping her for this major operation as we arrived and joined Zara.

"I called Christine," Zara said, "and she'll be on a flight down first thing in the morning."

Then they wheeled Mum out of the ward she'd initially been placed in, and she smiled at us.

"Wish me luck," she said.

She was on the bed with a drip connected to her arm.

She smiled bravely and then mumbled something about saying goodbye in case she doesn't make it.

What can you say in circumstances like that?

"She'll be fine," one of the nurses wheeling the bed out assured us.

We watched as they took her down the corridor and into the area where the operating theatre was located.

There was nothing else we could do except sit around and wait until the operation was done.

What was hard to reconcile was the suddenness with which it had happened. One day she was fine, perfectly normal, or so it seemed, and the next; she was in hospital having major surgery to replace a damaged heart valve.

That same nurse came back to reassure us that everything would be okay, and she guided us to a small reception lounge where we could wait. There was coffee and tea available as well.

"They're very good surgeons," the nurse said. "They'll do a brilliant job. I'll come back and let you know the moment they've finished. She'll be in the Intensive Care Ward for a few days, but I can take you in there to see her as soon as it's done."

And then we were left in the waiting room.

A couple of hours later we were taken into the ICU where Mum was on a special; bed with tubes and monitors hooked up to her in several places. The screen beside the bed showed her blood pressure, heart rate, and had half a dozen other scrolling graph lines that were incomprehensible to us. Obscured machines emitted buzzing sounds and regular beeps with different tones came from the monitors on both sides of the bed. Mum was conscious and she smiled at us. I can't remember what any of us said to her or what she said to us. What was important though was that she'd come through the operation and considering all the stuff still connected to her, she didn't look too bad.

"She's done well," the same nurse told us. "In two days, we'll transfer her to the recovery ward."

Everything looked good and there was nothing else to do but to go back home. Christine would arrive from Queensland in the morning and Zara was going to pick her up at the airport. After that we would all come together at the hospital to see Mum.

"I feel terrific," Mum said when we saw her the next afternoon.

She did look a lot better. There was good colour in her cheeks, and she was alert, cheerful. She complained her chest (where the stitching used to close the opening made for the operation) was itchy, but she wasn't allowed to scratch it.

"They're going to shift me into the recovery ward tomorrow," she told us.

We weren't allowed to stay in the ICU for long because it disturbed the patients recovering from major operations. There were two other patients in the ICU as well as Mum, but both were not conscious. Nurses fussed about them. One of them, a man in his late forties, had undergone a complete lung and heart transplant. There'd been nothing wrong with his heart, but it was easier to give him a lung and heart transplant and take his good heart to use for another transplant recipient, the other of the two patients in the ICU, thus doing two operations at the same time, giving two people the chance of a better life rather than just one. Being told that, we had great expectations that Mum would have quick recovery.

We were quietly ushered out.

On the third day, Monica and I turned up in the evening after I'd finished at the factory. Zara and Christine were there with Mum in a private room. Mum looked quite good, sitting propped up in bed, she was cheerfully chatting with the girls when we walked in. She'd just finished the evening meal and the table on wheels with the leftovers had been rolled to one side. Mum still had a drip connected to her right arm feeding fluids directly into her vein or artery. She still had wires connected to a monitor beside the bed which monitored her heartbeat, which looked steady and regular on the graph displayed on the screen.

Although this was encouraging, she began to deteriorate a day or so later.

The nurse in charge of the recovery ward told us that Mum had contracted a Golden Staph infection, probably through scratching.

I thought that was a doubtful explanation. Most likely this dreaded disease was everywhere in this older hospital, and unavoidable for patients like Mum, who at 77 and not the healthiest to begin with, was susceptible. Golden Staph was a severe menace in hospitals as it had evolved to become immune to all antibiotics used in hospitals to counteract it. It wasn't prevalent in new hospitals but was a big problem in older well-established hospitals across the country.

Another drip had been inserted into Mum's other arm, and this we assumed was to feed antibiotics into her to counteract the newly acquired infection. To be honest, she looked terrible. It was most upsetting to see her like that.

The antibiotics must have had some effect because a couple of days later she came good again and was sitting up in bed feeling cheerful. We could see she was hopeful of recovering soon. When we got to the hospital that night, she had finished her evening meal. Phillip was there, because it was his week on at the factory and after finishing work, he would come straight to the hospital to see Mum before making the long drive home out to Bacchus Marsh. Apart from Christine who had flown down from Brisbane to be with us, the rest of us lived in Williamstown and Yarraville and could come and go to the hospital at any time most days.

Over the next few weeks, this pattern repeated with Mum feeling good and hopeful that she would recover soon, suddenly alternating with a downward spiral where she was not doing well at all.

She got weaker each time, and never quite recovered to the same degree after each downward lurch. They kept increasing and changing the antibiotics, which each time saw her recover slightly, but very soon after she would go downhill again. By this time she was connected to a number of tubes feeding fluids and antibiotics into her, and others extracting urine, or blood samples for testing.

It was obvious that she wasn't going to recover, but not one of us admitted this. We tried to stay positive, telling each other that she would get better, especially at the moments when she rallied and became more conscious of us and her surroundings.

It was also close to her birthday and when the girls asked Mum what she would like she told them she wanted a piece of Zara's cheesecake. Zara made fantastic cheesecakes and she immediately went home and baked one for Mum. But when she brought it into the hospital, Mum was in one of her bad downturns and couldn't eat any of it. Zara gave the cake to the nurses and asked them to share it between themselves and any other patients who would like a piece.

Christine told me a long time later, that in one of the periods when Mum was feeling a bit better, she gave her back a massage, and not long after she saw all the skin across her back was dark coloured, bruised she thought, and blamed herself because of the massage. But the doctor told her it wasn't bruised, it was dead or dying. Her organs were breaking down and being excreted through the urine which was cloudy with stuff floating in it. The doctor told her quite bluntly, "Her body has already died, but her mind and her brain have not yet accepted that."

What a thing to tell someone!

One night, the doctors called us together and we sat in the visitors waiting room while they explained that there was nothing more they could do. The antibiotics hadn't worked, and the infection had ravaged her body, almost destroying every organ. As a last resort they suggested something which was basically a poison. They said it would kill the Golden Staph, but it would also most likely help in further destruction of her internal organs if they gave her too much. Nothing else had worked, which was a shame because the operation to replace the heart valve had been a success. But if they got the balance right, it might just get rid of the infection without doing further damage, and she might have a chance to recover. They needed our consent to try it.

The options were, do nothing and she would die within a few more days, or try this and she might still die, but there was the slimmest chance that she might also recover enough to be able to fight off the infection herself. And they stressed, it was a very slim chance. The fact that they needed permission to try it was clear that they really didn't think there was any chance at all but couldn't do it without us giving them permission to try. It was obviously experimental, and they were at their wits' end as to what to do next.

We had no choice really. No matter how slim a chance there was, it was better to try, rather than do nothing, so we reluctantly agreed.

It didn't help.

The next evening when we visited, Mum was conscious but weak. She kept trying to tell me goodbye, in a whispering voice I could hardly hear, and I kept trying to reassure her she would get better. I couldn't believe she would die. She had always been there for us. But she knew. I could see it in her eyes and in the way she looked at me.

Zara and Christine were there the next afternoon while I was at work. Mum died while they were with her, so at least when she went, she wasn't alone. It was the 5th of September 1991.

She had been 55 days in the hospital, and none of it very pleasant. I had to wonder afterwards, did the Golden Staph she contracted in the hospital kill her, or was it a combination of that and the Strep infection she already had in her bloodstream that did it?

It was the Strep that had damaged the mitral valve requiring the replacement. Perhaps it had weakened her immune system too much to allow her to recover properly after the operation anyway and the Golden Staph once it got into her was simply overwhelming. According to the autopsy, there had been other damage in the heart to the back walls where part of the structure had died, and some of the other valves had fibrous growths in them.

Perhaps it was her time anyway, and nothing the hospital did would have been effective. I think when your time comes, there is nothing anyone can do to prevent it.

She was buried five days later, the 10th of September, and was placed into the same grave at the cemetery in North Altona where Dad had been buried three years earlier. They were finally together again.

As it happens when you are in the midst of a funeral, you are not thinking straight. All the people attending had also been at Dad's funeral three years earlier. I assumed that they knew where we lived in Williamstown and I told them as we left the grave site that they should come around to our place where we had food and drinks set up in the studio, as we had for Dad, and that we would see them there. If they weren't sure where the place was, simply follow us. As we walked out of the cemetery, I saw most of them following us and getting into their cars. We jumped into ours and took off. I didn't think to wait long enough to make sure we were being followed and when we got home, only the immediate family arrived moments after us. No one else turned up, which was disappointing.

I will always wonder if they didn't care enough to come, or if they simply got lost between North Altona and Williamstown, and not knowing our address, or not remembering how to get there as they had three years earlier, finally gave up and went home.

Becoming Adult

They say that you only become an adult once your parents have died. I read this somewhere, I have no idea where, but it did make me think.

We were on our own now. With Dad gone three years ago and now Mum, there was no one we could ask about our early life or about events that occurred within the family before we were born. There was no one to help if we got into trouble, no one to give us advice (not that we thought we needed it… but just in case); all of that was gone. We would be on our own. It was our children who eventually would look to us for the same reasons we used to look to our parents. We had replaced them and the roles they played in our lives would now be ours to play in the lives of our children.

And this applied to Zara, Phillip, Christine and Paul, as well as to me. And so, Life goes on…

An invitation to a now-infamous party that led to a series of articles for *Tirra Lirra, and other magazines.*

At the beginning of 1992, I did a correspondence course (these days it would be an online course) on travel writing.

Why I did this, I have no idea because I didn't learn anything I didn't already know. Perhaps it was curiosity. There was always so much advertising hype regarding correspondence courses that I thought I would do this one to see what was involved. Part of the course included pitching ideas to various travel magazines, which the instructors evaluated, and writing an article, which I did on Williamstown as an Historic Seaport. I also included colour slides of historic places and relics in Williamstown.

I passed the course with good results and received a certificate and an Australian News Syndicate Press Pass which looked official, but which turned out to be useless the one time I actually tried using it to get into a venue with other members of the press. I also sent a couple of the articles written during the course to selected travel magazines, but both were rejected. Politely, of course, but it seemed the editors had their own stable of writers they relied upon and simply weren't interested in taking on new unknown writers.

Not long after completing this course, I received an invitation to Bruce Gillespie's Garden party. He and Elaine had recently bought the

— *Changing States* —

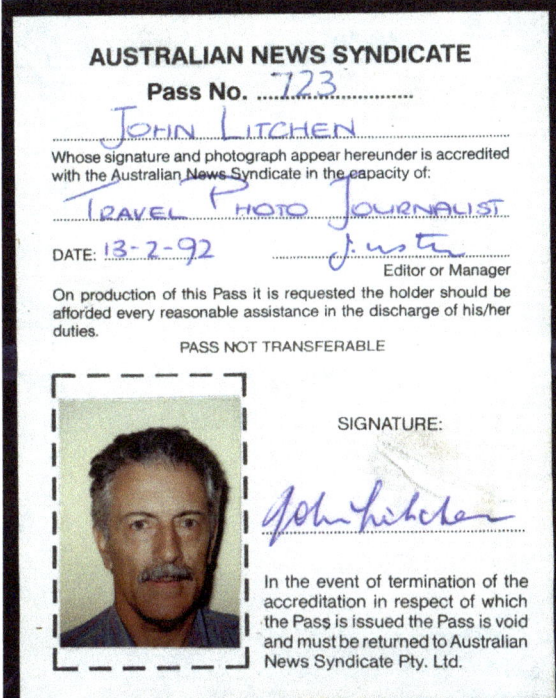

My useless press pass. At least it looked like a real one. It folded in the middle and looked like a miniature passport.

adjoining block to the house they lived in Keele Street Collingwood and had turned the space into a vegetable garden. They invited heaps of people most of whom turned up on the day, a Sunday afternoon in May 1992. There were well over 100 people there which was a huge crowd for a party. A brilliant report on this party was printed in **Bruce's Metaphysical Review** (Issue #18 March 1993) written by Yvonne Rousseau. The report captured brilliantly the essence of the party and gave wonderfully written sketches of many of the people who were there. Ask anyone who was there, and they will swear that Yvonne was there, except for Bruce and Elaine who of course knew she wasn't. Bruce even told his readers this in his introduction to the article by Yvonne, yet still people argue over whether she was there or not. She spoke to many of the attendees by phone to ask them about it, she spoke to Bruce of course for additional details, and yet when she completed writing the report, anyone who read it would swear she had to have been there. That kind of writing is pure genius. But then Bruce was always very good at eliciting superb writing from his friends and associates world-wide which he published erratically in his two major magazines, **Metaphysical Review,** and **SF Commentary**.

On this day Bruce introduced me to a woman who edited a small literary magazine which he said was like a professional fanzine. It was ***Tirra Lirra*** the *Independent Contemporary Magazine,* which appeared quarterly, and for a time it had some government funding. It had lovely covers in colour and the interior was black and white, and contained stories, essays, memoirs, poetry, photos and other stuff. Some of it was academic which I found pretentious, but most of it was readable and enjoyable. The editor, owner and publisher, was the lovely Eva Windisch.

How Bruce met her I had no idea, but Bruce knew heaps of people in different aspects of the publishing and writing worlds both professional and amateur, so it seemed natural that she would be there. Bruce had also contributed a few articles to her magazine. We hit it off and over a few glasses of wine she asked if I would be willing to contribute something to her magazine, so I said yes. She gave me a few copies of recent issues to read to get an idea of the kind of material she published.

I had second thoughts once I got home. I had no idea what I would write about, but then what came to mind was a story Mum used to tell us about her father and how he obtained the gold ring with an opal setting that he always wore on his left hand. I thought, that's a good story. It had some creepy elements to it, and I wondered if I could write it well enough to be interesting, so I tried. Once I had the story done, I called it *A Promise Kept,* and sent it to Eva. Shortly after that I tried writing a poem in Spanish about Mum who had recently passed away.

I had written two poems in Spanish years before on the anniversary of the bombing of Hiroshima. One was about that bomb that was dropped and the other was one imagining what it must be like to be very old. I did this as a way of remembering the language I had learned while living for a year in Mexico, before I met Monica, but these poems vanished after being printed by John Bangsund in his *Philosophical Gas* fanzine of which that particular issue also vanished. A part of it appeared in a later issue, but the original issue was never finished or published. Once I'd met Monica, whose language was Spanish, there was no need for me to write poetry in Spanish trying to not forget the language. I could talk to Monica in Spanish.

Writing a poem about Mum in Spanish, (*Pensamientos),* shortly after she'd died seemed appropriate. I couldn't express what I wanted to say in English, it didn't seem right, so I thought about it in Spanish and the poem seemed to write itself. In my mind I always thought of Spanish as a poetical language. After that I translated the poem into English, and it didn't seem too bad after all. I also sent this to Eva, and 'blow me down' she published the poem in the December 1992 (*volume 3 #2)* issue of

Tirra Lirra. In that same issue she also published the first of a series of memoirs that I was writing, *Life and Death along Stony Creek*. The earlier story I'd sent her, *A Promise Kept* she had published in the July 1992 issue (*volume 2 #4*).

What I loved about writing for Eva was all her authors and many of her readers were always invited to a launch of the magazine held at a pub in Johnston Street Collingwood, a few streets away from Bruce's place in Keele Street. Bruce and Elaine would always be there, since Bruce had also contributed articles to ***Tirra Lirra*** as well as being a friend of Eva, and we would enjoy a pub lunch with them and the various people reading extracts from what they had published in that issue of the magazine. Eva would give everyone a copy or two. We didn't get paid, there wasn't enough funding for that, but it was nice to be published and recognized by others. There was quite often, some entertainment with folk singing or someone playing the piano. They were delightful afternoons and everyone attending felt special as well as being part of a community of artists and writers.

I followed that with a series of short memoirs; *Our last Summer in Williamstown* (***Tirra Lirra*** *Volume 3 #4*) *Hide it under the Axe* (*volume 4 #1*) *The Great Flood* (*volume 4 #3*) *You are my Sunshine* (*volume 5 #3*) *Peril of Pauline* (*Volume 8 #1*)

The Great Flood was a short story that evolved over time into a slightly longer story and then into a novella which in turn became part of a much larger novel in two parts, but more about that later.

I also thought of a story Dad often told us regarding the day he arrived in Melbourne on the ship *Re D'Italia* in 1924. I called it *The Day of Arrival* and sent it to a Melbourne publication called ***Australian Writer***. They accepted it and published it in November 1994.

It was during this time that I discovered a magazine in Perth that started off looking like a small newspaper but evolved into a magazine and a series of anthologies. They published short stories and articles about writing. The publication was called ***Reader's world***. They paid for the stories published. I sent them a copy of *The Great Flood* hoping they would accept it. I figured they would since Eva had already thought it good enough to be published. It was sent back with a note asking me to change the ending to make it more dramatic. I promptly rewrote it with a different ending which also expanded the story so it was 500 words longer than the version published in ***Tirra Lirra***. They paid me $40 for the story. It went into their first anthology called *Readers Paradise*.

Meanwhile, I also contributed more articles to Neville Coleman's ***Un-***

derwater Geographic Magazine in 1990. *Greenhouse*, a brief piece on the effect of climate warming, and in 1993 *Abalone: King of the Molluscs*.

Neville was kind enough to add to my article, some biological information regarding the species of Abalone found in Australian waters.

Then there was a brief article for **Australian Photography**, *The Alternative Album*. (*April 1993*).

What was the name of that Film? I wrote for Bruce who published it in his **Metaphysical Review** (*July 1994*) about the making of the film which won us the right for the World SF Convention in 1975.

So, when I wasn't working at the dry cleaners in my alternate week off, I would be working on writing and photography, and was gradually beginning to see work being published. It gave me some expectations that when I finally retired, I might be able to get by with my writing.

That's a dream many of us have, but very few of us can make it a reality. Writing and publishing will always be a hobby, or a pastime, for most of us, myself included... but it was nice to dream a bit.

There were two short stories after we'd moved to Queensland, *A Last Abstract Cry* (**Reader's World** *Volume 2 #7, February 1999*) and *A Beach Too Far*, (**Winter Warmers** *anthology from Indian Ocean Books. August 2000*), both of which earned me a small fee and a couple of copies of the publications. There were also a couple of articles on writing published in **Australian Writer**, and **Stet**, the same magazine after it changed its name.

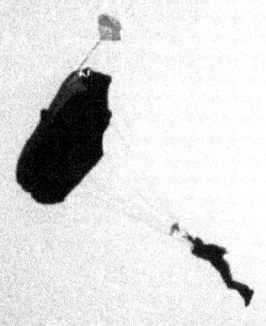

Jumping out of an aeroplane, who would want to do that?

Brian of course.
He thought it was a great idea and kept talking about it until we finally agreed to take him out to Pakenham, once a country town off the Princes Highway after leaving Melbourne's outskirts at Dandenong. Driving through Berwick (where a major scene in the film *On The Beach* had been filmed in the 1950s) Beaconsfield, and Officer, we arrived at Packenham, and had no trouble finding the large acreage of paddocks that housed the Skydiving school and a rough unpaved airstrip. Packenham and all those other small country towns are now part of Greater Melbourne. The city has sprawled out in extensions along all the major highways absorbing small towns and creating new suburbs. We could have gone there by electric train, a suburban train, but for us it was easier to drive because we could go right up to the Skydiving school's front gate. The train station was a long way from this place.

Because Brian was under 18, we had to sign papers agreeing to let him participate in the training sessions on the Saturday afternoon as well as the pre-flight preparations and the actual flight during which the skydive would take place. He was excited about staying there overnight as well. After watching him do some initial training in a group we left him there and went home. He was going to jump by himself, not make a tandem jump like many beginners do. He wanted to be in control of the parachute and the jump. This meant he had to do several hours of specific training which is why he had to stay overnight.

Brian looking on as parachutes are examined and folded in preparation for the next jump. Below: Brian stepping outside to take part in training exercises for his jump on Sunday.

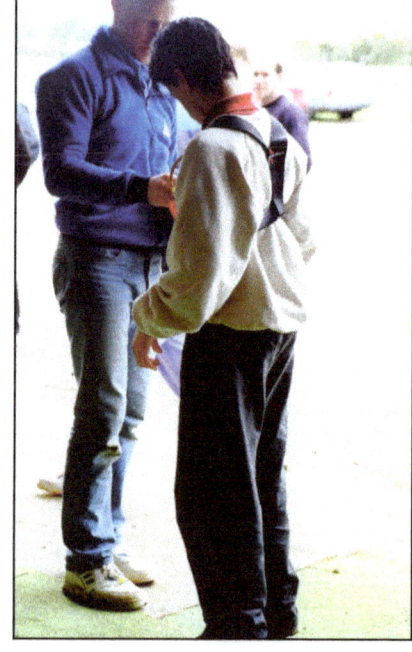

— Changing States —

His jump was scheduled for late Sunday morning, if the weather permitted. And the weather was patchy with intermittent showers, typical Melbourne weather. As the saying goes; 'if you don't like the weather, just wait a few minutes…' It was Springtime, and Melbourne's weather was always changeable.

We got there around ten o'clock the next morning and watched Brian being fitted out with a jumpsuit and his parachute, helmet and goggles. He joined a dozen people lining up to board the plane. All of them were doing individual jumps, some like Brian, for the first time, while the others were making their second or third jump. The weather was stable, not too windy, cloudy, but no threat of rain.

 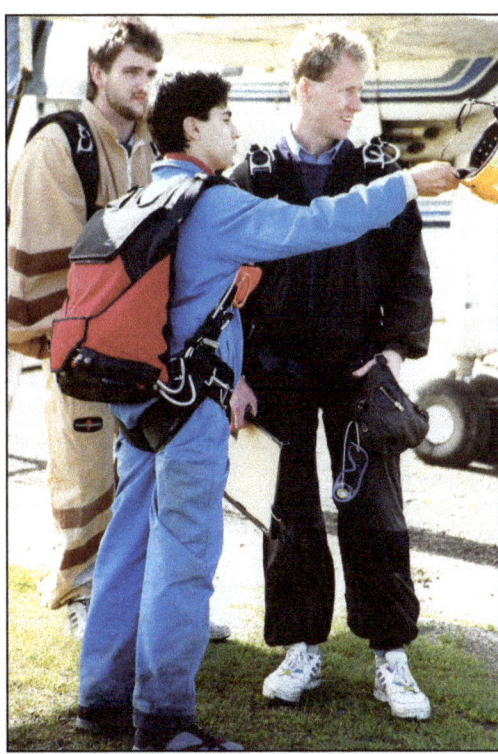

Discussing final details of the jump with his instructors while waiting beside the plane. They would shortly be joined by the rest of the guys making the jump. They would line up in the order of who would go first, second, and so on. They would exit the plane in the reverse order of entering.

— John Litchen —

Final checks before boarding... Brian is the one wearing the yellow helmet.

Taxiing at the end of the runway on the far side of the paddock, ready to take off.

Off they went. We watched as the plane taxied out to the far side of a huge paddock where the packed earth runway was located. With roar the plane took off and passed overhead. It made wide circles gradually getting higher and higher until after about twenty minutes it had reached a suitable height for the skydivers to take their plunge. It was almost invisible against the darkening clouds.

One by one they emerged; tiny little figures silhouetted against the threatening sky, falling away behind the plane and rapidly enlarging as they came closer to the ground. Once they were all out, the plane stopped circling and flew off a short distance to give the divers plenty of space. One by one their parachutes opened and the whole group drifted slowly downwards towards the huge adjoining paddock. There was a big cross in the paddock next to the where the runway was located, and this was the spot the divers aimed to land on.

Monica never said anything, but it was obvious how anxious she was. I hardly had time to get anxious because I kept trying to get photos of Brian coming down, but it was hard to tell which one he was since they were all silhouetted against the sky. When we finally figured out which one was Brian he was close to the ground, adjusting his parachute for landing. His landing was not as elegant as some of the guys who'd done more than one jump. But he landed without mishap, gathered his chute and walked back to the shed where the chutes would be laid out to be inspected and folded for another later skydive.

— Changing States —

Waiting at the edge of the field where the sky divers would land, watching anxiously as Brian came down.

Brian was delighted with the experience and talked all the way home about making more dives after additional training, but much to Monica's relief, after a few weeks he lost interest, and we never went back to do it again.

Gathering his chute and walking back.

From one extreme to the other

From Skydiving to Scuba diving.

Brian had already dived a few times in the water using Fred's hookah setup on his abalone boat, and together he and I had been diving in some of the safer spots along Victoria's wild southern coast. I had been teaching him how to use a snorkel, how to use a wetsuit and fins to skin-dive, which I had written about for Neville Coleman's Underwater Geographic magazine, but now it was time to learn scuba diving from a reputable school.

We went to Dive Experience, a business and diving school run by the Marks Brothers in Williamstown. Not only did they teach scuba diving courses, they also organized dive tours usually around the Port Phillip Bay Heads and had two excellent boats based at Queenscliff which they used for training new divers as well as taking more experienced divers on tours to dive on a sunken submarine just outside the Port Phillip Bay Heads. Brian had completed the theory, (at Dive Experience's headquarters in Ferguson Street in Williamstown, just down the road from where we lived in Douglas Parade) as well as the practical work done in the local swimming pool and in shallow water by the beach, and now it was time for the first dive in ocean water. He was part of a group of twenty beginners making their first ocean dive.

He didn't need his own scuba gear because that was supplied by Dive Experience. He of course took his own wetsuit, mask, snorkel, flippers and weight belt, as did everyone else.

It was a gorgeous Sunday Morning when Brian and I arrived at Queenscliff at around 8:30 in the morning. We were lucky to find a spot to park almost beside the two dive boats.

Once he had his wetsuit on he went and collected the equipment, the scuba tank, vest and regulator he was going to use.
Note in the trailer above where the scuba tanks were stored, there was also a compressor to refill the tanks once they'd been used.

About 50 metres away was Dive Experience's van with a covered trailer loaded with scuba tanks, a compressor, vests and other equipment. Divers were already transferring the tanks and vests they were going to use onto the dive boats. Brian went over to let them know he was there, and the dive master told him to go and get dressed. He came back to our van and started to get into his wetsuit.

There were crowds everywhere. People getting onto yachts and motorboats, people standing around watching the activity of which there was plenty to see. Boats leaving the moorings and heading out along a channel towards Swan Bay and its calm waters. Fishing boats returning after being out at sea much earlier or overnight, cars backing trailers with boats on them down the local boat ramps, fishermen cleaning their catch by the water's edge and seagulls flapping raucously around chasing scraps thrown into the water; fishing and seaports in coastal towns are endlessly fascinating.

The dive master was trying to hurry everyone because the tide had almost finished coming in and they wanted to be away and to get the divers into the water while the sea was relatively calm, and before the tide turned to go out. They were to do a drift dive with the divers doing their first ocean dive drifting along the inside of the Queenscliff coastline towards the heads where a buoy with trailing ropes to grab onto in the water marked the pickup spot. It would be a one kilometre drift dive in water up to ten metres deep.

Brian had collected his scuba tank, regulator and vest, was wearing his wetsuit and was about to go over to join those waiting to go down onto one of the two boats. He would be on the Calypso, the older of the two boats.

He nudged me. "That's Peter Russell-Clarke isn't it?"

It was him. He was standing on the pier just ahead of us, watching the activities going on as the many divers prepared to board their dive-boats moored beside the pier. Apart from the Calypso being readied for its dive run, there were yachts leaving the harbor and heading out into Swan Bay, there were guys in small dinghies heading out for a day's fishing. It was a perfect day, and everyone was out and about. I had heard Peter lived on a farm in the country not far from Melbourne; maybe it was on the Bellarine Peninsula and was simply out for a morning's walk.

Brian went over to him and said hello.

Peter was happy he had been recognized. And then when I reminded him about the Don Lane Show and how he had cooked a steak and two eggs on top of a hot car engine, he burst out laughing.

I don't remember what else we talked about, but Brian asked if he

At every stage there were constant checks, to make sure equipment was right, that each diver was getting onto the right boat.

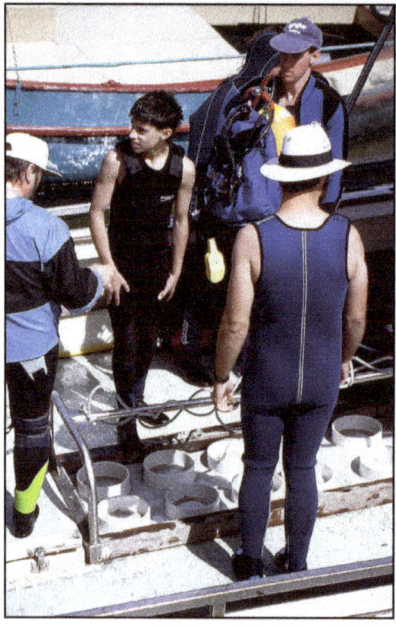

could have a photo taken with Peter.

"No worries, mate," Peter said. "Happy to do it." He grabbed Brian around the shoulders and gave me a thumbs up. I snapped a couple of shots then got Brian to take one of Peter with myself. Again, he was happy to oblige. Then we had to go and get Brian sorted on the Calypso in preparation for his first ocean dive. When I looked back, I couldn't see any sign of Peter. He had moved off somewhere else.

Passing equipment down. Each diver is responsible for the equipment they use on the dive.

— John Litchen —

Boat harbours like Queenscliff are always fascinating, and Queenscliff with its fortifications on the bluff overlooking the Heads and The Rip, has a history that goes back to the beginning of settlement in and around Port Phillip Bay. While Brian was getting dressed and getting onto his dive boat, the Calypso, I wandered about taking photos. Boats being repaired, boats in the water moored beside piers... I never get tired of looking at them and taking pictures. You could take several pictures of the same boats from the same spot and every time the picture would be different. The water moves, and consequently the boats move, and the light reflected from the water changes; it's endlessly fascinating. No wonder so many onlookers can always be found wandering about enjoying the activities on any day, but especially on a weekend's day.

The Calypso heading out.

On the Calypso

Once the divers were all on board, the Calypso made its way along the channel and out into Swan Bay. A short dive was done for beginners like Brian to familiarize themselves with the gear they were using. They went through the exercises of taking off their scuba unit and putting it on again, taking off their mask and putting it on again, blowing the water out of it to clear it, and other similar things. Once the instructors were happy the students knew what they were doing, they came back on board. The Calypso moved to the location for the start of the drift dive, and after a brief explanation of what they were to do and that they were to stay in pairs in a group where everyone could see each other, they went back in. The water here was clear so there would be no problem with visibility.

The tide was beginning to turn, which meant there was an outward drift of water that would carry them towards Port Phillip Heads. Buoys had been anchored at a spot well inside the Queenscliff side of the Heads and this was where the dive boat would be waiting to collect the divers who would drift along the bottom, allowing the current to carry them towards the pickup point.

The Calypso moved ahead in front of them and positioned itself in the location to catch them as they drifted along.

This dive lasted around forty minutes and Brian was one of the last ones up. He really enjoyed it.

Although I didn't go into the water, I had a great time taking photos of the divers getting ready, getting into the water and later returning to the boat.

Brian preparing to enter the water.

— Changing States —

Once everyone had gone over the side, the Calypso went to the pickup spot to wait for the divers to drift along to the buoy where they hung onto ropes while waiting to get back onto the dive boat. Brian, is in the middle of the group below, waiting their turn to get back onto the Calypso. Because there were two boats with our group, as well as other dive groups there, it seemed chaotic, but the dive masters had everything under control, and it all went smoothly without any mishaps. A great day was had by everyone involved.

Brian climbing back into the boat at the end of the dive. It's a lot harder getting out of the water than going in... There were two guys on the transom to help the divers back on board.

Peter Russell-Clarke

I had encountered Peter on the Don Lane Show which at that stage was running only once a week. He was a chef on the show and often presented outlandish methods of cooking ordinary food. I might remind readers that from time to time I was employed with the band on the show as a replacement for Garry Hyde the resident percussionist. When Garry couldn't make the show, he would often call me to fill in for him. On one of these occasions, Peter Russell-Clarke came onto the set driving a car. He then proceeded to joke around with Bert Newton and Don

Lane as he said he was going to show everyone how to cook steak and eggs with the car engine. The idea was that if they were driving around somewhere in the country and were hungry but couldn't find a place to cook, they could always pull over and use the car's engine.

He did it, with much hilarity. He opened the hood and proceeded to cook the steak and two eggs on top of the car engine which was obviously extremely hot. Whether he used a frying pan or laid the steak directly on top of the engine block, I couldn't see from where I was sitting with the orchestra. The live audience were enthralled. It didn't take long before he served Don and Bert the steak and eggs on a plate ready to eat.

He often appeared on the Don Lane show. Perhaps it was a stepping-stone that led him into having his own TV cooking show on the ABC, **Come and get it**. Or perhaps it was the other way around, and that short cooking show on the ABC is what gave him the notoriety to be asked to appear on the Don Lane Show. I'm not sure anymore. **Come and get it** was only five minutes long and geared towards kids to make them more conscious of eating good food, and how much fun it was to prepare and how quickly it could be done. This little cooking show ran for 900 episodes during the whole of the 1980s.

Brian watched it every night. It was on just before the evening news at 6pm. It inspired him to cook one of Peter's recipes, which he called the Peter Russell-Clarke egg. It was an egg fried with bread. The egg sat in a hole cut in the bread and they were fried together with melted tasty cheese on top. It was one of Brian's favorites for a while.

It could be said that Peter Russell-Clarke was Australia's first Celebrity Chef. He wasn't the first to have a cooking show on TV, that dubious honor goes to another chef who had a program on channel 7. Peter was the second chef to have his own show, and it is that show, **Come and get it,** that people still remember today more than forty years later.

I remember the controversy he caused when he cooked a steak with strawberries during the 1977 Silver Jubilee dinner for the Prince of Wales, (now King Charles 111) who was in Australia for a short visit to represent the Queen. The Silver Jubilee commemorated her 25th year since her coronation as Queen. People talked about it for a long time afterwards. No one did stuff like that back then. Now with celebrity chefs by the hundreds with shows on TV 24 hours a day, any and all imaginable food combinations are promoted, and some of them work very well. But I still remember it was Peter who first cooked fruit with meat in Australia.

Before he was a chef, Peter was an artist and a cartoonist. He drew cartoons for magazines and for companies to promote their products, and in 1969 he got the job of drawing the cartoon characters for the **Ben Bowyang** strip which appeared in the Herald newspaper every night. If anyone was suited to draw this strip, it would have to have been Peter. He was as much an *Aussie Larrikin* as the characters in the strip. He did this for ten years or more. He also illustrated children's books as well as writing many cookbooks. But it is probably as a chef that he is still remembered.

I hadn't seen or heard much about him for some years, apart from sometimes getting home early enough to catch his five-minute show on the ABC. It was a nice surprise to bump into him beside the harbor in Queenscliff.

Brian with Peter Russell-Clarke at Queenscliff.

— Changing States —

Although we'd only met a few times, (during his appearances on the Don Lane Show), and that was a long time ago, Peter was so friendly, and chatted so amicably you would have thought we'd known each other for years. I actually felt as if I'd been a mate of his forever. He had that way with people. No matter who you were, he made you feel that he was the best of mates, and that's a rare quality indeed.

Since Brian had finished his dive by early afternoon and everything was packed into the van ready for us to come home, I decided to have quick look at the Queenscliff Fort before returning home.

Fortifications

As the colonies in Port Phillip Bay became established a report was sent to England in 1858 about the possibility of defending the shipping in Port Phillip Bay. It was suggested that an iron plated floating fortress should be considered for protection of shipping since the ships were mostly owned by English companies. With the French actively exploring the southern Pacific, establishing colonies not far from Australia, as well as exploring the Australian coastline, the British needed to protect their investments. Floating defenses would principally be for protection of shipping. If foreign warships couldn't get into Port Phillip Bay, then the nascent colonies would be safe.

At first the fortification of the Heads was rejected, but this decision was later reversed and three 'sixty-eight pounders' were installed on the bluff at Queenscliff that overlooks the entrance to Port Phillip Bay. Forts built in shallow water alongside the main shipping channels were also built including a fortified artificial island near the South channel. Cannons were also placed around Williamstown at Point Gellibrand as well as overlooking Hobson's Bay in case foreign warships managed to get by the fortifications at the Heads. In 1854 HMS Nelson was converted into a steamship, one deck was removed, and the newest guns were installed. She took 170 days to sail from England to Australia where she anchored in Hobson's Bay.

As the Russians were becoming aggressive in Europe, fears they would attack the colony in Port Phillip (in 1870) added to the local paranoia, so another deck was removed from the Nelson and new '64 pounders' were installed. A twin propeller was added giving the ship a speed of 7 knots. Also in 1870 further fortifications were considered and a fort was built at Queenscliff as well as on the opposite side of the Heads at Point Nepean. Batteries of guns were installed, especially newly developed swivel guns which could cover the entrance to the harbor as well as Swan Bay and the start of both main channels. The South channel fort was built, and work was started on building Pope's Eye Shoal Fort to protect the West channel, but it was left unfinished once the channels were mined with electric controlled explosive devices that could be set off with the push of a button.

In 1892 a moat was constructed to surround the Queenscliff fort. *Who knows why?* Located on top of a flat hill overlooking the entrance and Swan Bay it seemed ridiculous to construct a moat like ancient castles in England once had. Perhaps because the fort on Swan Island was surrounded by water, as were the ones constructed on nearby shoals, they thought the fort on the hill also needed to be surrounded by water. The moat was later filled in. There were tunnels connecting the batteries built into the bluff (Shortland's Bluff) with the fort. With more modern improved guns, the forts took over the need for fortifications in the water. The fort had twenty-one-centimetre and twenty-five-centimetre guns as well as sixty pounders installed.

Paranoia often prevails, especially when people are cut off from their countrymen by huge oceans and enormous distances that took months to traverse. The fear of invasion by a foreign power, or of attacks by pirates if that's what you want to call them, resulted in massive amounts of fortifications being established which made Port Phillip Bay relatively safe, if not impregnable.

Inside the fort are lighthouses, the original telegraph station, and barracks accommodation for the infantryman who manned the fort. Underneath the surface are rooms where powder for the guns and the shells were stored.

The guns were never used at Fort Queenscliff, though one shot from Fort Nepean was fired across the bow of a German cargo ship exiting the Bay during the first World War. The captain had been unaware that War had been declared. He was going to continue on but the pilot on board convinced him that the next shot would destroy the ship, so he surrendered. During the 2nd World War after Pearl Harbour had been attacked it was decided that Port Phillip Bay fortifications were inadequate and that a squadron of fighter planes would be better protection.

The guns at Fort Queenscliff were removed in 1946. *

*For more information on Port Phillip Bay defences, refer to **Port Phillip Pilots and Defences** by Captain J Noble. (1973 – 9)

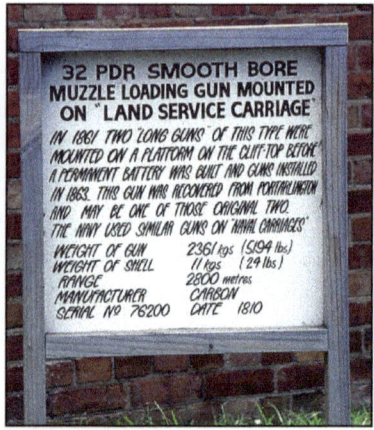

A small group of tourists looking at the smaller guns still on display on the other side of the lighthouse.

The Bay no longer needs the protection the fortifications once promised. Visitors are allowed to visit the fort, even though the Army still has a contingent there and it is used for training purposes. We were only there an hour before we had to go home, (Brian found it boring,) so I didn't get a chance to explore the underground parts of these fortifications but managed to get some photos of the place. I did intend to come back another time with Monica for a more leisurely look, but for reasons I can no longer remember, we never did.

Before driving up to the fort we stopped to have a look at the ferries coming and going. In previous years, you had to drive from Queenscliff, or anywhere on the Bellarine Peninsula back through Geelong and on to Melbourne then across Melbourne and out onto the Nepean Highway to take you to Portsea and Point Nepean, which is right across the heads on the opposite side to Queenscliff and Point Lonsdale. As the seagull flies, the distance across the heads is only 4 to 10 kilometres, but to drive there it was a round trip of almost 200 kilometres and took hours since one had to go around the Bay following the coastline to get to a point only a few kilometres away from where you started. Although expensive for the trip across from Queenscliff to Point Nepean and back, the time saved driving is well worth it. The ferries opened the areas around Port Phillip Bay Heads and brought an influx of tourists both local and from parts further away, which benefited the towns on both sides of the Bay near the Heads.

— *Changing States* —

The channel out is very close to the shore. Nobody swims in this area because of the dangers of the sudden drop into deep water, and the strong currents as the water goes out or comes in with the tide. It is not far from the Rip and there is an 8 knot current with the water moving very fast at the peak of the tidal movement.

Frigates at the Williamstown Naval Dockyards

This dockyard was one of Australia's main shipbuilding and refurbishment dockyards (under various names) from the 1870's onwards. During the Second World War it was requisitioned by the Commonwealth of Australia being named HM Naval Dockyard Williamstown, or more commonly Williamstown Naval Dockyard.

After the war and while I was growing up and later working in Williamstown, the dockyard was a major employer building survey vessels and fuel lighters during the 1980s. Two Frigates commenced building in 1988 and 1989, *HMAS Melbourne (FFG 05)* and *HMAS Newcastle (FFG 06)*.

There was something special about *HMAS Newcastle*. It was the first of the Adelaide-class guided missile frigates to be built at Williamstown for the Royal Australian Navy. It would join the peacekeeping forces to serve in the Persian Gulf. My recollection is that it also was sent to Fiji during the coup d'état in 2006. And it did eventually get sold to the Chilean Navy in April 2020 where it was renamed *Capitan Prat*.

She was laid down by Amecon (the private contractors building the frigates) on the 21st of July 1989 and was launched on the 21st February 1992, then commissioned into the Royal Australian Navy on the 11th of December 1993. Our previous Adelaide class frigates had been constructed in the United States, but Newcastle was the first to be built entirely in Australia, and it was at Williamstown, and that's why there was such a big fuss made of the launch.

I remember the launching of FFG 06. It was accompanied with great fanfare and huge crowds of locals turning up to watch. It was a hot summer's afternoon and as I headed towards Nelson Place, the streets were packed with cars and people walking along towards the dockyards. I had to turn off and go up as far as Cecil Street to find somewhere to park. By the time I got to the dockyard there were long shadows cast across the open areas which were jammed with so many people it was impossible to count them. I had never seen so many people packed together so tightly before. Who would have thought so many would be interested in watching a navy frigate being launched? A dais had been set up beneath the bow, and all the scaffolding and other stuff that surrounded it during its construction had been removed. Against the people crowded into every available space, the frigate looked enormous, towering above them. It was 138.1 metres long with a beam of 13.7 metres. That's 453 feet long with a beam of 45 feet. The keel of the ship would be fifteen feet or 4.5 metres below the waterline. Fully loaded it would displace 4,100 tons. Massive when you got up close to it. But I could get nowhere near it.

I thought it would be a good idea to take photos of the event for possible use in a later article and had driven past the dockyards a few times

It was unprecedented that people were allowed inside the dockyards where the ships were built, which is probably why so many turned up for this launch, apart from knowing it was the first of the Adelaide Class Frigates built entirely in Australia.

— John Litchen —

There was a loud cheer as FFG 06 slid down into the water it hit the water hard and fast, throwing up a wave that spread out across the harbour rocking the hundreds of boats moored there. It rapidly drifted towards the shipping channel but two tugboats were on station and they caught up to it and stopped it drifting further out, They towed it back to another pier further inside the dockyard where it would undergo internal fitting and weapons installation.

during its construction to see how it was progressing. It wasn't a secret site, but it was a construction site and no one who wasn't involved with it or who didn't work at the dockyards was allowed in, but anyone driving or walking past could see it.

Having a new 'press-pass' I approached the officials and asked to be allowed to go to the press gallery beside the dais where the traditional bottle of champagne would be smashed against the hull to initiate its launch, and which gave a great view of the proceedings. To get close shots of the launch from a privileged position would be fabulous. I was refused entry and told my pass was a fake pass and useless. To say I was pissed off would be an understatement, but there was nothing I could do.

I ended up in Commonwealth Park on the other side of Gem pier, well away from the dockyard piers. Everyone crowding the park got a

reasonable view from a distance as the frigate slid backwards down into the water, making a huge splash when it entered, producing a miniature tsunami that rocked the small boats and yachts anchored at nearby jetties. The frigate drifted quite a distance before two tugboats towed it back to another section of the dockyard hidden from view, where internal fitting out was completed. It would take another year for it to be completed and officially handed over to the Royal Australia Navy (Commissioned) on 11th December 1993.

I didn't write the article, but at least I got some photos of the event.
I never tried using that 'press card' again.

Tugboats stopping FFG 06 from drifting into the shipping lanes, and slowly bringing her back to where she will be docked for completion of the fit-out.

Beside the dock where the fit-out was to take place.

No one stopped me as I stood by the front gate of the dockyard to take photos of FFG 06 while under construction. It was an impressive sight to see, this towering ship, covered with scaffolding, surrounded by massive cranes with swarms of people working around it.

*Incidentally, another 10 frigates were built after that with the last being launched and commissioned in 2006.

It's all downhill

That's what everyone tells you after you turn forty. Now they tell you when you hit fifty or sixty. I never believed it for one second.

How you feel is how you think you feel. If you start thinking you are getting old, then more than likely you will start acting as if you are old, and the downhill slide begins… It's all in your mind.

All of us at times feel invincible, not consciously, perhaps not even sub-consciously, but the feeling is there, which is why young people do crazy things older and wiser folks would never contemplate. I never thought I was getting old at fifty-three. I was fitter and healthier than I was in my mid-thirties. But then unexpectedly something happens that is a shock, and the sub-conscious realization of 'invincibility' is shattered forever as reality intrudes.

I had started martial arts (Karate) at the age of forty-eight and mixed in with people half my age and younger. A couple of injuries decided me against continuing with Karate. In Chile I discovered Aikido, a martial art that can be both destructive, but also gentle. It's an art that people can practice from a young age to a very old age and was exactly what I needed. Again, in Chile all those we trained with were half my age and quite dynamic. Continuing with this training on our return to Melbourne, I found the group I trained with were much closer to my age, mostly in their forties, more relaxed and softer in their approach to practice, and that suited me.

Now whether the falling and rolling we do in aikido, or the fact that at work we often had to move and lift heavy equipment or carry heavy loads of clothing contributed to me having a hernia, or whether it was simply something that happened to a lot of men after a certain age, I don't know. But one Saturday morning after we'd finished and had locked up the shop, I felt an odd sensation at the base of my stomach, beside my right hip. It felt like there was a ball of gas trapped there. A strange feeling. Going to the toilet I discovered a protrusion of soft tissue about the size of a small egg. It was just below where my trouser belt sits, and just above the groin on my right side. It wasn't painful but it was squishy when I touched it.

This is not good, I thought.

I had no idea what it was.

But I immediately went around to see Dr John Silver, whose surgery was around the corner from us. John was a school friend from my later years at University High School and had recently moved to Williamstown where he took over a well-established general medical practice. I knew he would still be there, and that I would have no trouble getting to see him.

"You've got a hernia," he said the moment he saw it. "It's an inguinal hernia and you'll need surgery to fix it."

"Shit!" This was not something I was looking forward to.

It was the nail in the coffin of invincibility.

"Don't worry," John said. "It's easy to fix."

I had previously had a few reminders of the frailty of a human body, when I tried to open an old window at the factory that had been jammed shut for years, and pulled several muscles in my back that needed a physio therapist to fix, and during a hard karate session, the left calf muscle tore in half and the doctor who strapped it up said to let it heal by itself. I hobbled around for weeks with a walking stick until it healed, and during a later intense session testing for a provisional black belt, I was thrown onto the floor and finished with several cracked ribs, but none of those affected the subconscious sense of invincibility; they were accidents, and accidents happen to everyone. But this was something different. This was something broken inside which resulted in the hernia. This was the first sign that my body was aging, starting to fall apart.

At least that was what I was thinking as Dr John scribbled an official letter.

"See Howard and give him this letter." John said.

Howard was Dr Howard Parker, who as a boy lived practically next door to us in Douglas Parade. We went to school together as kids, but once he'd done his secondary school he went to university where he trained to be a doctor. He then went to England where he specialized in surgery involving men's urinary tract, prostate, hernias, and other problems. He had recently returned from England and had opened his specialist office in Newport.

"He's the best specialist surgeon that we have in Williamstown."

John picked up the phone and called his number. I couldn't hear what he was saying, but I was sure it concerned me because the only thing I heard was inguinal hernia.

"I've made an appointment for you on Monday morning."

I worried about it for the rest of the weekend and come Monday morning I was at Howard's office in Newport a minute after it opened. The receptionist took me straight in to Howard's examination room.

After an effusive greeting, we hadn't seen each other in some time, he got down to business. One look and a gentle examination of the squishy bulge was enough for him to confirm John's diagnosis of an inguinal hernia.

"You'll need an operation to fix that," he said. "And the sooner the better. Now that I've got you here, when was the last time you had your prostate examined?"

"Never."

"Well, I think it's time we did that."

He got me to pull down my pants while he put on a rubber surgical glove. Told me to bend over against the examination bed in his office while he put a lubricant on the glove."

"I'm going to stick my finger up your bum," he said. "Try and remain as relaxed as possible."

Not easy to do when you know someone is going to stick their finger up your arse.

I forced myself not to clench my buttocks as I felt him insert his finger.

"That's very good," he said.

It was a weird sensation as he moved his finger over and around my prostate gland. When he pulled his finger out it momentarily felt like I was having a shit.

"Everything is fine. No problems with your prostate. Have a wash in the bathroom."

He peeled the glove off and dropped it in a medical waste bin. While I was washing and redressing, he made a phone call and when I came and sat down in front of his desk, he smiled reassuringly.

"You have an inguinal hernia and need an operation as soon as possible. The longer you leave it the worse it will get. And there can be dire consequences. If the muscles surrounding the split which allows the intestine to protrude stiffen and lock, the material trapped in that part of the intestine will start to rot because it will be unable to move down the intestine as it should. This causes peritonitis. It also prevents material from moving through the intestine as it should. The whole lower intestine could start to rot and would have to be completely removed."

This was terrifying…

"You don't want that to happen."

I stared at him, lost for words as what he said sank in.

"It's a simple operation," Howard continued. "Takes about forty-five minutes, and you can go home the same day if we do it early in the morning."

"Okay, well, the sooner the better, I guess."

"Good. I've already booked you into the Williamstown Hospital for surgery tomorrow morning. It's the only day this week I am at Williamstown. I've put you in as a public patient, so it won't cost anything, but you must go to the Hospital tonight or late this afternoon to be checked in. They need to prep you for the surgery in the morning."

That was sooner than I had expected.

"I'll come around to see you there about 8 pm. I have one other patient who is also having a hernia fixed tomorrow morning, so you will be done right after him. Okay?"

And that was it. I went home and told Monica she would have to come with me to the hospital so she could bring the car back. She seemed freaked out at the idea of me unexpectedly going into hospital for an operation. After her experience of giving birth at the same hospital, she hated the thought of going there, or to any hospital. They were very good, it was only because she was 36 when Brian was born that she'd a had long and painful birth, not the fault of the hospital. The nurses, the midwife, and her doctor had looked after her with great care.

"I'll be fine. It's an easy operation, I'm told. You don't need to worry." But I was nervous which I didn't let Monica see. She was upset enough.

This would be the first time as an adult (at 53) that I was going into hospital for a medical procedure. I had been at the Williamstown Hospital when I was sixteen to have the little finger on my left-hand fixed after breaking it in multiple spots during athletics practice at school. I remember them using chloroform to put me under and how horribly sick I was after I'd woken up. I was not looking forward to it. When I mentioned this to Howard in his office, he just chuckled.

"We don't use that stuff anymore. That was in the dark ages. You won't feel a thing, and you will wake up without being sick or having severe headaches."

When he saw that I was skeptical, he added, "Trust me."

Nevertheless, I was nervous when I got to the hospital to check in. There were no problems, and I was taken to a ward with two beds. The other guy having a hernia operation in the morning was sitting up reading a newspaper. I was told to undress and put on the supplied hospital gown and that a nurse would be along soon to prep me.

It was a male nurse and he asked which side I was to be operated on and when I showed him, he took an electric razor and shaved off the hair on that side of my groin and lower stomach. No sooner had this guy finished when Howard and another doctor arrived. Howard introduced me to the anesthetist who got me to step on a set of scales so he could calculate the dosage he needed according to my body weight. While he did this Howard had a chat with his other patient. He then came over to me and made a mark with a *Texta* on the side where the cut was to be made. He put a circle around the hernia which wasn't protruding as much as it had two days earlier.

"Nothing for you to eat tonight, but you can drink a bit of water. You should have a good shower tonight, and another one when you wake early in the morning. We want you nice and clean before we start."

"No problems."

"Good, then we'll see you in the morning."

With that they left. I did as required, got back into bed thinking I wouldn't be able to sleep, being in a strange environment, but I actually slept well. I read a bit from a book I'd brought with me before falling asleep.

I woke with all the noise hospital staff make to wake up patients, had my shower, urinated heaps even though I'd hardly drank any water. I was nervous. They came and took the other guy away leaving me alone in the room. I took a sip of water and almost immediately had to go to the toilet again. Then they brought the other guy back and he was barely awake. With help from three nurses, he got back into bed and lay there on his back with his head propped up with several pillows. He started snoring.

"We'll be back for you in five minutes," one of the nurses said.

Another came over to me with a needle. "This is injection to relax you before the operation."

A few minutes later they came back with a wheelchair, and I sat on it without their help. They wheeled me off to the operating theatre where Howard, the anaesthetist and two other nurses waited.

"How are you feeling?" Howard asked.

"Not exactly looking forward to this."

He chuckled. "Of course."

The nurses got me to stand up and held my arms as I turned and sat on the edge of the operating table. The did the usual thing they all do repeatedly, they asked me my name and date of birth and confirmed that it was correct. I was given another injection. "This should make you feel drowsy," the nurse said.

Laying back on the table the other nurse inserted a cannula into a vein on my left arm. I watched her do it but felt nothing. She connected a small tap and a tube filled with a clear liquid to it. I was very relaxed by then.

Certainly more relaxed than I would have imagined considering I was about to be cut open.

"In a moment I am going to switch you off," the anesthetist said.

Switch me off… that was an odd expression.

"When you wake up it will all be over," Howard added.

"Are you ready?"

I thought they would ask me to count backwards from 10 like they had done years before when giving me chloroform that I had to breathe through a mask, but there was nothing like that. I was looking up at Howard and one of the nurses who were both smiling reassuringly.

"In five seconds," the anesthetist said. He reached towards the tap on the cannula. 'Three, two, one,"

And instantly everything went black. Like a light in a room had been switched off plunging it into darkness. Everything vanished instantaneously.

Someone was shaking my shoulder. I struggled to open my eyes. As my head cleared, I saw Howard smiling and looking down at me. "It's all done," he said. "You can probably go home this afternoon."

The nurses helped me to sit up. To swing my legs off the bed so I could stand up for them to help me into the wheelchair. I was very wobbly. I was numb and drowsy and didn't feel any pain. Once in the wheelchair they again asked for my name and birth date. Which I told them.

"You seem okay," the one who had asked said.

"You could have wheeled me back and left me in the bed to wake up later."

"We have to wake you up," Howard said, "to make sure nothing went wrong while you were unconscious."

"And?" I mumbled.

"It's all good. They'll put you back into the bed in the ward and I'll be around to see you later. You'll sleep for several hours which will help with the healing process. If you feel up to it later this afternoon, you can go home. But if you are still in pain when you move, then you can stay overnight and go home in the morning."

I was barely conscious as they took me back to the room and got me into the bed. I was asleep before my head hit the pillow, and the next thing I knew it was three in the afternoon and my mouth was so dry I thought it would crack if I tried to say anything. There was a bottle of water on the bedside set of drawers with a curved straw sticking out. I picked that up and sipped the water. It was heavenly. After lying there for an hour, I decided I had to go to the toilet but when I tried to sit up so I could get out of bed the pain was excruciating. I called the nurse, and she brought me a container to piss in. What a relief!

The guy in the other bed had woken up and he left in a wheelchair. He had decided he would go home.

Monica arrived around five o'clock ready to take me home, but it was too painful to stand up and go out to the car, so I decided to stay overnight.

Howard turned up around that time and I told him it was still very painful when I tried to move.

"That's fine. Stay overnight. You should be much better in the morning."

About an hour or so later I was able to get out of bed and walk very slowly to the toilet beside the room. I should be much better in the morning.

Meanwhile, Monica went home because she had to prepare something for Brian to eat for dinner. She came at nine o'clock the next morning, (Wednesday) and although it was painful getting into the car, I felt much better. I was glad to be going home.

At home I didn't do anything except sit in a straight-backed chair. I couldn't sit in a low lounge chair because getting back up was extremely painful. You don't realize how often you need to use stomach and associated muscles just to do a simple thing like standing up and walking. I could drop down slowly into a low chair, because I could support my weight as I lowered myself, but I couldn't get up again.

Another thing I discovered was never to laugh at anything after you'd had an operation for a hernia. I was feeling pretty good by the late afternoon; walking about without obvious pain as long I as went slowly. I could even go up and down the stairs from the ground floor to the fist floor. That evening I decided to watch TV with Brian and Monica. They sat in the low lounge chair while I sat on a straight-backed kitchen chair which was easier for me to stand up from. We were watching Seinfeld, and of course, Kramer did something ridiculously funny and I burst out laughing. We all did. But it was something I shouldn't have done. The pain was instantly frightening. I thought for sure the incision that Dr Parker had made, and so carefully stapled together (which made the incision look like it was zipped shut), had burst open.

"I can't watch this," I gasped through the intensity of the pain. "It'll kill me."

I stood up slowly and left the room where more laughter exploded from Brian who was thoroughly enjoying the show.

Concerned, Monica followed me out.

"*¿Estás bien?*"

"I'm okay, I can't watch anything funny because it hurts too much when I laugh."

She gave me a hug.

"Go back and watch the rest of it. I'm going downstairs to have a cup of tea."

The next day I was much better. In fact, the site of the incision was starting to get itchy, and the staples stuck out a bit because the swelling had gone down. It was a sign it was healing quickly, and that was good. I had no trouble moving about the house, and could even sit in the more comfortable lounge chairs. There was the occasional painful twinge to remind me to be careful when I stood up suddenly. It had to be slow and careful. I wouldn't be able to do anything strenuous or lift anything heavy either for a few weeks. I was told not to go back to Aikido training for at least twelve weeks, to make certain the incision was fully healed inside. On the coming Monday Dr Parker would remove the staples.

I was back at the shop on the Saturday morning but only sat by the register where I could give change to customers or write down orders left for cleaning.

Howard came in with his wife (Jenny) to pick up his dry cleaning and was surprised to see me there. It had been four days since he'd operated on me.

"You back already? How are you feeling?"

"Really good. Don't tell me any jokes though."

"You see," he said to his wife Jenny, "when you work for yourself you can't afford to take time off, even to be sick."

I got the impression that he was continuing a discussion that he and Jenny had been having at some earlier time. He smiled, and before taking their dry cleaning and leaving, he reminded me of our coming appointment.

He removed the staples on Monday. They were standing up as the flesh around the incision had shrunk back to a normal state. I was wondering if it would hurt as he took them out, and how he was going to do it. He did it with something that looked like a small screwdriver. He simply put the flat part underneath each staple and flipped it out.

I didn't even feel them come out. There were fourteen of them and he did it in a few seconds while he was talking to me to distract me form what he was doing. After it was done, he got me to do a couple of exercises that used the lower abdomen muscles.

"You're as good as gold," he said afterwards. "Just remember, nothing too strenuous for the next twelve weeks."

John Litchen

Bits and pieces

Zara's and Fred's 30th anniversary

In May 1993 we would be celebrating our 20th year of marriage. But Zara and Fred beat us by 10 years. They were married at the beginning of 1963 and were getting ready to celebrate their 30th anniversary.

As usual, they had a big party to celebrate. Being more extrovert than us, Zara and Fred often had big, sometimes even elaborate parties. A huge tent was set up in the backyard, a wooden floor laid over the grass for guests to dance on, a DJ with a gigantic sound system blasted the latest as well as the all-time hits for not only the guests but for the whole neighborhood to hear. George and Karin came down from Sydney for the celebration. George had been Fred's Best Man at the wedding. There would have been 200 people there including for the first time in years, all my brothers and sisters as well as one cousin, a good many Greek associates from Dad's side, as well as Zara's friends from the Ballet and the theatre. It gave Zara a chance to show off and be the centre of attention, and this time her reasons for doing so were genuine. It was her (and Fred's) special celebration. She had become interested in Belly Dancing around this time and hired a group of the girls she danced with to give a performance, which of course gave her the opportunity to join in and show off her ability as belly dancer.

Christine came down from Brisbane. Phillip came in from his acreage at Bacchus Marsh, and Paul and Lynne who were living in the family home in Yarraville, and Monica and I were there. We were the only ones apart from Zara and Fred who were still living in Williamstown. I thought it was a good opportunity to get us together for a photograph, since it had been many years when the last group shot was taken. There was a lot of dancing, lots of food consumed, some very fine wines and spirits lubricated everyone, and the party went on, after a series of speeches, well into the night.

Left to right: Phillip, Zara, Me, Christine and Paul. Below: Cousin Shirley (Bridget) and me. We are now in 2022 and not another group shot of us brothers and sisters has been taken mainly because we all live so far apart from each other. So, this shot will have to stand for all time, having captured a moment when we were all at our best as far as age and health was concerned.

Fred just getting started while his best man George Olah and Zara's Godfather Bill Mazouris Look on. Bill also participated in their wedding ceremony.

Nothing like a few drunken anecdotes to liven up the guests.

Fred with George going strong telling stories and remembering exciting moments.

Fred's brother Heinz and his wife Sibylle came over from Germany for the event and a couple of days after this party Fred invited us to a very expensive and very special Chinese restaurant in North Melbourne. There are only two of these restaurants in the world, and the other one, the main or original one is located in Beijing, China.

I drove the people mover, a Toyota Tarago, so Fred could be more relaxed during the evening.

Outside LILI's restaurant in North Melbourne, Me, Karin and George, Monica, Zara, Sibylle and Heinz. Fred is not in the picture because he was behind the camera taking it.

It was a sumptuous dinner, very exclusive which most of us enjoyed. Unfortunately for Monica, the plates served were mostly seafood, which she is allergic to and couldn't eat much at all. Sibylle also didn't feel too good after the meal because what was served were things she had never seen or even considered eating before. She felt sick afterwards but I think that was mainly psychosomatic brought on by unfamiliarity with the food served— like *beche de mer* or sea slug, a delicacy in Indonesia and China, and jellyfish, to name two, which I must admit gave me some difficulty as well being extremely slippery and hard to pick up with chopsticks. Monica had trouble using chopsticks, but she gave it a good try before asking for a fork. She only picked at a few things that were not sea food.

Karin, George, Fred and Zara, 'diving' in to the first course of fifteen plates. The asparagus in the plate in front was the only thing Monica took from this course. They also served abalone which Fred brought in for them to cook.

Below: before going in to sit at the table we had a drink together, Sibylle, George, Fred, me, Karin, Monica and Zara. Fred had also invited two friends of his from Singapore who joined us for this sumptuous meal. Heinz took this photo.

They brought out fifteen plates at a time, and each time twelve or thirteen of them would be sea-food, the other couple would be vegetables, or a rice dish, which were the only plates Monica took food from.

Big Balls

A few months later, May 19th, was our 20th anniversary and we didn't have a party. We celebrated quietly with a nice fancy dinner at an elegant restaurant in town.

Basically, it was an unremarkable year with nothing that really stood out or was worth remembering.

We did go to a charity ball just past the middle of the year with Zara and Fred, and Christine who also came down from Brisbane for the occasion. Monica and I weren't fond of these kinds of events and rarely went to them, but Zara and Fred were enthusiastic enough to convince us it would be good night, especially when he said he'd hired a stretch Limousine to take us there and to bring us home.

We met at their house in Cecil Street and were taken to the venue, at the Exhibition Centre in Carlton which was the only place big enough for four hundred people to be seated and still have room for dancing. We went in the stretch limousine that Fred had ordered. It was the first and only time Monica and I had been in such a vehicle. It was a rare experience to be seated in beautiful leather armchairs toasting each other with glasses of champagne while we drove from Williamstown to Carlton. The weather was threatening, and didn't seem very pleasant as we left, but at least it wasn't raining. It was cold though.

The ball was a huge success with luxury cars, cartons of rare wines, and heaps of other stuff being raffled off to raise funds. There was a huge popular band that played dance and rock music which echoed in the immense space of the Exhibition Buildings, so it didn't sound that great, and for me was not inspiring enough to want me to get up and dance. There were too many -people, and too much noise. You couldn't hear yourself talking and to have a conversation meant you had to be yelling at each other to be heard. Meanwhile, the weather outside had deteriorated. It had turned so bad you could hear the rain or possibly hailstones pounding on the roof far above us over the noise of the guests and the loud music.

A photographer went from table to table, group to group, taking photos of the guests. They would be ready within fifteen minutes of the Ball finishing and would be on display near one of the exits for people to see and buy on their way out. I got him to take a couple of Monica and me as well as one of me with Zara and Christine (my two sisters).

With Zara and Christine, my two sisters.

With Monica.

— *Changing States* —

The heavy rain and wild wind had diminished by the time people started to leave. What was left was a steady light rain washing over everything. Fred got onto his phone and called for the stretch limo to come and get us, and we went out near the entrance to wait for it.

There were people lined up and as a limo or taxi arrived, several would grab it and off it would go. It went on like this for a while, and the limo we were expecting didn't show, or perhaps another group had grabbed it before we realized it was there. There was a lot of confusion. After twenty minutes or so, the numbers of people waiting had gone to almost zero, and still were there. We waited a bit longer until it was obvious no more taxis or limos were coming.

Monica was shivering so I wrapped my jacket around her. I told Fred we would start walking down Exhibition Street into town, it was only a few blocks, and would find a taxi to take us back to Williamstown. Off we went, with Christine following us. Fred and Zara trailed along behind, with Fred still trying to call someone on his bulky mobile. Within a hundred metres we were thoroughly soaked. My shirt stuck to me, and with Melbourne's icy wind blowing I couldn't stop shivering. By the time we got into town and stood near the top of Bourke Street and Exhibition Street, we found a taxi and piled in gratefully.

Back at Fred and Zara's, after we dried off to a degree and had a couple of glasses of Cognac to warm up, we felt much better. We didn't stay though; we got into our car and drove home.

A costume ball

As the end of the year approached Fred again suggested we should go to a ball with them. I was reluctant but when Zara told Monica it was to be a fancy dress ball, she seemed enthusiastic and wanted to go. Fred Had hired a Merlin the Magician costume, and Zara dressed up as an elegant lady of the Court. Monica decided she would wear a pink kimono and looked quite Japanese once she had dressed. I decided I would wear my Aikido Gi with a formal Hakama. I also wrote some kanji wishing everyone a Happy New Year on a headband and wore that. It wasn't much of an effort, but I hated the idea of dressing up in elaborate costumes for something as boring as a ball. This Ball was sponsored by the Victorian Opera and was to raise funds for that institution. The Guest of Honour was the new Premier of Victoria, Jeff Kennett who was also a patron of the Victorian Opera. He had won the election from Joan Kirner who was the first, and so far the only, female premier of Victoria.

She had taken over the premiership from John Cain Jr and was premier from August 1990 until October 1992 when Jeff Kennett won the state election to become premier for the next seven years. He had been premier for just on a year when as Patron he attended the Ball for the State Opera that took place on new Year's Eve, 1993.

Zara looked good in her heavy velvety costume, Fred as Merlin, I thought, seemed a tad flamboyant, but then that suited his extroverted character. Premier Kennett and I made a good pair dressed in formal black and white, although, I thought when alongside Monica who was comfortable in her kimono, my wearing a Gi and Hakama was a cop out. I should have put more thought into what to wear, perhaps something more Samurai-like to match Monica's kimono.

A step sideways and a jump forwards into an unabashed advertisement

Joan Kirner and her husband Ron lived in Williamstown and had done so before she became a politician. They were customers in our dry-cleaning shop, as was her aide Steve Bracks, who later took over the leadership of the parliamentary Labour party in Victoria when Joan resigned as leader of the opposition having lost the election to Jeff Kennett.

Ron and I often had interesting chats at times when we weren't busy, if he happened to drop in. He had seen a couple of my short memoirs published in *Tirra Lirra* and suggested I should write a few more and maybe a book of them could be published. So too did Eva Windisch, the editor and publisher of *Tirra Lirra*, she said she would like to publish it if and when I had enough stories to fill a book.

Ron lent me a book he had by an American writer who had done just that, writing short memoirs about living in and growing up in a small, isolated community. I enjoyed the book, but it was very different to what I had been doing.

But I always kept in the back of my mind what Ron and Eva had suggested and so fifteen years later, once we'd settled down in our house in Robina, on the Southern Gold Coast, and had published several more pieces in *Tirra Lirra,* I added more stories; a few Mum used to tell us as well as a few more of my own recollections when we were growing up in Williamstown and Yarraville and did publish them as a book, ***Fragments that remain.*** It took fifteen years to come to fruition and this book is dedicated to Mum, with a lovely picture of her as a young woman on the back cover of the revised edition.

It wasn't the first book I produced after arriving on the Gold Coast. ***Fragments from A Life,*** which I did as a private special edition for family only, was the first. This was a fragmentary biography using the notes Dad had written of his life and which he gave to me, fleshed out with collective recollections of my brothers and sisters regarding Dad's life and the stories he told us when we were kids.

It was an experiment structurally since it jumped back and forth in time over the entirety of Dad's life, and was told from three different viewpoints; his first person narrative, close third person from our collective memories, and a few short bits of a distant third person point of view relating to historical moments that influenced Dad's early life.

Leather-bound with a gold embossed title it was a limited edition of 12 copies published in 1997.

The Fragments that Remain was completed and published in 2010 fifteen years after moving to the Gold Coast.

This first edition, published in 2010.

In 2020 after revising the original and correcting a few mistakes in the text, a revised edition was published with a new cover that I think better reflects Williamstown where I grew up for the first seven years, and later worked and lived, as well as gives more credit to Mum whose stories are told here as well as ours in which she largely is featured.

Now, (in 2022), this book forms an introduction to a sequence of six ongoing memoirs which follow my life and travels from when I left school at the end of 1957 up until the present day.

Only in the first of the six, **Ephemeron**, am I by myself, since it covers the 1960s, travelling to Darwin and working in the rice fields of Humpty Doo, travelling to Europe where I spent 18 months, and then later to Mexico where I spent 12 months and learnt a little bit of Spanish.

All of the other five are of my life with Monica whom I met in 1971. Our meeting is detailed in **Grab that Moment,** and the rest of our life together is covered in the subsequent volumes including this one. I can't imagine what my life would have been like without Monica. Although the harsh reality is now, after fifty years together, she has sadly passed away, and that it is exactly what I have to do.

Something to think about

I had mentioned to Monica as 1993 drew to a close that if she wanted to go back to Chile to visit her family again, there was enough money in the bank. Not enough for the two of us, but enough for her to take a trip.

She seemed taken aback.

"Its close on three years now" I reminded her. "You did say to everyone there you would come back in three years."

"But not by myself. I meant both of us."

"It's not possible for me to come this time. Phillip and I are still discussing whether to sell the business or not, and on top of that we can't seem to find a buyer. Not too many people want to be a dry cleaner, or would be interested in running that kind of business. It's hot, it's smelly with chemicals and stuff, and it is a specialized trade. It's hard to find a buyer. Besides, he's happy where he is and doesn't really want to sell it."

"I don't want to go by myself..."

It seemed that she lacked confidence.

Youthful enthusiasms disappear as you get older and more reluctant to do things you wouldn't have thought twice about twenty years earlier.

It is a long trip and takes a number of changes of planes at Sydney, and perhaps Auckland, but certainly in Tahiti if you use *Lan Chile*, unless you fly directly from Auckland to Buenos Aires, with *Aerolineas Argentinas*, as we did before together when coming home from our stay in Chile. And there would be another plane change in Buenos Aires to get to Santiago in Chile. It's a long flight however you do it, especially if you go direct from Auckland to Buenos Aires; eleven or twelve hours for that one stretch, with a couple of extra hours on the way back since the flight then is against the jet-stream.

"But you did it when you came to Australia back in 1970."

"I wasn't alone. I had Laura and Alicia with me. This time I would have no one. I'm not thirty anymore either, I'm fifty-three."

"Talk to Hernán next time he rings and see what he says. I'm sure he'd be happy to see you again. They all would."

We had been thinking of going next year but the way things were at the moment it didn't seem likely. It would have been good with just the two of us. Brian would be old enough to stay home and look after himself by then, so the two of us could really enjoy the holiday.

But since I couldn't go, I thought it would be good for Monica to go. She might not get the chance to see them all again. They were much older than she was, Hugo being fourteen years older, Hernán 12 years older and Max, about 9 years older. She was the baby of the family. Anything could happen and while she had the chance, another visit to see them would be good. She'd missed seeing her mother before she passed away, mainly because we couldn't afford to go there together at the time. I didn't want anything like that to happen again while there was a possibility that she could make the trip.

"I will think about it," she finally said. "I'll talk to Hernán next time he calls. I'll only go if I can stay with him and Max in their flat. I don't want to stay in a hotel."

A couple of months later just before Christmas she told me she had decided she would like to go and visit Chile again, but only if it was okay with Hernán and Max whom she would speak to on Christmas day.

Monica's trip diary 1994... Extracts

Sydney Airport March 25 1994.
I arrived here at 9:30 am. I'll continue to Buenos Aires where I'll stop in transit again before finally flying to Santiago where I'll be staying with Hernán and Max for about 6 weeks.

John told me last year about September or October that he had enough money in the bank for the fare if I wanted to go and visit my family on my own.

I wasn't very enthusiastic at the beginning, because I couldn't imagine travelling without John and Brian. He told me it would be a while before he could come with me, not until he could sell the business. Perhaps then we could go together, and Brian would be old enough to be left behind since he was not so fascinated with Chile.

Then I said I would think about it.

I would go only if I could stay with Hernán and Max. This I told him before Christmas.

On Christmas when I talked to Hernán and Max on the phone the matter came up and I asked them if I could stay with them. They seemed willing and happy, so I decided to fix the date for March, not the beginning, but towards the end which would include two weeks of school holidays over Easter for Brian which of the six weeks I'll be away only four would account for possible problems with Brian's school attendance and transport.

So here I am looking forward to this holiday, a little bit dopey for only a few hours sleep, but still enthusiastic. I got up at 4:30 to be at the airport by 6 in the morning.

Once again Monica kept a diary of her trip and activities in Chile but they mostly concerned visiting family and old friends, shopping and other activities. She started writing it in English but switched to Spanish after a few pages.

The reason I have included a few extracts here is that she had some health problems during this trip which I feel are relevant to how she was later once she was home.

Not mentioned in her diary but told to me afterwards was that she twisted or damaged her back lifting her luggage down from the overhead rack in the plane on the way from New Zealand to Buenos Aires. It reminded me of what had happened when we arrived at the *Ramada Hotel* on the Gold Coast when she tried to lift Brian's heavy bag out of the van and twisted her back. Those first few days were agonizing, but with the help of a chiropractor to realign her spine she was okay for the rest of our 10 day stay. Something similar must have happened on the flight, even though her hand luggage was no where near as heavy as Brian's bag had been, but reaching up, over-extending, and twisting as she took the bag from the overhead rack was enough to throw her spine out of alignment.

Her back wasn't that good when she left anyway. She had been doing aerobics at a local centre a short walk from our place and one of the exercises involved a stretch, sideways. The floor was very slippery and as she stretched her feet slid out from under her and she finished inadvertently doing the splits and falling back on her bum. She damaged the upper leg muscles and could barely walk for several days without a lot of pain. It must also have affected her pelvis and lower spine.

She was pissed off with the instructor because he took no notice of her and basically dismissed her complaint as not worth considering. He should have been watching all the students, especially the less experienced ones, and not making them do stuff the younger more flexible women could do. Monica was fifty-three so he barely took any notice of her. Happy to take her money in advance for the class, but didn't bother with her after that, leaving her to follow the others as best she could.

She never went back to those classes again.

> **Santiago**
> March 28, Monday.
> I got here at the scheduled time last Friday. Actually, the flight arrived ten minutes early, 8:40 instead of 8:50, a long tiring trip of 27 hours with the following stops: Sydney, 4 hours, New Zealand 1 hour, and Buenos Aires 2 hours.

It didn't take long to go through customs. Max and Hernán had arrived as I was going through. I waved at them from a distance.

Hernán was looking the same as he had three years ago, but Max had aged since the last time I saw him. He had a nasty version of some sort of ulcer on his upper lip which he called a *fuego*. He said it was Psoriasis. I hope it isn't Herpes or some other catchy thing.

Comments on April 7...
Monday was a bad day for my back which has been aching since March 7th after that aerobics class that included the slide, which caused me to do the splits and injure my groin and lower back. I never went back to aerobics after that. I had some details for a *Kinesiólogo* from Ximena and the father of Michele's boyfriend but couldn't make an appointment. So I looked in the phone book and found Clinica Echaurren where the receptionist told me the *Kinesiólogo* could see me that evening at 5;30 and that he would assess me and see whether I needed to see the Traumatólogo.

Jorge López, the *Kinesiólogo*, examined me and applied heat, infra-red rays, and gel, and told me I really needed to see the *Traumatólogo* which I did that same night. A nice guy, Dr Guilott. After examining me he said that he thought I had *lumbago doloroso* or something like that and it was due to tension of the muscles and blabla bla babble... He made an appointment for an X-ray to determine if I had a tumor, or a deformation, or a dislodged disc, etc. He really didn't know. But I had to be on a strict diet for the next day Tuesday.

On Wednesday I went to have my X-rays taken. I thought they were to be two, but they took 5, then three more. I suppose some didn't come out clear enough.

Later that day around 6 pm I went to see Dr Guilott for my results. He said the X-rays showed that my spine was all right, that it showed no damage, but my spine wasn't straight, and my pelvis is higher on the right than on the left, so John was right when he said I stand crooked. I wasn't surprised because of the fact that I always had to shorten slacks on one side and not the other. All this is weakening and putting stress on the muscles in the area. He gave me some tablets to take for 10 days and advised me to have some sessions with Jorge the Kinesiólogo. I had already decided I was going to do that.

Again, he applied heat with infra-red rays and gel and gave me exercises to add to the ones I was already doing.

*A **Kinesiólogo** in Chile is a health practitioner who deals with movement and functioning of the body's bones and muscles - a cross between a chiropractor and a physio therapist. A **Traumatólogo** deals with physical and psychological injuries.*

> I felt as lot better after that. The exercises and the tablets made a big difference.
> A few days later...
> I went to the *Kinesiólogo* and he said that I was progressing nicely. During his manipulation of my back he heard, and I felt a crack, and he said that was a sign that the misplacement of my spine and pelvis had been corrected. I hope that's true.
> He said that after twisting my spine that my flexibility was all right and that everything was falling into place.

From this point on the diary is all in Spanish since she was (alone) in Chile and Spanish is her language. But, once she came home, after a few days to recuperate, she wrote the last few pages of her account once again in English.

Some concerns

The rest of the holiday went really well for Monica. She was enjoying herself once her back had healed enough to not bother her. She did tell me when we spoke on her birthday by phone that Max had aged a lot since she'd last seen him three years earlier when we were there together.

Max had looked older than his two brothers back then. He was the youngest of her three brothers and was about eight years older than Monica. I remember him being as white as a sheet of writing paper, skinny enough to look scrawny, and he always dressed in black which made his paleness more intense. He mostly stayed up at night and slept during the day *(which Monica reported in her diary of her stay with them)*. If he went out during the day, as he did a few times when we were visiting together, people on public transport would defer to him as if he was a priest and often gave him their seat out of mistaken respect.

She was worried about him.

She worried about Brian too, thinking he was in many ways a lot like Max, especially with his sleeping habits. He always had trouble sleeping at night and would stay awake hours longer than he should have. And in the mornings it was difficult to get him up so he could get ready for school. He would dawdle and take far too long getting ready and when we tried to hurry him up he would get angry and say he was going as fast as he could. On top of that, he hated school anyway. There were no subjects he particularly liked, He didn't have any idea of what he might want to do as she got older, so choosing subjects suitable for an evolving career wasn't possible.

What made things worse in my view, was that the Federal Labour Government had initiated a program to give high school students a fortnightly sum of money to help towards things the students would need at school.

Most of the kids who applied for this allowance spent the money on cigarettes, alcohol and soft drugs, they didn't buy schoolbooks or pay for excursions or use if for travelling costs to get to and from school or whatever the money was supposed to be used for. And for those like Brian who had no idea of what they wanted in the future simply transferred across to receiving the dole and never bothered looking for any kind of work. "Why should we work?" They collectively said. "The government gives us enough to live on."

Yes, if they are living at home and their parents are the ones paying for their living. They don't pay rent, they don't buy any food. The money they got every fortnight went on the same shit they'd spent their allowance on while at school.

That soon became more difficult once the government realized how many were taking advantage of the system. But it was too late. The government had created a whole generation of people who would forever be dependent on welfare.

Fortunately, two of the weeks while Monica was in Chile coincided with the Easter school holidays so I didn't have to get Brian ready for school during those weeks. He wasn't too bad the other weeks she was away.

A long flight

It took just over ten hours to fly from Rio Gallegos in Argentina to Auckland in New Zealand. It was a short stop in transit, enough time to have a quick wash and comb her hair which made her feel better, then it was back onto another plane to fly to Sydney, another two and a half hours. In Sydney she had to join the queue of people checking onto ongoing flights and making sure her luggage was transferred so it could be collected in Melbourne. She was one of the last ones to be processed and had to rush to board the flight to Melbourne. As with us before, (in 1991) the luggage couldn't be addressed directly to Melbourne because Aerolineas Argentina's flight finished in Sydney, and it was Qantas' responsibility to get the luggage to Melbourne from there.

May 13th, Melbourne.

It was 9 pm when I arrived in Melbourne, and I had this thought in the back of my mind that maybe my suitcases wouldn't make it to Melbourne. So, when I got to the carousel and could see only one of my bags, I wasn't surprised. I asked one of the airport fellows if there was any more luggage coming and he said that was it. I told him one of my suitcases hadn't arrived and he said to go to luggage claims, a short distance away. I was pushing a trolley with my one suitcase and my hand luggage and when I got to baggage claims there were five other people there, also missing luggage. One of them was a little old Chilean lady who asked me to translate for her. It took a while before I got my chance After filling in the info on the form given to me, I tried to help the old lady. It was getting late, and I was worried that John would think that I hadn't arrived on that flight and would go home. It turned out I couldn't help the old lady much because she couldn't find her airline ticket which had the details of her luggage numbers, and she asked me when I went out to see if her daughter who was waiting could come in and help. So when I went outside, after hugging and kissing John, I found this lady's daughter who then went inside to help her mother.

I was so happy to see John who looked very smart wearing a blue shirt and a suede vest, but at the same time I was annoyed about the missing luggage. They told me it could be in Melbourne the next day, or if it was still in Santiago it could take several days before it turned up. They gave me a number to call the next day to see what the situation was. There was nothing else we could do so we went home.

It was 1:30 am when we finally got home, and Brian was in bed. I didn't see him until the next day at lunch when he came downstairs. He wasn't going to kiss me at first, but then changed his mind and gave me a hug and a kiss.

The suitcase was delivered the next day by a jolly little old lady in a mini truck full of suitcases. It had been in Sydney and not left in Santiago after all. I bet there would be a lot of relieved people that evening. I was relieved that they had found it and delivered it so quickly. And best of all, everything was in one piece, and nothing was missing.

On Monday, I went to the travel agent who had booked the flights for me to see what to do about a claim for medical expenses incurred as a result of the incident on the plane with the hand luggage. I had records of all the expenses as well as the X-rays of my back and spine. I had four weeks to lodge the claim and since my expenses were around $250, and the insurance would keep $50, I might get back $200 which would be okay, but these insurance companies are notorious for not paying claims, so we will have to wait and see.

May 14th.
Now I'm at the end of my account of a terrific holiday, *gracias Johncito*, I had such a good time, but sometimes I missed John badly and I worried about Brian. It was an anguish that invaded me at the most unexpected times.

Here I'm back home to enjoy John's company and Brian's also even if his is not so enjoyable at times. But regardless of my good and loving relationship with John, I still missed very much my family and friends back in Chile. Especially I miss Hernán and Max. It was so good to stay with them... so many reminiscences, laughing so much at times. Of course, there had been a few arguments with Max. I miss very much Christina, and Patricia and Cecilia. How I wish that I had at least one friend like them here in Melbourne.

Betty and Cheryl were good friends whose company I enjoyed but unfortunately, they don't live here anymore. I must not forget Gladys and Sonia, but even if they don't live here, I can communicate with them on the phone.

At the moment here in Melbourne I have no friends and my social life is almost nil, and I'm the only one to blame for it. I must reach out to other people even if I think some are not very responsive. I think one of the reasons I've isolated myself is because I cannot be bothered with entertaining which goes hand in hand with friendship and socializing. I'm not just talking about going to people's places for dinner or going out on other social events (even if I'm not very good at mixing at these events) but to invite people to our place. I must work on this.

So, John and I have isolated ourselves and since it is me who is affected by this, (and Brian also I'm sure) then it is up to me to do something about it.

I must come out of my shell.

In Santiago I seemed to be a different person. I don't know if it is only because I was on a holiday with my brothers and their families and my old friends to relate to, or because Santiago and Chile are where my roots are.

But I'm here, the place where I chose to live, where my husband and son and home are. I must not forget Chile, which is such a huge part of me, but it is here where the main part of my life is taking place.

A moment aside...

Monica left Chile when she was 30 years of age and spent the subsequent 51 years in Australia, 50 of them in Melbourne after her first year in Sydney. Of her two closest friends whom she encountered in that first year in Sydney, both who had immigrated to Australia from South America, Sonia and Gladys, Sonia who was Peruvian moved to Perth where she married and started a family, remaining there until she passed away, and Gladys stayed in Sydney for 30 years before moving to Melbourne to be near relatives who like her had migrated from Chile. We visited Sonia in Perth, and she came to visit us on the Gold Coast after we'd moved here. Gladys who moved to Melbourne about the time we left for the Gold Coast has kept in contact with us all these years.

The thing is, Monica never told me how she felt regarding her friends, because had I known, I would have encouraged her to get out and to meet more people. It didn't bother me so much being alone, but then I grew up here and knew lots of people in all walks of life even if only a very few would I call close friends. It might very well have been different had I stayed in Mexico or migrated to another country where a different language was spoken, but I didn't. I was always home, and comfortable. But it was Monica who struggled at times, out of her depth, but always she put on a brave face. She seemed so happy I never imagined that she missed her friends and family so much, or that she sometimes felt depressed because she had difficulty in making friends here. It was sad to read those last diary entries.

She made me very happy, and I miss her terribly now that she has passed away.

A special night out

She returned from Chile second week of May, having missed our wedding anniversary as well as our birthdays. But she was back in time for Brian's eighteenth birthday which was on the 2nd of June. We took him for a special night out at Dracula's theatre restaurant/cabaret.

We went in a small group with Zara and Fred, David and Dione, (*Brian's cousins*), and Paul, my youngest brother.

David and Dione had gone to school with the children of the owners of Dracula's, and of course Monica and me. The Newmans, who had both worked in theatre at the Tivoli and The Lido, knew Zara who had worked as a show girl and dancer at both those places. They also knew me because they lived in Williamstown and were customers at our Dry cleaning shop, so they made sure we had a memorable night.

Dracula's was a family venture with the children performing in the shows while the parents mostly managed the business rather than performing. The show was spectacular, very funny and extremely entertaining. The place was packed every night and there were long waiting lists of people wanting to see the show and enjoy a dinner with a difference.

We were lucky to have obtained a table on such short notice.

Brian in the kitchen at Zara's and Fred's place the day after the night out at Dracula's.

— Changing States —

Lynette and David, Dione and Zara, Brian with me behind, Paul and Fred. Monica is sitting down next to one of the characters from the show.

Part Two

Easter Island, Isla de Pascua,

Ile de Paque, Paasch Eyland,

Rapa Nui.

A spur of the moment decision

I have mentioned elsewhere that there are times when an opportunity arrives that is unexpected, and you should *grab that moment* and *run with it*.

This was one of those moments.

Monica had returned from her six weeks trip to Chile to revisit her family and we had settled back into our normal daily routines for a few months when I saw an advertisement in the newspaper about *Air New Zealand* opening a route to Chile via Tahiti and Easter Island in conjunction with *Lan Chile*, Chile's national airline. In order to get people interested in flying this route, *Lan Chile* had created a special fare to encourage people to visit Easter Island from Australia. It was $1700 return from Melbourne or Sydney. Normally it would have cost much more, since Easter Island is such an isolated destination.

Easter Island is a Chilean territory and Monica and her two companions had stopped there briefly on her original flight to Australia in 1970. They didn't need to go through Customs because it was Chilean territory and while the plane stayed there for two or three hours, the passengers had an opportunity to exit the airport and make a brief visit to see a couple of the Moai that are close to the only town on the island, Hanga Roa, which was a five minute drive from the airport.

She didn't object to me making this trip, she encouraged it.

It would only be a short trip, I would be there for ten days before coming back.

It was a place that had interested me, especially after reading Thor Heyerdahl's book ***Aku Aku***, on his discoveries and adventures on the island, but that had been many years ago, and the idea of ever going there never materialized. It was a place I never thought I would see.

I had almost forgotten that it existed until I saw the ad in the paper for a special return trip there.

It was an opportunity not to be missed so I grabbed the phone and made a return booking...

— Changing States —

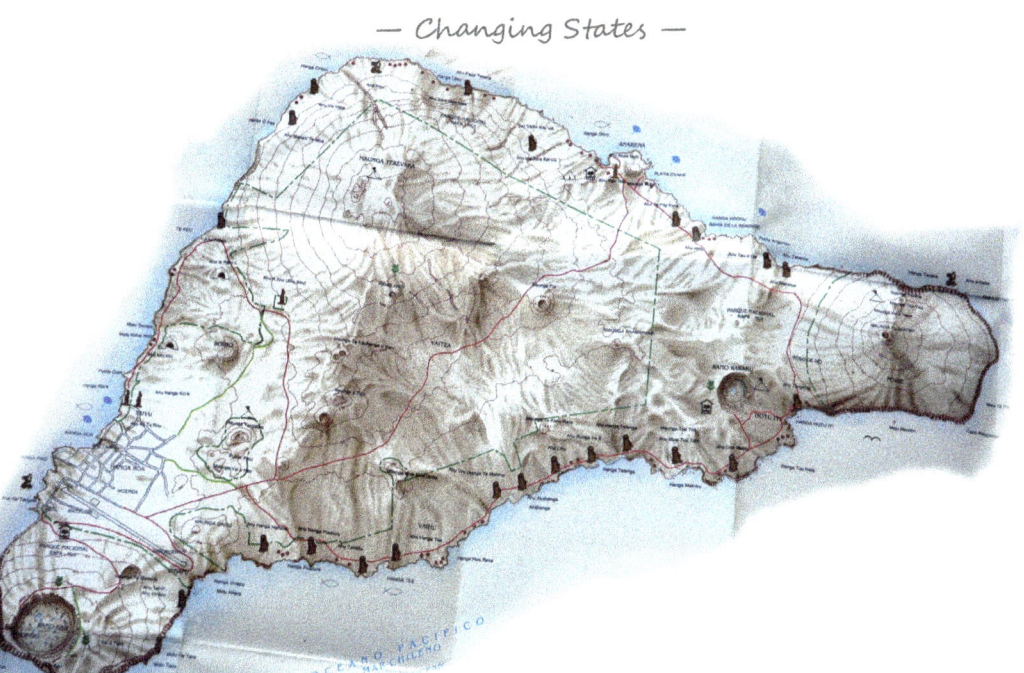

Hard to get my head around...

It's difficult to imagine how isolated Easter Island is unless you go there — six or more hours flying from Tahiti in the dark across a vast empty ocean in search of a tiny speck of land.

I had left Melbourne at 9 am on a Thursday, flown to Sydney and changed planes to go on the New Zealand. An hour or two in the transit lounge at Auckland and then onto a flight to Tahiti which arrived at 11:30 pm my time but early in the morning their time of the day before since the plane had crossed the International Date Line somewhere between Auckland and Tahiti. There were a couple of hours in the transit lounge in Tahiti where I had to go through Customs entry and exit and take my luggage to another check in before boarding the Lan Chile flight from Tahiti to Santiago which stopped at Easter Island on the way. After flying all day and on into the night, more than fourteen hours in the air not counting transit stops, I would arrive in the morning of Thursday, the same day I had left only an hour later than the time I had departed. I had gained a day, which was hard to get my head around.

What if the plane couldn't land and had to go on to Chile another five hours away? Or back to Tahiti? There is nowhere else it could go. Did it carry enough fuel? What if we had to ditch?

I knew when I started having those thoughts that I was over tired. I can't sleep comfortably on long flights and usually stay awake with gritty eyes, and by the time I get where I am going, I am feeling totally exhausted.

We were flying into daytime towards the east and as the sky rapidly brightened, I looked down at an impossibly far away ocean that looked as if it was frozen with microscopic ripples. A slight sinking feeling in my stomach indicated the plane starting its long descent.

I looked out the small oval window into the distance. There was no division between the sea and the sky. Other people in the plane were waking up and moving along the aisle to the toilets or simply standing up to stretch cramped legs.

Ping! The seatbelt light came on and everyone moved back into their seats.

The plane banked, and far down I caught a glimpse of green outlined with a thin white line where waves smashed against a black rocky shore. Then it disappeared as the pilots positioned the plane for landing and again all I could see was an endless expanse of deep blue ocean.

I was relieved. The pilots had found it! One tiny spot in the middle of a vast empty ocean. Very soon I would be walking on that little speck of land in the middle of nowhere.

The tip of a giant mountain

The glimpse of green I had seen was nothing more than the tip of a giant mountain extending three thousand metres from an unstable crust at the bottom of the ocean.

Many millions of years ago the Nasca and the Antarctic Plates nudged the Pacific Rise and the Earth's crust split open.

This new hot spot was part of a ridge of sub-sea mounts and active volcanoes extending for thousands of kilometres across the sea floor towards the coast of South America. At first the weight of the whole ocean above prevented the lava from flowing, but even the mighty ocean could not stop the Earth from venting its internal pressure.

Molten lava forced the crack wider, vomiting out in sluggish glowing waves across the sea floor only to cool rapidly and solidify in water that could not boil because of the intense downwards pressure of the ocean above.

For centuries it continued flowing over and beyond that which had solidified. Another crack appeared many kilometres further along the ridge and more lava flowed across the ocean floor. When the two lava flows joined, a third crack opened. Fresh lava oozed out between the two main erupting points to form a huge trapezoidal base 130km x 90km x 60km x 100 km.

Upon this base a mountain grew.

Three million years ago the first part of this mountain (*Poike*) was thrust above the surface of the ocean, and the black lava that was to become known as Easter Island was exposed to the sun, the wind and the battering waves of the Pacific.

It did not rise too high above the waves before it stopped. Over the next half a million years this tiny island rumbled and spewed small amounts of lava until finally the larger second volcano (*Rano-Kau*) burst forth boiling the ocean surface. It threw mountains of steam and gas into the atmosphere. This joyful reunion caused the first volcano to come to life again and the twin lava flows joined. Parts of the island split. Vents and fumaroles opened. More than seventy volcanic cones grew, the biggest of these (*Terevaka*) forming the third volcano that gives Easter Island its triangular shape. One other small volcano, (*Rano-Raraku*) though its parent was *Terevaka*, grew beside *Poike*. This cinder cone exploded to form a crater of more porous material and it was here, once the island was inhabited, where the quarry for the great stone carvings was located.

At the other end of the island *Rano-Kau* also exploded, leaving a crater 1.5 km across. *Terevaka* is the youngest and the highest mount on the island even if it is only 510 metres above sea level. Its last eruption was a mere 12,000 years ago. Since that time the island has been geologically quiet.

The more porous volcanic tuff weathered by rain and the effects of the heating and cooling from the sun broke up and formed soil. Wind-borne grass seeds took root. Birds came from South America and other Pacific islands. They deposited guano and the seeds of trees and palms and in time the island was forested. Some birds stayed; others maintained their migratory habits. The island became a small paradise until the arrival of Humans changed it forever.

The navel of the world - Te Pito o Te henua

Easter Island is the most remote inhabited island in the world. Nothing but the vast Pacific Ocean surrounds it. 3700 kilometres to the East is Chile, the long thin edge of South America. Mangareva at the bottom end of Polynesia is 2300 kilometres northwest, and due west is Pitcairn, an even tinier inhabited speck of land 1900 kilometres away, famous because of the mutiny on the Bounty. There is nothing South of Rapa Nui except the frozen continent, Antarctica.

Yet people found this extremely remote island, perhaps not once but two or more times, which speaks volumes for those early seafarers and their ability to travel over vast distances of empty ocean. Once they came, they never left.

According to the oral history of the island, Hotu Matu'a came from the East and landed at Anakena, the only place on the island where there is a white sandy beach. These were the long ears. The short ears were part of another group that came later, from the West. Inevitably these two groups would fight each other until, just before the Europeans' arrival, most of the long ears were eliminated by the short ears in a huge battle that took place near Poike.

It was suggested by Thor Heyerdahl that Hotua Matu'a came from Peru, and he cites the similarity of stone walls and the styles of carving on some of the stone figures as obvious evidence. The existence of words similar to those used by tribal Indians in Peru, as well as vegetables found in South America but not in Polynesia is claimed as further evidence to prove his theory that people also migrated into the Pacific from the west of South America, moving westwards eventually meeting people from Polynesia who were moving Eastwards. He maintains there was a second wave of people from Polynesia who also found Easter Island as Europeans call it. There may even have been some travel back to Polynesia from Easter Island during the early days of colonization. Modern Archaeologists dispute Heyerdahl's theories, but there is still enough mystery to allow Heyerdahl some credence.

When Hotu Matu'a and his people arrived, they found forests of giant palms and an abundant bird life. Sunflowers grew in clumps with tall grass across the volcanic steppes, and Totora reeds had been growing in the crater of Ranu Raraku for 30,000 years. Toromiro, a stunted tree unique to Easter Island, grew inside the craters of several smaller volcanoes. They built small canoes from the reeds of Ranu Raraku, and large sea going canoes from the trunks of the giant palms, similar to the Chilean wine palm, that grew in clumps all over the island. They fished for tuna and porpoise.

They lived well. Huts were built with oval stone bases covered by a wooden framework thatched with bundles of grass. The vegetables they had brought with them to the island, *Camote, Manioca, Uhi, Kumara*, all similar to sweet potatoes, and *Pukapuka*, a kind of banana, grew well in the shallow but rich soil of the island. The chickens that came with them flourished, as did two species of small lizard said to have been stowaways on the canoes that brought Hotua Matu'a and his people.

Happy in their isolation, they called their island Te Pito O Te Henua, The Navel of the World.

They did not call it Rapa Nui until much later.

As the population increased, more and more of the island's resources were used. When new arrivals came, battles were fought over territory. Once this had been established, there was peace, at least until the population grew to such an extent that it could not be supported by the resources of the island.

Rapa Nui is a small island, only 120 square kilometres. It is twelve kilometres across at the widest point by about twenty-five kilometres long. Once the population reached over 6000 resources started to run out. Birds disappeared; fish became scarce. There were not the tropical reefs around the island to support large populations of fish, and without trees to build sea going canoes, pelagic fish could not be hunted. Intense gardening couldn't supply enough food for such large numbers, so the people descended into savage warfare and cannibalism.

Everything stopped while they fought and killed each other. No more Ahu were constructed, no more Moai were carved, and those in progress, some of the biggest carvings ever made, were left still attached to the bedrock in the quarry at Rano Raraku.

People hid in caves. The island is riddled with lava tubes and caves. The population fell to about 2000 which was all the island could sustain. It was at this point in the history of Rapa Nui that Europeans discovered the island.

First contact

Late in the afternoon on April the 5th 1722 three Dutch ships commanded by Admiral Jacob Roggeveen arrived. Because it was the Easter weekend Roggeveen named the island *Paasch Eyland*. It appeared to be a low barren sandy island, but the sight of smoke told him it was inhabited. Unwilling to attempt a landing on a completely unknown coast so late in the day they spent the night hove-to several kilometres offshore. During the night the weather deteriorated so they did not attempt a landing the next day either. By the morning of the following day the weather had calmed, and a single islander paddled out in a canoe to meet them.

The ships followed the canoe and anchored near Anakena. 114 Dutchmen went ashore and lined up in a military formation. Hundreds of Islanders appeared. Perhaps the Europeans were nervous at the sight of so many naked fierce looking warriors, so as a show of strength, the sailors were ordered to fire their muskets. A dozen people fell dead, and many were wounded. The natives quickly dispersed taking the injured and dead with them. The Europeans were left alone.

First contact had been made.

The Dutch reported in their log that they had been baffled by the giant Moai and could only conclude that they were of religious significance.

It would be 47 years before another European expedition arrived. Gonzalo de Haedo claimed the island for the king of Spain and renamed it *Isla San Carlos*. With much pomp and ceremony, the Spanish came ashore and marched to the top of the nearest hill where they erected three large crosses. The priests sang litanies and the sailors carried colorful banners and Spanish flags. From the top of the hill they fired three volleys from their muskets. The ships anchored in the bay near Anakena answered with a twenty-one-gun salute.

A mere four years after the Spanish had left Captain Cook anchored at Hanga Roa Otai, still on many maps as Bahia de Cook. He noted the resemblance of the people to other Polynesians. He had already explored much of the Pacific. He even had with him a man from Bora Bora who could almost understand the islander's language. He noted that many of the Moai had been toppled over as if deliberately destroyed and correctly concluded that a war between factions on the island had been the cause of the destruction.

Final disaster

It would be 88 years before the final disaster when Slavers arrived from Peru.

They forced people to sign papers giving Easter Island to them. They tricked all the able-bodied men and women they could find to board their ships for a ride around the island, then took them to Peru to work in the guano mines along the South American coast.

At the start of the voyage when the people realized they were not going be put back on Rapa Nui, they started to jump overboard, to swim back to their island. The Spanish chained them below decks to prevent any more losses.

In the harsh climate along the coast of Peru the islanders suffered severely from homesickness and malnutrition, they died from measles and smallpox. Missionaries were sent to Easter Island to convert the remaining people to Christianity. The whole population was baptized. Tattooing was forbidden, and European clothes had to be worn. Within a few years measles, influenza and malnutrition had reduced the islanders to a few hundred people living in wretched conditions.

Chile annexed the island in 1888 after winning a war against Bolivia and Peru. They didn't colonize but leased the island to a businessman from Valparaiso who grazed sheep there. He later sold his interests to a Scottish consortium known as Williamson Balfour and Company which ruled the island with an iron hand. Many of the workers married islanders and the population began to diversify genetically. Due to harsh treatment by the company the workers staged a revolt in 1914 which was put down by the Chilean navy.

In 1953 the Chilean government revoked the lease given to the English and took control of the island.

Though it encourages some migration from the mainland the government restricts population growth and development to the area around the village of Hanga Roa where about 2000 people now live.

The rest of the island is designated as an archaeological park.

Touchdown

As the plane came down to land, I caught a glimpse of the crater of a large volcano. Light sparkled off the water in the crater. Then we were past it, the wheels bumped, and the plane settled smoothly onto the runway. The engines reversed with a roar and the plane slowed rapidly. Everyone relaxed. We had arrived.

Stepping out of the plane I could see low grassy hills rolling away from the long runway. Only a few years earlier it had been lengthened with the help of the US Government and NASA. It is now long enough to take an emergency landing of the Space Shuttle if that ever becomes necessary.

It was good to stretch my legs after the cramped flight from Tahiti, and the short walk across the tarmac to the moribund terminal building was a pleasure. Most of the people on the plane headed for the transit

section of the building. Only a few followed me into the incoming passenger terminal. Going through Customs was a breeze. I only had a camera bag and one small overnighter slung over my shoulder. A perfunctory glance, a quick stamp in my passport, and I was through, stepping out onto a wide veranda bordered by a dusty car park.

Several local people approached me and asked if I had somewhere to stay. When I said not yet they offered me a room at their house or residencia. Prices were quoted and I selected *El Tauke*, a place I remembered reading about in Lonely Planet's **Guide to Chile and Easter Island**.

There are hardly any hotels on Easter Island so most accommodation is in extra rooms people have added to their homes. Breakfast is taken with the host family. Other meals too, if you want, but it is better to eat in the many little cafes at a time that suits you rather than eating at fixed times. I don't keep regular hours for meals, so bed and breakfast suited me.

Hanga Roa is less than two kilometres from the airport, so it didn't take long to be ferried to my room at *Residencial Tauke*. I took a few moments to freshen up and change the clothes I had slept in while travelling from Australia. Although tired I didn't want to go to sleep and wake up sometime in the middle of the night. I would stay awake until it got dark then go to bed and that way when I woke up the next day my body clock would be back to normal.

For me it was still the same morning as it had been twenty hours earlier when I had left Melbourne, yet I had been flying all day and all night. I always found it hard to believe that crossing the *International Date Line* would give me an extra day going eastwards and that I would lose it when I went westwards to get back home.

I left my cameras in the room, locked the door and went for a walk.

It was warm and sultry, so I headed downhill towards the water. The road was dusty but paved, one of only two paved roads in the town. All the other roads are dirt tracks. The vegetation by the roadside was lush and green, sub-tropical and redolent with the scent of frangipani and bananas. There were no shops like anything familiar, but a number of homes had verandas and large doors open to a space that was filled with stuff for sale and I saw groups of people chatting and looking at things. Other places had what at home would be a garage, which was used as a shop since there were very few cars on this island. Signs painted on the side and above the open door indicated what was being sold.

There are only two streets in Hanga Roa that are paved with cobblestones cut from red scoria; the main street through the town as you come from the airport, and the road that goes from the church on the hill down to the harbour. It forms a T-junction with the main road. Every other road is nothing more than a graded track often with red scoria as a base.

Every person I passed said *Hola* or *Buenas Tardes* and would readily fall into conversation if I hesitated. I asked about places I could walk to from Hanga Roa and was directed to a site, Ahu Tahai, about a kilometre along the coast from the tiny fishing harbour that was protected by a groyne from big waves that rolled in from the Pacific. I could see several Moai silhouetted against the late afternoon sky.

I could smell warm salty air as I got closer to the water where a few fishing boats had tied up. Several men were unloading yellow-fin tuna.

*The small boat harbour at Hanga Roa. It is the only boat harbour and only for small boats. Larger vessels visiting have to anchor offshore, and goods and passengers or tourists are ferried to this harbour. A short walk along the foreshore in the direction the horse rider in the above photo is going will take you to Ahu Tahai, which is the closest example of **Moai** to the only town on the island (Hanga Roa).*

— Changing States —

*It is a beautiful and serene location. It is clear to see here that the **Moai** have their backs to the sea, and are looking inland towards the centre of the island. Every one of them, all around the island does the same. Their backs are to the sea as they gaze inland. I think, because of this, whenever you get close to see them in detail, there is this incredible feeling of loneliness when you look past them at the sea and know that it extends for thousands of kilometres in every direction away from Rapa Nui, and there is absolutely nothing there. No wonder the people turned inward and the **Moai** reflect this.*
Because of their proximity to Hanga Roa, a short walk of about thirty minutes, Ahu Tahai is probably the most visited and photographed site for people who are stopping over one day while in transit.

A pleasant encounter

As I strolled towards the *Moai* in the distance I found myself accompanied by an old lady who was walking to the cemetery which I had to pass on the way. She wanted to know where I came from, what I thought of *Rapa Nui*, where I was staying. I told her I had just arrived, and already I loved the place. She beamed happily. When I told her I was staying at *Residencial Tauke*, she said the owner was a friend of hers. His wife had died last year. She was *Rapa Nui** and was buried here in the cemetery. She offered to show me her grave.

The cemetery is on a bluff overlooking the great ocean in the direction of the setting sun. It was full of white and red flowers which stood out against the deep green of the cut grass around each grave. I could see it was a place looked after with love and affection. The old lady showed me the grave she had mentioned and gave me a flower to place there. After I had done that, she thanked me then wandered off to do whatever it was she had come to do.

At Ahu Tahai there is one group of five Moai on the nearest bluff and two other Moai on separate Ahu on the further adjoining bluff. Between the two groups there is an ancient stone harbour with a stone boat ramp leading down to a narrow channel that twists and winds between jagged black rocks that just stick up enough out of the water to break the force of the waves. It looked a very dangerous place to bring in a small boat. But it must have been used at one stage or it would never have been built. I imagined that only someone who knew it well would have dared to bring a canoe through that twisting channel to the stone ramp.

Ahu Tahai, because of its proximity to Hanga Roa, is one of the most photographed archaeological sites on the island. It was Restored by archaeologist William Mulloy who first came to Easter Island with the Norwegian expedition led by Thor Heyerdahl. I was quite excited to see up close some of the actual statues I had only previously seen in photographs. I wished I had brought my camera with me on this first walk. But then I thought, if I had done that, the old lady would not have spoken to me assuming I was a tourist in transit. I would come back tomorrow to take photos.

** **Rapa Nui** is the name they use for Easter Island, It is also the name used to refer to inhabitants born here of ancestry that can be traced back orally, it is also, as one word, **Rapnui** the name of the language spoken amongst themselves. For outsiders, ie visitors and people from Chile, the locals use Spanish.*

— *Changing States* —

As I was examining the remains of an oval shaped *Hare Paenga* or stone house, a minibus arrived, and several American tourists hopped out.

Festooned with compact cameras, they scrambled all over the site taking as many pictures as they could before the guide called them to get back into the bus so he could take them somewhere else. Because of the way the flights connected between Chile and Tahiti via Easter Island, they only had a day and a half, and it was a scramble to see all they could in that time. I was happy I had another ten days to go, so I could take my time.

Looking past Ahu Tahai towards Hanga Roa the edge of which can be seen in the left hand corner of the picture above.

*Right; the best looking fully restored **Moai** at Ahu Tahai. Those eyes really bring it to life, and as you walk around you can't help feeling it staring at you.*
*What is surprising is that each individual **Moai** has a unique face. Though they look similar or even the same from a distance, up close each is an individual with a different face.*

— Changing States —

I walked back from Ahu Tahai to Hanga Roa passing many people on horseback. People on motorbikes rode by at a leisurely pace, with sometimes as many as three people on the one bike.

Nobody went fast. Twenty-five kilometres per hour was the speed limit in town, and you had to stop at every corner before proceeding.

Out of town the roads were so rough you would be lucky to get to twenty-five kilometres per hour before having to slow down to negotiate deep ditches or sharp rocks.

Too elegant and too expensive for me

That evening I had dinner in an elegant restaurant which was part of a residencial catering to tourists with money. By local standards it was an expensive place. I was the only customer and the meal had been specially prepared for me. I had met the proprietor, Raul, earlier that afternoon as I walked along the main street. He was cutting a clump of bananas from a tree growing in his garden. Seeing that I was a stranger in town he called out to me, and we started a conversation. When he found I had recently arrived he asked where I was going to eat that night.

"*No se. Todavia no he pensado en eso,*" I told him.

"*¿Que te gustaria comer?* What do you like to eat?" he asked. "Meat, Chicken, Fresh fish."

I thought about it for a moment. This was an island, so the fish should be fresh. I remembered the Yellowfin Tuna I had seen down by the pier.

"What about Tuna?"

"Ah, an excellent choice. I can cook the best tuna you will ever taste. I do it with a local sauce so you can try true *Rapa Nui* food."

"Sounds good."

"What time do you want to eat?"

It was only three in the afternoon, but it felt like midday. I never think about the evening meal so early. I'm a late eater. But I didn't want to put him off, so I asked if 6 pm was not too early.

"Perfect." He beamed. "I will have everything ready."

At 6 pm the sun was still very high in the sky, and I didn't feel the least bit hungry, but I had made an appointment, so there I was at the restaurant, and there was no one there. The place was open, and all the tables inside had white linen tablecloths over them. Only one table was set with two wine glasses, a basket of fresh bread rolls with a small tub of butter, bread plate and cutlery. In the centre of the table was a small vase filled with sweet smelling frangipani flowers.

Raul came rushing from the kitchen.

"Sit down please." He gestured to the set table.

"Is no one else eating here?"

"No. It is very quiet. No tourists come this time of year."

And that was the reason I was there. I had seen in the paper that *Lan Chile*, in collaboration with *Air New Zealand*, was running a special off-season promotion to encourage people to holiday on Easter Island. The return airfare was inexpensive, and since Easter Island was a place, I had often thought I would like to see, I jumped at the chance and went and bought a ticket.

Raul poured me a Chilean chardonnay that was first class. I sipped this and nibbled on a fresh bread roll. Suddenly I felt immensely tired. It had been a long, virtually nonstop trip from Melbourne to Auckland, on to Tahiti, and from there after changing planes, to Easter Island. I left Melbourne early in the morning, travelled all day and night only to arrive on Easter Island at midday of the same day I had left. After walking around the town as well as the few kilometres out to Ahu Tahai and back, I was now ready for bed, but it was still early. Too bright and sunny, like it was the middle of the afternoon. It was well after 6 pm local time.

Raul arrived with a huge plate. It had on it two very thick slabs of tuna marinated in lime juice and herbs after which it had been grilled. A whole avocado had been cut in half, each half filled with marinated fish and salad. There was mound of rice steamed with coconut milk, baked sweet potato or *kumara*, and a variety of green vegetables. It was too much. There was enough food on the plate to satisfy three people.

"*¿Todo esto es para mi?*"

He nodded enthusiastically.

I started on the fish which was delicious. Raul came and sat with me. He talked about *Rapa Nui* and the *Freedom Movement*. How, like the Tahitians who want to be free of the French, the people of *Rapa Nui* want to be free of the Chileans. He asked what I thought, but the moment I started to answer, to tell him I had no thoughts on the subject having arrived only that day, he pointed out that I had stopped eating,

"*¿Hay algo malo con la cena?*" (Is there something wrong with the dinner?)

"The food is delicious," I said.

"Please, eat. I will do the talking."

He was a little overpowering. After every two or more sips of wine, he would grab the bottle and top up my glass. He told me about how much the locals wanted to develop the tourist industry, but that the Chilean government held them back. He was one of the founders of the *Free Rapa Nui Movement* and had organized the protest banners erected in the grounds of the island's only church.

I had seen them, a bit further up the street from *Residencial Tauke* where I was staying.

Finally, I had eaten as much as I could, not quite two thirds of what I had been served. I asked for the bill.

"Will you be eating here every night?"

And when I hesitated, he added, "because if you do it will be cheaper."

"I don't know. I'd like to try some other places too."

"In that case it will be seven dollars."

That's US dollars of course. He could have asked for pesos but he knew as a foreigner I would be carrying US Dollars. I gave him five and two ones and thanked him for the delicious meal.

The sun was only just starting to drift down towards the Western side of the island, when I left the restaurant. It was almost 8 pm. I walked back to my Residencial and went to bed.

A pleasant breakfast with new friends

The next morning, breakfast was waiting for me in the residencia's dining room. A plate with three flat bread rolls called *hallullas*. I had eaten these some years before while Monica and I had visited her family in Chile. *

On the road out of Santiago, the capitol, to the Maipu valley there are hundreds of roadside bakeries where *hallullas* are baked in clay or earthen ovens, and on Sundays these little bakeries are packed with day trippers stopping for a fresh coffee and a hot roll straight out of the oven. They are unbelievably delicious.

And these ones before me were like that. Cut in half, one was with cheese, one with marmalade, and one with ham. There was a cup and saucer, a selection of tea bags, a small tin of instant coffee, and a thermos of very hot water. There was also fresh fruit. Bananas from the trees in the front garden, an orange, and a piece of melon.

After wishing me a good morning the owner's sister who had come over from Chile to help after the owner's wife died, left me to help myself. I ate the bread rolls, the melon, and had two cups of coffee. Two inquisitive little girls kept running in and out of the dining room to ask me all kinds of things. The younger, about five or six, repeated everything her older sister said. She thought it was funny and laughed a lot. They were the owner's granddaughters and were there every morning.

In the afternoons too, whenever I came back from somewhere and sat down on the patio in front of my room, both would miraculously appear as if out of thin air, again asking questions or telling me stories about what they had done at school or seen on television. I was their only guest in the time I was there, so I guess I was a novelty for them. I thought it was nice.

After breakfast I got my camera bag and walked down the road to the harbour. There was a soccer match in progress on an oval opposite the

*See **Between the Mountains and The sea.**

small, protected boat harbour. The crowd was enthusiastic, cheering and yelling at every move any of the players made. There were people surfing beyond the groyne that protected the harbour. I photographed the fishing boats in the harbour and some old wreckage nearby, then went to Ahu Tahai to get some shots of the Moai I had seen the evening before.

Not much to look at

On the corner where the road from my residencial meets the road running along the beach by the harbour there is a dilapidated little restaurant. It doesn't look much, but I discovered later that their food was delicious. This time I stopped for a cup of coffee so I could watch the boat harbour and whatever was happening there. The coffee was served as a thermos of hot water, a tin of instant coffee (Nescafe) and a bowl of sugar. You make your own.

Since I was the only customer this early in the day the lady who had served me sat down opposite and we had a long conversation about where I came from and what I was doing on *Rapa Nui*. She told me she had an artifacts stall in the craft market by the church and that if I wanted some good souvenirs I should come and have a look at what she had for sale. I told her I would do that.

There seemed to be a lot of people coming and going into and out of the house next door to the restaurant and I asked her what was happening.

"My older brother," she said, "is very sick."

At that point another customer arrived, a tourist with a local man acting as a guide. He told his guide in English with a German sounding accent that he wanted to eat fish. The guide ordered in Spanish. When I saw the meal, they served I decided then I would come back that evening for dinner.

I ate there most evenings from then on. The food was always excellent and the price a quarter of what I had paid for the meal I had the day I arrived.

Why the days are so long

The sun was barely above the horizon when I got up on Sunday. It was 7 o'clock in the morning but it felt and looked more like 4 am. The sun was barely lightening the sky and looking up I could still see stars twinkling.

At breakfast I asked my host and was told it is because the Chilean government makes them keep the same time as they do in Santiago. It is a permanent three hours of daylight saving which means working hours on Easter Island or Rapa Nui coincide exactly with those in Chile, and makes for business between the mainland and the island simultaneous. But that explained why at three in the afternoon yesterday it was as hot as midday, and why the sun was directly overhead.

A long walk

By the time I had finished breakfast the sun was up and already the air was warm. I went back to my room and grabbed my camera bag and set off to walk to Rano Kau, the volcano on the other side of the airport.

Perched precariously on the rim of the crater overlooking both the caldera on one side and the endless Pacific Ocean on the other, is the Bird-man village of Orongo.

All along the crater rim for about 500 metres are 47 low houses no more than a metre high which were constructed with flat slabs of rock to make the walls. To form the roof, larger flat slabs were laid across the top from wall to wall then covered with earth and planted with grass. From a distance they are completely invisible. The doorway into each house was a small square tunnel not much wider than average shoulder width. Inside you could only crawl or sit. You could not even walk crouched over. It is pitch black inside, not a bit of light getting in through the walls or the roof. Only through the tiny entrance would any light get inside. It must have been claustrophobic in there.

— Changing States —

Tourists walking along the narrow path at the top of the rim overlooking the ocean where the village of Oromgo is located.

The lookout point which gives a fantastic view of Rano Kau. The fresh water for the town of Hanga Roa comes from this lake inside the caldera. No one knows how deep it is, but all the patches of green visible are floating islands of grass, reeds and matted algae.

It was a long walk, about six kilometres, and once I had gone through town and around the end of the airport runway, it was all up a steep incline. It got steadily warmer, but a cool breeze off the ocean disguised the intensity of the sun. There was not a cloud in the sky.

I passed through a clump of small Eucalyptus trees, part of a reforestation program, and began the long winding walk up to the rim of the volcano. Here I could see a fair distance over the island, and it looked barren. The grass was beginning to dry, and the low rolling hills in the distance looked more like sand hills than grass covered knolls. I tried to imagine how it must have looked a thousand years ago when there were still forests and large groves of palms.

All the original trees had been cut down and used for firewood, for building huts, and for transporting all over the island the giant stone carvings or Moai with which the people of Rapa Nui had become obsessed. The Moai who represented kings, priests, and other important people were erected on top of burial chambers or stone platforms called Ahu. I suppose at that time the islanders could not have imagined the forests would all disappear. Seeing such an abundance they must have thought it would last forever. They never knew what a rapid expansion of a population could do, and by the time they did realize, it was too late.

There are lessons here for all of us if we take note, but the world is more interested in the mystery surrounding the construction and transport of the giant statues or Moai, than they are in the destruction of the environment by overpopulation and overuse of resources.

A couple of hire cars (small Suzuki 4-wheel drive vehicles) and a minibus of tourists passed me. I could see further up the track others walking, and there was another couple about a kilometre behind me. It was harder than I thought, and by the time I got to the point where I could look over the rim and down into the crater of the volcano the camera bag was very heavy. My shoulders ached from the weight of the bag, but I was glad I had brought my cameras because the view across the one-and-a-half-kilometre crater was superb.

Islands of reeds and matted algae floated on deep blue water. It was said you could walk across, from island to island, but if you fell in you would disappear forever.

Parts of it looked very swampy to me, but you would have to be crazy to try walking across. There is a story that a scientist taking water samples from the middle of the crater, after having walked across the floating reed islands, fell in, or got trapped in a boggy section and sank beneath the surface. He was never found, and few people have ventured out into the crater on foot since then. I could not confirm this, though many people talked about it. No one seems to know how deep the water in the crater is.

Because of all the lava tubes and the porosity of the soil which rapidly absorbs surface water left by rainstorms the whole island appears semi-arid. The only surface water available that is fresh is found in the craters of the three main volcanoes, Rano Kau, Rano Raraku and Rano Aroi. Rano Kau, the largest, is the only one where a village was established, Orongo, the village of the Bird Men.

The only way to photograph the whole crater would be from the air, or to use a fish eye lens. Since I didn't have one of those I had to be content with taking a series of shots that I could later join together to form a panoramic view.

About 500 metres past the viewing point is the village of Orongo. There is also a car park and a small office where a fee is collected from visitors. This fee covers the costs of maintaining the various archaeological sites all over Rapa Nui. The ticket issued entitles you to visit any site anywhere on the island. If you come across a park ranger elsewhere on the island he may ask to see this ticket and of course if you don't have one he will immediately issue one and collect the fee.

"Please, do not stand on the roofs of the houses," I was told as I purchased my ticket. "Follow the paths."

The paths were narrow, like mountain goat tracks. There were a number of people strolling along the paths between the low lying houses.

One path ran along the very edge of the cliff on the ocean side of the crater rim so I followed this. The path was so close to the edge that without leaning I could look down over a shear drop of perhaps 300 metres to where reefs of jagged black lava took the brunt of huge waves crashing into the shore. I tried to visualize the young men of the tribe climbing down these cliffs, making their way through those massive waves so they could swim the kilometre out to a black needle of rock beyond which lay the islets of Motu iti and Motu nui. They swam out there to await the arrival of the first sea birds for the season. Each year Sooty Terns would return to nest on these three wild islets

No doubt the men would fight over who got the first egg laid, and perhaps many would be broken. Eventually each would get an egg, and gently holding it in his mouth so his hands would be free, he would swim back and climb the cliffs to the village. The jagged rocks at the bottom of the cliffs had to be negotiated while the waves pounded, a path had to be found up the cliff, then a short race along the crater rim to the king's house, the one with the petroglyphs carved into the stones by the entrance. More eggs would be broken, but the first man to have the honour of carrying an unbroken egg back to the house of the king, would himself become king for a year.

Orongo was not a permanent village, although it appears very permanent being all built of stone. It was only used during the season when the sooty terns' migration across the Pacific brought them to Rapa Nui to breed. Orongo was probably abandoned about the same time as production of the giant Moai ceased, just before discovery of the island by Europeans.

Motu Iti and Motu Nui, as seen from the top of the crater near the village of Orongo.

It was at least a five hundred metre swim from the base of the cliff to the two tiny islands where the sooty terns laid their eggs. The top of the cliff edge was also grassy and crumbly with loose stone and dirt making it a dangerous climb down and probably a worse one coming back up after swimming out to the islands and back. They had to hold the tiny eggs in their mouths as they swam and then scrambled back up the cliff in a race to be the first.

On my way back down the road well below the rim of Rano Kau I was out of the wind, and I could feel the sun burning my face. I broke a branch off a bush and held it over my head to try blocking the sun. I wished I had bought a hat and resolved to do so as soon as I got back to Hanga Roa.

As I came around the end of the runway a Suzuki pulled up next to me. The driver asked if I wanted a ride.

"*Si, por favor,*" I said. I climbed in, relieved to be out of the sun, and not having to walk the last 2 kilometres into town.

"*Te quemaste la cara,*" he said. "Your face is sunburnt."

"I can feel it."

He drove carefully, stopping at every corner, never exceeding the speed limit of 25 kph. At first this slow speed gives the impression that life on Easter Island is laid back, lazy, that everything happens in slow motion. But after a while this becomes the normal pace and I found myself relaxing. Tension dissipates easily here, and it becomes difficult to imagine how we can sustain the rapid pace we live at in the big cities all around the world.

He asked the usual questions: where was I from? What did I think of Rapa Nui? Where was I staying? Would I post a letter for him when I got back to Australia? He had a friend who lived in Sydney, someone he met while they were filming the movie, **Rapa Nui,** with Kevin Costner.

"Certainly, I 'd be happy to post your letter."

"I'll pay you for the stamps. How much do they cost?"

"Don't worry about it."

He told me he was a sculptor, that he had a stand in the handicrafts market opposite the church on the hill, that I should come and see his work, not to buy but just to talk. He also worked for the local council when he wasn't selling his handicrafts.

"Why do I work so hard," he said, "when every *Pasquence* has his own land? The land provides food and there is fish in the sea. No one has to work. When people ask me that. I say because I'm not lazy like you. That's what I tell them. The truth is I have three daughters and one is at school in Tahiti, and the other two are in Chile, one in Iquique, the other at Viña del Mar. It costs a lot to keep three kids at school overseas."

I had to agree. He made a U turn in front of my residencial.

"I will bring the letter before you leave," he told me.

"*Hola* Luis," the owner of the residencial called out. He was fixing the engine of an old Volkswagon Kombi in his driveway and his hands were covered in grease.

"*Hola* Tauke," Luis called. To me he said, driving off, "*Ahi nos vemos,*"

"I'll see you around."

"*Es un buen hombre,*" Tauke told me. "*Trabaja duro, como un Chileno.*" (He's a good man. He works hard, like a Chilean.)

Tauke was originally from Chile, and was always working, fixing old cars, hot water systems, anything mechanical or electrical. He was always gone early in the morning before I had breakfast.

"Your face is burnt," Tauke said. "You should wear a hat."

Out again, this time with a hat

I went to my room, showered and changed clothes. The water stung where I was sunburnt, so I put some oil on it to ease the skin. Then I went out and bought a hat. I walked down to the little restaurant overlooking the boat harbour and had an instant coffee and a cheese sandwich for lunch.

There were a lot of people at the restaurant. People kept coming and going to the house next door too, visiting the man inside who lay sick and dying. When my sandwich arrived, I asked how the man next door was.

"He will last perhaps another day, but he is old. There is nothing anyone can do. When your time comes it is best to go with dignity. He did not want to die in the hospital. He is happy to be home where his family and friends can be with him."

There was no one at the other restaurant over the road, closer to where the fishing boats tied up. Both these places are mentioned in *Lonely Planet's guide*. Both of them have good food. The only reason I could see why no one patronized the other place much, was that where I was, the owners who both cooked and waited on the tables were charming ladies with wonderful outgoing personalities. They made you feel at home, that they were old friends, and they loved to gossip. Mostly they spoke *Rapanui* with a few Spanish words mixed in, but to people like myself, visitors to the island, they used Spanish.

When I finished my sandwich and coffee, I walked over to the fishing harbour but the only activity there was a man washing out a boat with a bucket of sea water. A road ran along the top of a ridge below which was a small beach protected by the groyne There were a few kids out surfing but the waves were not big. Several schoolkids were taking swimming lessons in the shallow water. There was a lot of laughter and splashing. A couple of kids sat in the shade of a giant head sticking up out of the grass verge by the roadside.

The only beach at Hanga Roa was on the other side of the small harbour where the fishing boats moored. A very small beach. Hardly any sand at all. The only other beach with light sand was way across the other side of the island at Anakena. Most of the island has jagged rocky shores with no beaches, and usually the water drops off into a great depth, a dangerous coastline. Visiting ships anchor off the only harbour, this one above, which is still called **La Bahia de Cook,** Cook's Harbour. Captain Cook anchored offshore here when he was on his way to discover Australia.

I walked along the road and followed a different path back into town. I discovered the telephone office, and the bank where I could change some money. I also found the tourist information centre where I obtained several excellent maps. Tomorrow I would rent a car and visit all the sites shown on the maps.

Renting a small 4-wheel drive

On our drive back into town from Ranu Kau, Raul had introduced me to a man who ran a general store in the main street.

This man also hired *Suzuki Sierras* to tourists wanting to visit the less accessible archaeological sites. He assured me the man would rent one to me at a good price. I went there, and after negotiating a price, not as low as Raul said, but a good third off the normal rental price, I got the vehicle for the day.

Following the rules, I didn't exceed 25 kph, and I made sure I stopped at each corner. I drove back to my residencial and collected my cameras and the hat. There was a little shop next door, so I went in and bought some mineral water and a couple of oranges to take with me. The lady was very friendly. She told me she has a daughter who is married to an Australian and lives in Sydney. She went there last year to visit her. She was very impressed by the size of the city. It was the first time she had been anywhere other than Tahiti.

When I went to pay for the drinks and oranges, she discovered she didn't have enough change. "Why don't you pay me later," she suggested, "when you get some smaller money?"

My little rental car

I drove out the way I had walked, around the runway to the airport, but instead of taking the right-hand track and going up Ranu Kau to Orongo, I went left and followed the track to the far end of the runway to the other side of the volcano. The track degenerated into two-wheel ruts as it went down a steep slope towards the ocean.

Coming around behind Rano Kau the land leveled and there was Vinapu. There was a Moai here that had fallen, or had been toppled over, and was broken into several pieces. The head was staring at me as I got out of the Suzuki and walked towards it. But it was the walls of the Ahu beyond the fallen head that caught my attention.

Like the Inca walls along the road at Tiahuanaco in Peru, here was a wall made of accurately cut blocks of stone that are of immense size but fitted together so smoothly that you could not find a gap wide enough to poke a blade of grass through.

There is no other stone wall like this on the island.

*The head of a toppled Moai stared at me as I walked from the Suzuki to towards the cut stone wall above. The precise fitting of the stones together in the enlarged image above shows what Thor Heyrdalhl claimed in his book **Aku Aku**, that the people who made this wall were probably the same people who made similar walls in the Andes in Peru, and that they brought this technology to Easter Island, but it was later lost as other Ahu do not show this degree of precise fitting.*

All the other Ahu are made of stone that is not cut and shaped to fit. They are much rougher and more primitive looking. Thor Heyerdahl claimed that Vinapu was built first while the early settlers retained the stone mason skills brought with them from Peru. That the other Ahu all were degenerated and less skillfully constructed as subsequent generations lost the art of the original stone masons, until the final and most recent Ahu were simply made of piles of stones stacked together without any skill whatsoever.

One of the walls of this Ahu at Vinapu had been extended at a later period and the stones were not as well made as the original ones. These Ahu at Vinapu were not used as burial chambers as were the more recent constructions but were simply bases upon which to stand the Moai.

Other archaeologists claim the reverse: that Vinapu shows the final development after centuries of learning to work with stone.

Carbon dating has not provided any evidence one way or the other, since only the rock can be dated but not the work put into the construction.

I took the photographs seen here, and sat on the grass as I contemplated the Ahu and tried to imagine how stones as immense as these could be cut and trimmed to such precision without power tools.

A cool breeze blew off the water and the sun shone in a deep blue sky.

Across the island to Anakena

After a while I got back into the Suzuki and drove diagonally across the island to Anakena, where Hotu Matu'a was supposed to have landed.

I did not see another vehicle on the drive across the island and there was no one at Anakena. I parked in the shade by a clump of coconut palms and walked past several new picnic tables and stools that seemed new. Once I had walked through the grove of coconut palms, which had been planted many years ago as part of the rehabilitation of the beach, I could see the beach. Glittering white sand lapped by water so clear and calm it seemed to be invisible. But what dominates this beach is a huge Ahu on which stand seven Moai, four of which have red topknots balanced on their heads. With their backs to the beach these Moai stare inland towards the coconut palms.

On a small knoll further away from the beach is another single older Moai. This was the first Moai to be replaced on its pedestal. Thor Heyerdahl had asked the islanders assisting his archaeological expedition how the statues were placed on the platforms, so the mayor at that time gathered a group together and over a couple of weeks they showed him how it was done.

The Moai was lying face down. The men jacked the face up off the ground using long poles. Small stones were placed underneath to keep the giant statue off the ground.

It was then jacked up a little higher. More stones were gathered and placed under the statue. Little by little, the pile of stones grew taller, and the statue was raised higher and higher.

When the head was a bit higher than forty-five or fifty degrees off the ground, ropes were tied around the head and the statue was pulled from behind until it rocked back onto its base. After three hundred years or more of lying on its face, it stood proudly once again staring inland.

Just around the bluff from Anakena is another small beach of golden sand surrounded by black lava rocks, Ovahe. There are a lot of caves beside this beach and it was here in these caves that Hotu Matu'a and the first settlers stayed. These are the only two real beaches on Rapa Nui. Anakena is popular during the tourist season but nobody swims at Ovahe because there are too many sharks in the water.

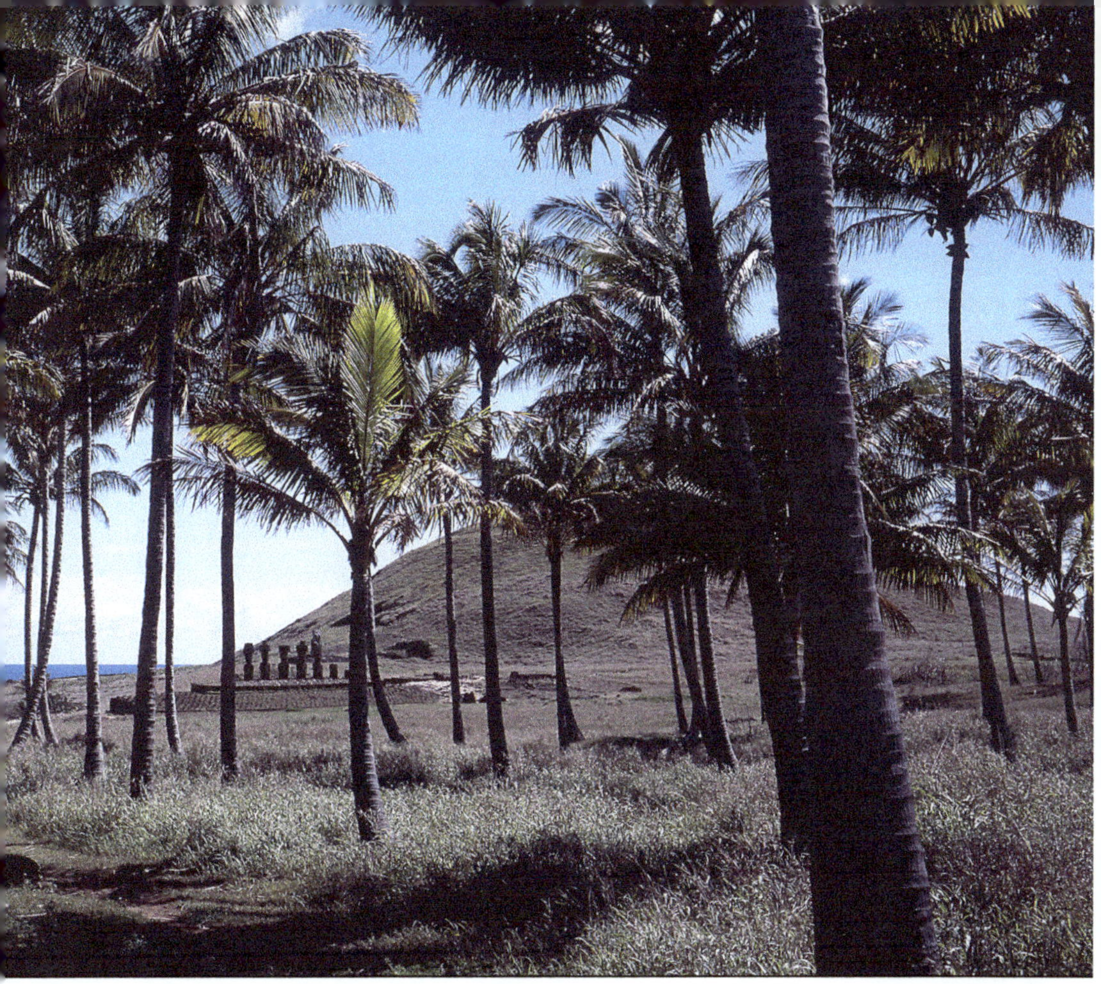

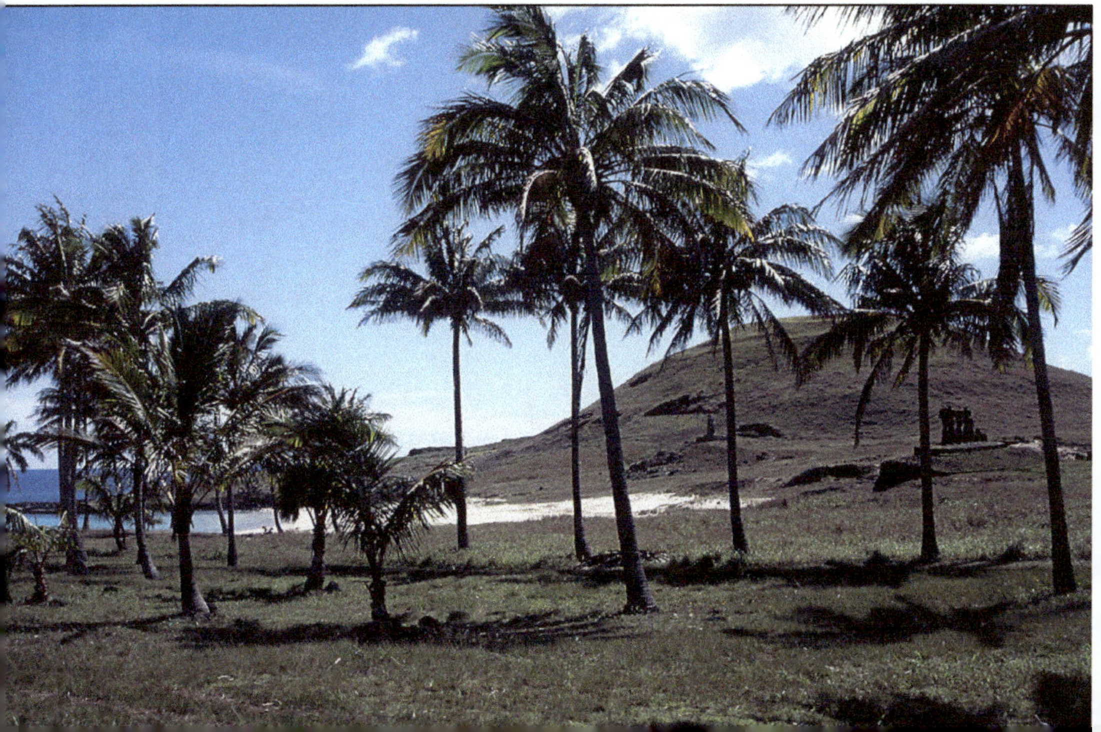

Front and back views of the main group of seven Moai at Anakena.
One can also see the Ahu on which they stand has been well constructed with rocks and stones carefully fitted together. Later Ahu were much less well constructed. The palm trees are coconut palms and were planted to rehabilitate the area. All the original palm trees and other trees had been cut down hundreds of years earlier leaving the island a barren windswept terrain, with every Moai toppled over or knocked down and broken, which is what the first Europeans saw when they came here.

— Changing States —

A close look at the faces of the Moai will show you that each one is different, unique.

I followed the track around the coast, losing count of the number of times I stopped to look at broken fallen Moai. There are hundreds of platforms all along the coast, each one having at least five and often seven fallen Moai.

Two sites I passed with toppled and broken Moai. There were hundreds like this.

Not far from Ovahe is Tongariki which is in the process of being restored. Tongariki is the largest Ahu on the island with the most Moai. There are thirteen huge Moai standing here, the biggest I had seen so far. Two more are lying on the ground quite a distance away from the platform. Tongariki had been partially restored when in 1960 a huge earthquake off the coast of Chile triggered a massive tsunami which hit the east coast of Rapa Nui. The force of the water lifted the giant Moai off the pedestal, toppling them all, carrying several of these eighty to one hundred tonne statues as much as fifty metres inland

A man on a small motorbike pulled up as I was trying to get back far enough to photograph all of Tongariki in one shot.

He was the only person I had seen since leaving Hanga Roa two hours earlier. He was a park ranger, but he didn't ask to see my ticket, the one I had bought at Orongo the day before.

He just wanted to say hello, and to remind me not to forget to visit the quarry which was nearby at Ranu Raraku. It was a couple of Kilometres directly in from where we were standing. Its jagged volcanic rim stood out sharply against the soft rounded hills surrounding it. I thanked him and he rode off towards the quarry leaving a trail of dust to show me where the track was.

At Tongariki, one of the Moai still to be restored, laying on its back with the Ranu Raraku crater rim in the background. It had been knocked off its pedestal by the 1960 earthquake and subsequent tsunami that carried these massive statues as much as fifty metres away from the Ahu that had been standing on.

Ranu Raraku

Rano Raraku is the quarry where the Moai were carved. The whole world knows this place. If not by name, they know of it as the place where the giant heads sticking up out of the grass can be found. It is synonymous with Easter Island because of the many photographs published in hundreds of magazines over the last half a century. It is an astounding place when you realise that there are over three hundred giant statues in various stages of completion scattered along the inner and outer slopes of this small volcano.

Changing States

The huge heads sticking up out of the grass, some of them as tall as six metres, are all statues that were stood up to await finishing touches before being transported to whatever part of the island they were to be erected. To walk amongst these Moai, to realize they were carved with nothing more than stone tools, to think that most of the island's population must have been involved in the carving and transport of these Moai, to wonder why they were so obsessed with carving them, sends shivers along your spine.

The statues of the lower slopes are all partially buried by rubble that fell down or washed down from higher up. As you climb about the more rocky heights there are probably more than one hundred unfinished statues. Some of them are complete, lying on their backs as they were carved but not detached from the bedrock beneath them. Others are mere outlines cut into the side of a rock wall. Some are in what at first appear to be caves, but closer examination reveals that the rock has been chipped away from around the statue to form a cave in which the carvers worked. Always, the last part of the statue to be chipped away was the back. As this was chipped away, the statue would collapse onto its back. Then it could be dragged down the slope, where the workers would stand it up so the final finishing could be done. The largest of the Moai is still attached to the bedrock. It measures twenty-one metres long.

The largest Moai ever carved, lies unfinished and still attached to the bedrock.

— Changing States —

Up close with a Moaie at Ranu Raraku.

Unfinished Moai. Some are left abandoned where they lay, with grass and weeds obscuring them, others are kept in a way that makes it easier for visitors to see them, like the one above where the grass is cut and the Moai looks as if it is someone sleeping in a bed.

Tortora reeds growing inside the crater lake at Ranu Raraku where the unfinished moai and the quarry they were carved in is located.

There are so many left standing that were waiting for finishing touches but all were abandoned and over the years rubble and dirt has washed down the slopes pushing some over, and partially or almost completely burying them.

I spent most of the day here, wandering along the slopes of Rano Raraku. I met the park ranger again and he told me that his people spent more than 500 years carving the 900 or so Moai that are all over Rapa Nui. It would often take 40 or 50 carvers over a year to produce one Moai. Many of them were carved simultaneously. I imagined there must have been teams of carvers working all over Rano Raraku, like ants swarming over an ant hill, then suddenly it stopped, and everything was abandoned.

The conflict must have been horrific. The population decimated itself. Thousands of people died, one whole group, the long ears, being completely exterminated. Most of the standing Moai were topped and deliberately broken, while those in transit were abandoned along the roadside. Families hid from other families in secret caves, and cannibalism was rife. But once the population had stabilized at a number the island could support, life returned to normal.

That is until the Europeans came. Through slavery and disease the population was rapidly reduced to little more than one hundred people who had lost the continuity of the culture that had existed before.

Things were forgotten. Stories were muddled, genealogies confused, and with team after team of archaeologists studying the island the natives told them what they wanted to hear rather than what they could truly remember. No wonder there was so much mystery.

But today, with the population back around 2000, the people are proud of their history no matter how bloody it might have been, and proud of the enigma of the Moai, those giant statues that have baffled the world for centuries.

They call themselves *Rapanui* and their island *Rapa Nui*.

And like the rest of Polynesia they want to be independent, tied to no nation but themselves.

Everyone is concerned with independence to one degree or another. Raul is leader of the protest group who erected the banners in French English and Spanish in the grounds of the church on top of the hill at the end of the street where I was staying.

One of the banners stated in bold red letters against a white background: ***El Pueblo de Rapa Nui solicita la restitucion de sus tierras usurpadas por el Estado de Chile:***

The people of Rapa Nui seek restitution of the lands stolen by Chile.

It was also written in French.

An encounter with a drunk

Everyone talks about this, usually politely, but I did meet a drunk who was rather blunt. I had just left the office of *Lan Chile* after confirming my return flight to Tahiti. The office is half way from the town to the airport. I had stopped out the front by the roadside when this drunk staggered across the road. He was the only person on the island I had seen drunk. He called out to me so I stepped forward to meet him. He grabbed my hand and shook it. "*Como te llamas?*" he said. "What's your name?"

"John. *Me llamo John. Soy Australiano.*"

"My name is John too. John Rapanui. You like *Rapa Nui*?"

"Yeah. I like *Rapa Nui*. Everyone is very friendly. *Muy amable.*"

I started to walk back towards the town. He kept right next to me.

"Where you going?" he asked.

"To the town centre."

He laughed. "There is no town centre here."

"Well, whatever there is, that's where I'm going."

"You like Chileans?"

"I don't know," I said diplomatically.

"*Rapanui* no like Chilean," he stated with a gesture crude enough to be understood by anyone. Then he said, "*Rapanui,*" gesturing with a closed fist thumb up, "Good." Then to make sure I understood him completely, he stood in front of me so I had to stop. He ran his fingers across his throat as if cutting it with a razor. "*Chilenos - afuera!*" "Chileans - out of here!"

He was angry but harmless. He was so drunk he could hardly stand up. Having said his piece his anger abated. He held on to my shoulder until he regained his balance before politely asking me for a cigarette.

"I'm sorry, I don't smoke."

"Ahh," he said. For a moment he seemed at a loss, then he let go of my shoulder. "It was good to talk to you."

"Yes. It was very nice to meet you," I said in return.

"I see you later, maybe."

"*Chao.*"

He sat down in the shade of a tree as I continued on my way.

I thought about this as I drove back along the coast. The land was grassy but extremely rocky. Broken black lava everywhere. There was no shortage of rocks to build Ahu or platforms, stone fences, and houses.

The only animal life visible were several scrawny horses I had seen grazing in a rocky paddock. I passed many large Ahu where all the Moai had been toppled over and broken. I stopped at each one to take photographs. The government is hoping to eventually restore most of these, if not all of them, an enormous task that will take a long time. There are over six hundred broken Moai at sites all around the island, and so far only a handful have been restored.

When this task is completed, Rapa Nui will be a magnificent place to visit.

Although I saw plenty of horses, I only ever saw two cows in one field. There had to be more somewhere because fresh milk was locally produced.

The day of the children

The next morning, I was woken early by the sound of children's voices laughing and yelling with excitement. I got up to see what was happening. There is a school on the other side of the road from *Residancial Tauke*, and there must have been thirty or more children between the ages of ten to twelve milling about with an equal number of horses. Some of the children were already sitting in the saddles, others were trying to calm the horses so they could mount them. There was a lot of laughter and good-natured jesting from those older ones watching the younger ones struggling with their horses. It took about half an hour before everyone was mounted, then the leader called something and started up the hill towards the church. The other children followed singly or in pairs, riding quietly along the wide grassy footpath. Now that they were moving the excitement seemed to have died down. They followed the road around the church and disappeared.

Not long after the bigger kids on horseback had disappeared there was more noise around the corner in the other street. Younger voices this time. I went back inside and grabbed a camera, then went down the street to see what was happening. There was a crowd of little children all dressed in native costumes, their faces painted with patterns in bright colours representing tattoos. They were children from the kindergartens, and there were several teachers telling them what to do, how to line up. There was a clown on stilts marching and swaying along the street in front of the children and they all started to follow him. They also started singing. A delightful song in *Rapanui*. I could not understand a word of it, but the harmonies were simply beautiful. One of the teachers, a man, played a mandolin, strumming the melody and singing counterpart in a deep voice to add a bass line to the children's high-pitched voices.

Some of the children held up signs proclaiming **El Dia de Los Ninos**, Children's Day. As they marched along others ran to people who were watching from the footpaths and handed them small cards with drawings and messages on them. They had made them at the kindergartens just so they could hand them out to people during their parade. A little girl gave me one which said: **Si un nino crece con amor, aprende a amar.** *If a child is brought up with love, he - she, learns to love.*

I followed the little parade along the street snapping quite a few photos until they turned by the market and headed towards the small beach down where the fishing boats were moored.

— *Changing States* —

How beautiful we are, The Children.

This delightful little parade lasted just over an hour.

When the parade had petered out I stayed by the market.

Stalls under thatched awnings were loaded with vegetables and fruit. There were piles of root vegetables I had not seen before, and others that were familiar. I asked the names and was told: "This was *Camote*, and that, *Manioca*. Over there was Taro," which I had seen before. There was *Uhi* and *Kumara*, which I also knew. They were all varieties of sweet potato. There was *Pukapuka*, a kind of plantain, and *Caña*, sugar cane that had been introduced from Tahiti.

Then there were the things you find everywhere else: peas, beans, broccoli, cabbage, cauliflower, pumpkin, carrots, and potatoes. The fruits were tropical. Mango, Papaya and Pawpaw, melons, and bananas. There were no apples, pears or stone fruits; these would have to be brought in from the mainland (Chile) and would cost too much. Oranges and *Pomelos* which I had seen in one of the general stores (imported from Tahiti) were not here in the market. They were also too expensive.

Towards the back of the market was a lady cooking something in a large wok over a gas burner. She was deep frying what looked like small pancakes, and when I asked her what they were she told me; "*Sopaipillas*." They were about the size of a fifty-cent coin.

She lifted one out with a pair of tongs and drained it on a paper towel. She put it on a small plate and handed it to me.

"Why don't you try it?"

I did, and it was delicious. I wanted to buy some, but she wouldn't let me pay for them. She cooked several more, and put them on my plate, insisting that I eat them. While I was eating the little *sopaipillas*, several other people came over and bought plates of them from her.

An old lady came and greeted the cook, then she sat next to me and started talking to me. Her voice was so soft, softer than a whisper, it was non-existent. But she talked and talked, and I nodded as if I understood, and she seemed very happy, smiling and nodding as she spoke.

Two young school girls came up to me. They were selling raffle tickets at 2000 pesos each. (About $5) The tickets were to raise funds for a child who needed an operation on her heart. I couldn't quite understand what the prize was, but it was to be raffled on Saturday, a week after I would be leaving. I didn't buy a ticket, but I gave them a 1000 peso note towards the fund for the operation.

"*Muy caballero. Muchisimas gracias senor*," the one with the tickets said.

"*Gracias*," the other repeated.

The old lady stood up and smiled. Her mouth moved, but I couldn't hear anything. She turned and left.

"She likes you," the cook said. "She wouldn't have talked so much otherwise."

I looked at her and shrugged.

" You know, she never talks to strangers."

Even though I had not understood anything the old lady had said, I felt privileged that she had taken the time to talk to me.

"*Mas sopaipillas?*" the cook asked. She was already scooping another lot out of the hot oil.

"Thank you, no. I've had plenty. I'd better be going."

"Come again," she said as I stood up to leave.

When I got back to the residencial the lady who runs the little shop next door came running out. She was very excited, almost jumping out of her skin.

"My daughter who lives in Sydney just telephoned. She's going to have a baby."

I could hear people inside her shop laughing.

"Come inside," the lady from the shop said, "and have a drink."

Inside the shop were the two young girls and the lady from the residencial, and another older woman. They were all laughing and joking, having a great time.

"I'm going to be a grandmother. Can you believe that? At my age!"

She went to the fridge behind the counter and took out a can of Cristal beer. She passed it to me, raised her own drink. "To my daughter, and to my new granddaughter," she said happily.

Everyone drank with enthusiasm.

Unable to stand still

"I'm too excited to stay here," the lady from the shop said.

She looked like she was about to jump out of her skin. She kept bustling about, making sure the other ladies had enough drink left. Then suddenly she turned to me.

"Would you like to go and see the *Siete Moai?*" she asked.

"Yes, of course."

I had the idea that the Siete Moai were a special group somewhere near the centre of the island. Most of where I'd been so far had been around the coast of the island and not anywhere near the centre.

So she closed the shop, and while I waited with everyone else from inside the shop, she went and got her car.

The Siete Moai

The ***Siete Moai*** are situated at Ahu Akivi, which is two and a half kilometres inland. Unlike all the coastal Ahu where the Moai all had their backs to the sea, staring inland, the seven statues at Ahu Akivi are staring East, out over the ocean towards the rising sun.

These Moai do not wear Pukao, the stone hats made from red scoria.

The seven statues at Ahu Akivi were the last to be erected before the great battles that decimated the population and stopped all work at the quarry. They too were toppled over and damaged. William Mulloy and Gonzalo Figueroa, who had been members of Thor Heyerdahl's original expedition had returned a number of times to Easter Island. They had in collaboration with Sergio Rapu and the Chilean University of Santiago excavated Ahu Akivi and restored the Siete Moai.

The lady from the shop took us out of Hanga Roa by way of several back streets. Clouds of red dust floated behind us marking our route through the streets. It was still dry season and there had been no rain for months so all the trees and bushes in the gardens of the houses along the way were covered with a fine patina of red powder, dust thrown up by passing cars and motor bikes. Only after the first rains of the wet season would the brilliant greens of these sub tropical plants be seen.

Out of town we bounced over ruts that jarred the car's suspension.

"Not too many people come this way," the lady from the shop said.

She wasn't exaggerating because the path we followed was nothing more than two-wheel ruts winding through knee high grass. I could hear the grass swishing along the sides of the car.

Suddenly she turned off the track and drove across a grassy swathe towards a dry stunted tree. This ancient stunted tree which was almost dead was the only one left of the original trees that grew on the island. Every other tree elsewhere has been brought in over the last fifty years or so to help with re-forestation.

The last Toromiro tree left on the island is barely surviving.

"Puna Pau," she said. "This is where they carved the Pukao."

There was a low hill on either side of us, both of which turned out to be small extinct volcanoes. She led the way up the side of the one to the left of us. A lovely cool breeze was blowing which masked the intensity of the sun. I was glad I had brought my hat along.

We passed one of the Pukao. It looked just like a huge stone wheel with a round hub in the centre. It was lying flat and was as thick as I was tall. It must have weighed tonnes.

"They transported these on reed boats to the Ahu along the coast," the lady from the shop explained.

We were standing on a ridge and could see down the slope. Beneath us was Hanga Roa and the coast. In a direct line it would have been a bit over a kilometre.

Puna Pau is the only place on the island where red scoria is obtained. Some of the Pukao had carvings made into them that could have been specific to a particular Moai for which it was destined. Not all Moai had Pukao.

"How did they get them down there?" I asked.

She shrugged.

"Maybe they rolled them down," I suggested.

The children had disappeared over the lip of the shallow volcano, so I hurried along after them. Looking back down the way we had come I could see several Pukao. Some were lying flat with the topknot or hub sticking up, others were on their side. It was just as if they had been rolled down the slope, tipping over as they went.

There were perhaps twenty or more of them inside the crater. Some were lying flat, some were on their sides, as if ready to roll away. All of them were as thick as I was tall with a diameter of maybe one and a half metres. I imagined it would have been one heck of job rolling them up the incline of the crater to the lip. Once over they could simply roll downhill until they tipped over. Was this how it was done? I don't know. Nobody could give me an answer either.

The women stayed on top of the crater rim where there was a cool breeze while I went down into the crater to take photos of the Pukao. When I had finished, we went back to the car to continue along the track to Ahu Akivi.

Once we arrived the women sat down on the grass and chatted while I wandered around the seven statues taking pictures with two different cameras from as many angles as possible.

These statues are the only ones that look out to sea rather than inland, and it is said that they are searching for others who were expected to arrive from the East. It is also said that they represent the seven explorers Hotu Matu'a sent out to explore the island after he and his people had landed at Anakena.

The thing is, if you put statues in the centre of the island, the only way they can look is outwards towards the sea. Looking east is logical since this is the direction from which Hotu Matua and his people came.

Once I had finished taking photos we all jumped back in the car for the drive back to Hanga Roa. Before opening her shop she asked me I would take a letter and post it when I got to Australia. "It takes so long from here," she said. "First it must go to Chile, then after sorting it gets sent to Australia. Some times it takes two months."

"It would be a pleasure. I'll take it and post in as soon as I get home."

"I will write it tonight."

Once people knew I was from Australia, quite a few told me they had relatives there, and asked if I would take a letter back with me to post when I returned. They would get the mail far quicker that way than if they posted the letters on Easter Island. It sometimes took as much as three months for a letter to get from Easter Island to Australia.

I was more than happy to oblige and ended up taking almost a dozen letters back with me to post from Melbourne.

— Changing States —

The siete Moai

A question from Raul

Raul who had cooked dinner for me the first day I had arrived strolled past. He had come from the church on the hill at the top of the road where Residencial Tauke was situated. He stopped to say *Buenos Dias*.

"Why have you not come for dinner again?"

"Well..."

I couldn't think of any real reason.

"Perhaps you will come before you leave."

"I'll certainly try."

"*Bueno entonces, ahi nos vemos.*"

"*Chao.*"

At the craft market

I decided to walk to the craft market opposite the church at the top of the street. I took my camera bag back into the residencial and changed into a fresh shirt. The market consisted of many stalls along each side and down the centre of a very large tin shed. There may have been forty different stalls inside. Flaps in the side walls had been opened to allow breezes to blow through. Without that it would have been too hot inside.

Some of the stalls were closed, their content covered by sheets of canvas, but most of the others were open for business. All of them were full of carvings, miniature Moai in volcanic pumice, or wooden statues called Moai Kavakava. There was some decorated shell jewellery, some masks and a few weapons like clubs and spears.

I looked at most of the work before coming the stall operated by Luis. There was a lot of variation in the skills exhibited by the different artisans. Some of the work was quite crude, while other work would be of fine detail or exquisite craftsmanship. There were a few buyers arguing prices at some of the stalls.

Luis was showing an American lady a book of traditional Easter Island art where explanations in English told her what the carvings he had made represented. While she studied the book Luis went behind the stall and brought out a wood carving.

"This is the one I was making the other day." He handed it to me. "It's for you, if you want it."

I studied the carving while Luis went back to his other customer. It was a lovely piece of work with fine detail. It was not very heavy and not too long. It would fit into my overnight bag without any problem.

"*¿ Que piensas?*"

"I like it," I told him. "I'll take it."

"And what about one of these stone carvings?" He indicated a large stone Moai that he had made. It stood about a metre tall. It would look great in my garden, but it must have weighed fifty kilos.

"I travel light."

"I can ship it to Australia."

"I don't think so."

"Only $100. It took two months to carve. That's good value."

"It's too big." That was the wrong thing to say.

"Something smaller perhaps." he pointed at another stone Moai about half the size. "You can take twenty kilos in your luggage without paying extra."

"I don't travel with luggage," I told him. "Only what I can carry. That way I don't get held up at airports with customs or lost luggage."

"I understand," he said. He grabbed a smaller carving and passed it to me. "This is the one. It weighs no more than five kilos. Surely you can manage that?"

It was a nice piece, and just big enough to look good. I decided I would buy that also."

"*Muy Bien.*"

A price was agreed, and Luis said he would bring them around to the residencial in the evening.

He never came that evening because that was the night his father died. His father was the brother of the woman who owned the restaurant opposite the boat harbour.

A funeral

I found that out the next morning when I went out into the street after breakfast. There were quite a few people coming slowly up the street from the waterfront. They were singing a slow rhythmic song. Perhaps it was a prayer. The men wore suits and the women had on what looked like evening dresses, the sort of thing they would wear if they were going out to the theatre, the opera or a ball. It was most unusual. I had never seen anyone dressed up like that during the time I had been here.

As they came closer, I realized that the knot of people in front of the procession were carrying a white coffin.

Most of those were the people from the restaurant by the waterfront where I regularly had dinner. Amongst them was Luis. He saw me standing by the front gate of the residencial and nodded. He indicated

I should join the procession, but I felt uncomfortable doing that. Even though people were beginning to accept me as one who lives on Rapa Nui rather than as a visitor or tourist, it would not be right for me to be a part of this procession.

There were a lot of kids running around the edges of the group walking up the road towards the church, and quite a few people had come out of their houses or shops to watch the funeral party go by. I joined them and stood in the shade of a tree to watch.

The church bells had started tolling. A deep sonorous sound that echoed along the street. I'm sure they were heard all over Hanga Roa. Once the funeral party had reached the church, a lot of others who had been attracted by the bells followed them inside.

The priest used a microphone so everyone outside the church could hear the mass. It was a long mass broken by much beautiful singing in *Rapanui* even though the priest spoke in Spanish. The prayers and chants were not Gregorian but were sung with that particular South Pacific islander harmony that is so beautiful it brings tears to your eyes. Some of the people outside the church, those who were the closest, also joined in with the singing. It was a very moving mass.

After more than an hour the mourners emerged from the church. They were led by a man incongruously wearing a navy-blue parka over his suit. He must have been very hot because it was the middle of the day and the sun was beating down. He held aloft a very long pole on top of which was a tiny gold cross. The pall bearers carrying the coffin followed closely behind him. There was a large number so they could keep

changing as those actually carrying the coffin got tired. The rest of the party tagged along behind chanting prayers and occasionally bursting into song.

It took an hour for the funeral party to go down the street to the waterfront, where more people joined the crowd following the procession, then along the cliff top to the cemetery overlooking the ocean.

There were more ceremonies at the graveside, and more singing under the watchful eyes of the giant Moai standing on the clifftops nearby. I didn't go into the cemetery, not wanting to intrude.

*The procession approaching the cemetery.
Below: at the grave site.*

    I walked back along the cliff top to the waterfront. I could still hear the singing from there almost a kilometre away. The sun was shining, and an intermittent breeze blew across the island carrying the voices far and wide. It was my second last day on Rapa Nui and I felt sad to be leaving the next day.

Later that afternoon I went to the craft market to see if Luis was there. He wasn't but his wife was looking after the stall.

When she saw me she knew who I was.

"These are your's." She picked up the wooden *Moai Kavakava* and the much heavier *Moai* carved from pumice. I gave her the money Luis and I had agreed was the price. She put each carving in a plastic bag for me.

"Luis will see you tomorrow, before you leave."

My last day

The next day was a Sunday. A French warship had arrived before dawn. It anchored about a kilometre offshore. The fishermen were ferrying the sailors back and forth. Many of the artisans from the craft market had set up stalls or had laid out blankets on top of which they displayed their carvings and souvenirs. Sailors were crowded around these stalls, studying the carvings and discussing prices. Several officers were supervising stores being loaded onto a boat to be taken out to the ship.

Others were climbing onto saddled horses to be taken on horseback tours of nearby places of interest. Everyone on the island who owned a horse must have been there because there were horses everywhere. I could see a long line of them heading towards the cemetery and Ahu Tahai on the cliff beyond. A trio of sailors on horseback headed up the street towards the church, while coming down towards the waterfront, were more islanders leading horses. All the restaurants and cafes near the waterfront were full of sailors out of uniform, having breakfast, drinking beer, laughing and shouting, having a good time. There were people in little jeeps, with the tops down, or on motorbikes slowly driving along the waterfront. They went no faster than walking pace because there were so many horses and riders wandering over the road. They waved at, or called out to friends as they went past. They would circle the oval where a soccer game was in progress, then come back along the road by the water again waving and calling to their friends.

Every so often when the wind shifted, I could hear the voices singing the mass drift down from the church at the other end of the street going up the hill from the waterfront. I suspected that apart from those at the church, practically the whole population of Hanga Roa was down here by the waterfront. It is not often a ship visits, so it is always something not to me missed. I bought some *empanadas* and sat by the oval to eat them and watch the soccer game. It was played with not much skill, but with lots of enthusiasm and loud encouragement from the spectators.

— John Litchen —

*A French warship anchored off shore.
A stall with local wooden and stone handcrafts to sell to the sailors from the ship.*

Once the Sunday mass was over, most of those people came down from the church to join the crowd watching the soccer.

I thought it was a good way to end my stay on Rapa Nui. It was like a carnival with people on horseback, crowds of enthusiastic soccer fans, people driving back and forth waving and calling to friends, families picnicking on the grass, All it lacked was a group of dancers and some singers.

After a while people drifted away to do other things. I went back to my residencial to pack my things and put my cameras away. I had used all the film I brought with me. All I had to do now was wait till midnight when the plane from Chile came in to pick up passengers heading for Tahiti and beyond. If it was on time I would connect in Tahiti with a flight for New Zealand and Australia.

Luis came by and gave me the letter he wanted me to post. He also gave me a shell necklace as a going away gift. When he left the lady from the little shop next to the residencial came over and gave me the letter she wanted me to send to her daughter in Sydney. She also gave me a fine shell necklace. "For your wife," she said. "She must be *Muy amable*," because, she told me, I was very a very nice person. She makes the necklaces while she sits in her shop talking to customers, or when there is not much to do on a slow day.

She took another necklace from her bag and put this one over my head. "For good luck," she said. "You must wear this when you leave."

I didn't know what to say.

"I will see you later, at the airport. I work as a cabin cleaner when the plane comes in from Santiago."

Later that evening while I was sitting out on the veranda in front of the residencial, waiting for the owner to take me to the airport, Luis came by again, this time riding a bike.

"*Hola* John," he called out from the street.

"How come you're riding a bike?"

"*Es para bajar el peso*," he said. "I'm ninety-four kilos. I should be eighty."

It was a nice-looking bike.

"I got this off a French sailor. He wanted to trade it for some carvings. They haven't been paid for a month and they don't have any money. I thought it was a good trade. What do you think?"

"I think it's great."

After we talked a while, he said goodbye once again and reminded me that if I ever returned to Rapa Nui to come and see him. "I'll look after you."

"*Gracias.*"
"*De nada, Chao.*"
He rode off into the dark.

My friend from the little shop next door to Residencial Tauke was standing beside the boarding steps as I walked across the tarmac.

She gave me a hug and a kiss on the cheek. She beamed when she saw I was wearing the necklace she had made. She reminded me not to forget to come and see her whenever (not if ever) I was on the island again.

I turned at the top of the stairs to take one last look at Easter Island and she gave me a thumbs up sign.

Much later as I was flying back to Australia I knew I would never forget Easter Island, not because I had seen the giant statues and learned something of the mystery surrounding them, but because of the people I had met. People who had made me feel welcome, who made me feel that if I had wanted, I could have been one of them.

A day lost

It was six hours to return to Tahiti in a crowded plane.

From Tahiti to Easter Island, it had only been four and a half, but this time we are going against the Jet Stream instead of with it. And it was the same from Tahiti to New Zealand, six and a half hours going back compared to the four and a half it had taken coming over 10 days earlier. Similarly, from New Zealand back to Melbourne, another four and a half hours instead of two and half.

It's amazing the difference going against the Jet Stream makes.

The plane's top speed coming back against the Jet Stream was 749 kilometres per hour, whereas with the Jet stream behind on the way over the speed was up to 940 kilometres per hour. A huge difference in time spent traveling in the air.

It was a Sunday when I left Rapa Nui, and this time after traveling through the night, I arrived back in Melbourne not on Monday as one would expect but on Tuesday instead. We lost a day crossing back over that infernal International Date Line between Tahiti and New Zealand.

I had managed a few hours sleep between Easter Island and Tahiti, and also again, a few hours between Tahiti and New Zealand. Arriving in Melbourne I discovered it was a public holiday, the first Tuesday in November, Melbourne Cup Day.

Monica collected me at the airport, and we were no sooner home than Fred rang to tell me that our cousins from Sydney, Owen, his brother Peter and his wife, were in Melbourne for the Melbourne Cup and he had planned a night out with all of us to celebrate. They had been in Buenos Aires for a medical conference and were on their way back to Sydney with a one-day stopover in Melbourne for the Cup, the biggest race in Australia. They were both mad horse racing fans.

Feeling revived after a break at home, we went out for dinner that night at a Greek restaurant in South Melbourne and had a great time. It's not often we get together with our cousins from Sydney. Owen, we managed to see whenever we passed through Sydney, but Peter, who lived in Newcastle, we had only seen once, when we came back from Queensland via the coastal highway a few years earlier. Before that, the last time I'd seen Peter was when we shared a cabin at *Humpty Doo** rice fields outside of Darwin in 1958 for a few months. We were eighteen at the time. Now we were in our fifties.

See my book **Ephemeron...*

Oddly enough, both of them had been on Easter Island for a couple of hours in transit on their way back from Argentina and were there at the same time as I was. It would have been nice to have bumped into each other when we were all on the island together. They left on the mid-week flight whereas I left on the Sunday flight.

Their group had taken a quick bus ride from the airport to see the Moai at Ahu Tahai, the closest ones to the town of Hanga Roa, a short drive from the airport. Most tourists in transit make this brief trip to see these Moai. We talked a lot about Easter Island over dinner.

Unfortunately, I never did see Peter again after that dinner in Melbourne. We moved to the Gold Coast the following year (1995), and in 2004, Peter sadly and unexpectedly passed away.

In a note to me after he died, his wife Marie said they often spoke about me and my travels, especially about Easter Island which must have made quite an impression on him, even though he was only there a short time.

A moment of sadness

The tragedy with living in a country where major cities are thousands of kilometres apart, means one rarely gets the opportunity to catch up with relatives who live in those distant cities. You always think you'll make a trip and see them, but too often this isn't possible. Life gets in the way and before you know it, years have gone by without you realizing, and sometimes, as with myself and Peter, you never do see each other again. And that makes me sad when I think about it.

A rude awakening

I slept profoundly that Tuesday night and had barely woken up on Wednesday morning when the phone rang, and it was Phillip wanting to know where the hell I was. He had expected me to be at work and was pissed off that I hadn't turned up.

I quickly dressed and headed to the factory and shop just down the road. It was the last thing I wanted to do, but Phillip was expecting to leave on a holiday that same day, so I had to be there. He had expected me to be back on Monday, but that was the day that disappeared as I returned from Easter Island.

Once we got things sorted, he took off and I settled back into the old routines as if I had never been away.

— Changing States —

Part Three

Moving to the Sunshine State

Problems with an old building

The building we lived in at 159-161 Douglas parade Williamstown was built around 1887 and was just on 100 years old when we moved in. At the time it was built there was very little in that part of Douglas Parade with most of the town's commercial buildings clustered along Nelson Place fronting the docks on Hobson's Bay and along Ferguson Street to where the Town Hall is located. Also, the junction of Ferguson Street with the start of Douglas Parade saw shops and other commercial buildings begin to cluster at this location. Amongst the many businesses were 120 *Public Houses*, with the majority within close walking distance to the docks or surrounding the several railway stations that brought travellers into town. Close to the railway stations were also heavier industry that required transport for their products and raw materials which meant there would be lots of workers who were no doubt thirsty and so it was natural that publicans located their businesses around these railway stations to catch the workers coming to and from work. There are still more pubs in Williamstown than in any other suburb across greater Melbourne.

The Rodgers family who had a grocery store in the centre of the business district of Williamstown decided they would build a new premises a bit out of town so they could incorporate a stable with the shop and residence above. They used horses and carts to deliver their groceries to customers around town, and they needed space for the horses. Douglas Parade was one of three main streets that exited Williamstown. Douglas

Parade wound around the river a bit further out of town and crossed the mudflats of Stony Creek to continue to Footscray as Hyde Street. One could also turn right where Hyde Street crosses Francis Street and travel closer to the river along Whitehall Street past much heavy industry that had been established along the Yarra River banks (at Yarraville) before it splits into the Maribyrnong River (*Saltwater River*) – a tributary to the Yarra River which itself which goes through a large dockland area before continuing through the middle of Melbourne.

Douglas Parade was therefore a superb location for this new store the Rodgers family built. It was on the main industrial through-way in and out of Williamstown connecting directly with the already established industrial areas.

The other road that ran parallel with Douglas Parade was known by two names, depending on where you lived along this street: Williamstown Road, or Melbourne Road. It went from Ferguson Street to Newport Station where it crossed the railway lines beside the station and then continued all the way up to Geelong Road where it exits Footscray.

When I was a kid in Williamstown in the 1940s Douglas Parade was filled with houses on both sides all the way along it until Newport where the Power Station stood by the river. Then only one side was with houses extending back away from the river to Newport, but they only went a short distance past the Power Station until they encountered Refinery tanks and other tanks for storage of petroleum products piped there from the refinery at North Altona along the far reaches of Kororoit Creek Road, which could be sent off by barges and lighters in the river.

The third road out was the extension of Ferguson Street after it crosses the railway line at North Williamstown Station, Kororoit Creek road. It went out to the west past the army's rifle range and the Williamstown garbage tip. No one lived out that way until only recently.

The building at 159-161 Douglas parade was then a licensed grocery, and they used to deliver food items to our place at 19 Douglas Parade where the Dry-Cleaning shop with our family residence behind it, was located.

I have detailed this in two previous books at some length so won't go through it again.

Having Moved back to Williamstown with Monica and baby Brian in 1980, I had plans to use the shops for a music studio as a well as a place to sell musical instruments. It was such a huge space, something had to be done with it. We had behind the shops a lounge room, a hallway with a wide staircase leading to the floor above, a kitchen and an area Dianne (the Previous owner) had turned into a laundry and washroom. Outside at the back was a large courtyard with public toilets for patrons who attended wine tastings. Upstairs we had a bathroom three bedrooms and a huge lounge, above one of the shops, which was more than enough space for the three of us. Dianne had also renovated the entire living space above the old shops, so we only had to move in.

From the outside, it looked nothing much, just an old shop with a secondary shop attached. Inside it was quite elegant and refined.

It was built with handcrafted bricks, three bricks thick, and cement rendered on the outside on a bluestone foundation. The wooden floors both downstairs and upstairs were made from Oregon imported from Canada a hundred years earlier when it was built. Internal walls where not double brick were the old lathe and plaster kind. Over the years, settling and movement had cause millions of tiny cracks in the lathe and plaster walls and so rather than try to re-plaster them it was easier to cover them with wallpaper, and that's what Dianne had done. The part that had originally housed the stable with horses had a bluestone cobbled floor, but this had been replaced with a concrete floor during the 1940s. These bluestones, the same used by council for gutters and kerbs, had been used to pave the courtyard at the back, when we moved in.

At first, I absolutely loved the place. Monica did too, but after a while the sheer size of it became a problem to maintain. Plans for a music store were forgotten and the old part that had been a bottle shop when we bought the place, was turned into a giant lounge room combined with my extensive library of four thousand or so books, my record collection, and my various drums and musical instruments. I also had a Hi Fi system with wall mounted speakers (we had fourteen foot high ceilings) and could record and play drums there without hardly any of the sound getting outside of the building, (because of the triple brick walls).

But the problem with old places that are 100 years old is maintenance. I'd had cracks opening in the back part of the side wall along Princes Street because the foundations had been sinking which open a tiny crack in the wall high up on the second floor. I got Mr Ward, a general builder, carpenter, repairman we had used at the factory for many years to come and fill it a repair it. This was fine for a while. I even cut down the trees Dianne had planted along the back wall thinking that as they got bigger the roots would go underneath the building and suck out moisture in the ground, and this could be the cause of the crack opening up. But twelve months later the crack opened again. This time it was much worse and if you went into the room upstairs, our TV room, you could see the same crack inside. But what was bad was you could see right through to the other side of the wall. I could see light from outside. Removing the trees had made no difference. The crack continued to open.

I was thinking I would have to get specialists in to examine the foundations to see what could be causing the rear part of the building to sink and cause this huge crack. I climbed up onto the roof and found the crack was about 30 millimetres wide and extended right across the triple brick wall. I patched it with cement to stop water running down directly into the wall when it rained, but still water could get in that ran down the walls and over where the crack extended downwards. At ground level it wasn't noticeable, but once you got up above the height of the ground or first floor it started to widen and got wider and wider the further up you went.

There was a down pipe on inside Courtyard side, of the building and this ran underneath the kitchen area to drain into the street outside. I thought this could be broken and every time it rained water could leak out to sit on the ground underneath the building, to soften it and make the foundations sink. I tested it and found there was nothing wrong with it, so that wasn't the cause.

Still pondering what the cause could be we went to bed one night and were woken by a tremendous hailstorm. It pounded down on the roof. There was lightning and thunder. And the hail belting the roof was worse than the thunder. It was a cold night, because of the hail and the icy wind, but the storm passed, and we went back to sleep, only to be woken not long after with water dripping on us and into the room from cracks in the ceiling and down the walls. Brian too was woken by dripping water in his room.

It was an absolute disaster. We moved out bed into the large lounge room at the front where no water was dripping. We moved Brian's bed to another side of the room away from the wall and the window on the street side. There was nothing else we could do except watch the water continue to steadily drip into the two rooms. Eventually we went back to our bed now in the lounge room, which became our permanent bedroom after that, and went back to sleep.

As soon as daylight came, I went up onto the roof to see what had caused the water to get in. I thought I would see partially torn up sheets of roofing iron which allowed the wind to blow water in under the roof, but what I discovered was a layer of hailstones at least thirty centimetres thick all along the gutter inside the outside wall of the building. It sat there, and as it melted slowly water dribbled inside the building because the gutter was blocked by the massive build-up of hail. And it couldn't go anywhere but inside onto the ceiling from where it dripped down into the rooms. I got a shovel and shoveled the hail out of the gutter and threw over onto the footpath below where it quickly melted. Fortunately, no one was walking along the footpath. Once the bulk of the hail was gone the rest of it soon melted and flowed down the drainpipe into a gully trap as the base of the rear wall, from where it drained out into the gutter along Princes Street. It was the aftermath of this hailstorm that allowed me to discover the problem of the sinking foundation and the crack in the side wall.

A few hours later I happened to look into this old gully trap where the drainpipe from the roof dumped the water and although it was dry by then there was water pouring into the gully trap from a small lead pipe, the kind used a hundred years ago as water and gas pipes, before water pipes were changed to copper. I found this pipe had been put in there to drain water out from under the building. A fine idea, and it had worked for years. But what I also discovered was that the mortar that held the bricks together that formed the box-like gully trap, was porous. Any cement or lime had been leached out years ago and the mortar was nothing but porous sand. Every time it rained, every time water drained off the building down the drainpipe and into the gully trap to be dispersed to the street outside, it also leached through the porous sand and went under building to sit right beside the bluestone foundations making the soil there soft and compressible. The stone were slowly sinking into the soft went ground and this was why the side wall started to crack as the back wall of the building slowly sank.

Water poured out of that pipe all day, so there must have been a lot of it under the kitchen lying against the bluestone foundations. When eventually the water stopped coming out, I went and got some waterproof cement render and sealed the gully trap completely. I also sealed the old lead pipe.

Several days later, the ground behind the back corner was still damp, soggy, so I thought the sewer pipe may be cracked. These pipes generally crack or break at either end rather than in the middle. As the ground compresses and moves over time the points where the pipe is connected to the toilet and where it goes down to the main sewer under the street is where breakages occur. The ground near the outdoor toilets was dry and firm, but near the fence behind the corner of the building it was wet enough to be suspicious. I started to dig a hole and the deeper it got the soggier it became. A metre and a half down, a huge hole by this time, I found the pipe had cracked and water would come out every time the outdoor toilet was flushed. With this added to the water from rainfall runoff, that was the reason the back of the building had started to sink. There was another sewer pipe under this one, coming from inside the house, another half a metre deeper but this one was okay. I called a local plumber, and he came and fixed the pipe in half an hour. Then it was up to me to fill in the hole I'd dug. I probably saved $400 by digging the hole to expose the sewer pipe. Plumbers charge by the hour and it would have been a huge waste to pay him to dig a hole. It took almost all day to dig that hole. Once the job was done and the ground had dried a bit, I refilled the hole., which was a lot quicker than digging it.

From that point on water didn't get under the back of the building, and the crack stopped expanding. Finally, I got my long extension ladder and filled the crack near the top with cement. I also filled the crack where it extended through to the inside of the wall with cement, and plastered over it, finally covering it with matching wallpaper. I had to repaint the wall outside where the crack was and since I couldn't exactly match the old paint, I ended up having to repaint the whole side wall. I also had to patch cracks in the ceiling of the two bedrooms and repaint those ceilings as well. This was an enormous job, considering the size of the buildings and the heights of the ceilings on both floors. I did it all myself using extension ladders, long handled rollers, and outside, I also had to get on the roof and lean over to paint the upper part of the wall. I finished painting the whole building outside and inside.

It was this kind of massive maintenance that made me realize it was a building too big for me to maintain properly, too big and too old; and too old meant that there would always be maintenance problems in the future. After we came back from our trip overseas, and especially after Monica had returned from her return trip to Chile in 1994, we discussed selling the property and looking for another smaller, more manageable place to live in.

The crack developed between the side door and the rear upstairs window. In this image of the building before we moved in there were no cracks. They appeared several years later. The trees that I thought had caused the problem were only saplings against the back wall.

Sitting and thinking in the backyard as it was the year before we moved.

The start of a major change

Phillip decided he would buy my half of the business and the property from me, and he would run the business with his wife Chris helping in the shop. This happened officially on January 10, 1995, six months before the end of the financial year (June 30) 1995.

He felt he was too young to retire, and wanted to continue the business operating as it had for so many years. He was happy working in this industry whereas I had grown tired of it over the years and was looking forward to a change.

It was a huge step for both of us to take, and no doubt there was some trepidation on both our parts, but a decision had been made, and we both moved forward as best we could.

A brief moment aside

Brian had finished school the year before and was on the dole. He went straight from his student allowance to the dole. As part of being on the dole he had to look for work and I often had to drive him to places for interviews. He never got any jobs but had to fill in forms and get them signed by those who interviewed him to maintain his dole payments. All his friends were in the same boat. A whole generation of people conditioned to be on government support. This I think was the biggest failure of the then labour Government led by the man who pushed the whole country into 'the recession we had to have'. Meanwhile. interest rates had peaked at 17% and many mortgagees went bankrupt and lost their homes.

We were fortunate that we had paid off our mortgage which started at 10%, and by the time we'd finished with it, had reached 13%. People in our situation with earlier mortgages had their rate fixed at 13%. Newer mortgages started at that rate and went on to hit 17%. It was an absolute disaster for the country, and this was the time when Brian left school and desultorily looked for work. He really didn't care too much because he was on the dole and living at home where it cost him nothing. At school, although some students were able to get work experience with various businesses, when it was time for Brian's class to do that, the program had been canceled. No work experience was available. I managed to get to help a bit at the dry-cleaning factor at an attempt to gain some work experience — I'd hoped he may become interested enough to want to work for a bit — but he was not interested. Another problem was getting him up and ready to go to an interview. He was never on time, and we always got there late, certainly not a good impression for a prospective employer. We would have arguments with him if we tried to hurry him, with him always telling us he was going as fast as he could. He just didn't care.

Having insisted on staying in Melbourne, we thought it would be good idea to be away from him, well out of Melbourne or in another state so he couldn't just drop in when he needed something. We wanted him to depend on himself, and what better way for him to learn how to manage things was having him live independently.

I helped him find a flat to rent in Sunshine on the corner of Ballarat Road and Hampshire Road. I paid the bond and the initial month's rent. It was a working-class area, and the rents were quite reasonable, something Brian would be able to afford while on the dole.

It was a short walk from the flat down Hampshire Road to Sunshine Station where there were heaps of shops, two major supermarkets, takeaway fast-food shops, hardware, clothing stores, a laundromat for him to do his washing, and other shops for him to buy the things he needed. It was a good location, with buses stopping in front of the units and the railway station a short walk away.

Being responsible for paying rent, buying his own food, doing his own laundry, remembering to put the rubbish out for collection once a week, keeping the flat clean would, we hoped, teach him how to live and be independent. Everyone does it to some degree sooner or later. And Brian was 18, old enough to be going out on his own.

He seemed happy, which was relief for us. He liked the flat. I bought him a small fridge to keep his food fresh. He got our TV set, which didn't work too well there because the plug-in aerial socket wasn't functioning, and he had to improvise an aerial with a couple of twisted coat hangers. He also got some pots and pans for cooking and eating utensils and other bits and pieces like a toaster and a jug to boil water for tea or coffee, necessary for a kitchen.

Once we were sure he was set-up, we felt relaxed about the idea of selling our place and moving to Queensland.

In the meantime

We'd been looking around Williamstown for a suitable house to buy but discovered they were all ridiculously high-priced. Sure, we could buy a property when we sell the one we were in, but would have nothing left over to live on and I would have to look for a different line of work in order to live. I wanted to retire, so that wasn't an option.

We started looking further afield and could find no nearby suburb that we liked or houses either for that matter. We were even considering going to Portarlington, way across the Bay or down the other side towards Mornington. There were houses there that were affordable and would leave us with money to live on for a while.

But Christine happened to be in Melbourne at that time visiting Zara and Fred and she suggested we should come up to the Gold Coast to see what was there. The houses were much more affordable than anything in Melbourne.

"If you are going to go as far away from Melbourne that it takes several hours to get there, you might as well buy a place on the Gold Coast."

The more we thought about that the more attractive the idea became. We didn't want to live in Surfers Paradise, but there is much more to the Gold Coast than Surfers. I think at the back of my mind I wanted to get away from the sometimes-freezing cold weather in Melbourne during the latter part of winter. I was sick of cold weather and Southern Queensland with the border of NSW has the best weather year-round of any place along the east coast, so it was the logical place to consider.

We started buying the Gold Coast Bulletin and looking at the quality of the houses for sale and the prices compared to Melbourne, it was no wonder so many were moving there.

By the end of that year, 1995, 16,000 people had moved from Melbourne to the Gold Coast. And it only increased each subsequent year.

Back to the Gold Coast

We decided to drive to the Gold Coast again, now that I wasn't working anymore to have look to see what was available

Christine was living just up the road at Tanah Mera on the southern edge of Brisbane and said she'd be happy to have someone else in the family living nearby.

We told Christine that we'd come up and have a look. We stayed at her place and of course she came with us as we went house hunting. Subconsciously, we had decided by then that we would move there. We had yet to sell our place, but we did have the money Phillip paid me for my share of the business and property at 19 Douglas Parade, so we could use some of that for a deposit if we found something we liked.

This time the drive north to Queensland was filled with anticipation mixed with a feeling of freedom. We could take our time to find something. We didn't have to be back in Melbourne at any specific time. We didn't have to worry about Brian because he was now 18 years old and could be left at home while we were away.

It was lovely, just the two of us, driving along a familiar highway through towns we'd been in many times over the years, but this time we could take our time, stop where we wanted for a rest or an overnight stay, or to do a bit of sight-seeing, and then move on at a leisurely pace. It was a whole different feeling, driving north this time. There were no time constraints, and I had to keep reminding myself that I didn't have to be back to go to work by a certain time.

It was August, and the further north we got the warmer it became.

When we arrived at Christine's place, she was complaining that she felt cold, but to us, who had been in Melbourne a couple of days earlier where the temperature never got above 12 C at its warmest in winter, to encounter 22 C where Christine lived, was fabulous. We ran around with T-shirts and shorts on while she wore a jumper and long jeans. There wasn't a cloud in the sky and a lovely cool breeze occasionally wafted over us.

"This is lovely and warm," Monica said.

"Just wait till you've lived here for a year. Next winter you'll be wearing jumpers and jeans, and not shorts and a T shirt. You're not used to it yet."

I found that hard to believe, but later, I discovered once you do become accustomed to the climate, you do finish wearing said jeans and jumpers in the few short winter months especially in July and August.

On the floor

Christine had a spare room in the house but no extra bed, so we ended up sleeping on a mattress on the floor, which was okay until you wake up and want to get up. It's a bit awkward. Christine gave us extra blankets which we didn't think we'd need, but it did get cold during the night, and we certainly needed them.

Christine was in the kitchen making coffee when we appeared.

"Good morning. How'd you sleep?"

"Pretty good," I said.

"Like a log," Monica said.

"And did you use the extra blankets?"

"We certainly did. You were right, it was cold."

"It got down to 11 C during the night."

"That's cold enough for me," I said a before sipping the hot coffee Christine offered.

The toaster popped up four slices of fresh toast. Christine passed them to us on a plate and said, "There's jam and cheese, or Vegemite to put on the toast."

The search is on

Once breakfast was over, we headed out to our Tarago and hopped in for the drive down to the coast. The weather was already warming up and I on its way to a top of 21 C.

"Where do you want to look first?"

"Why don't we just drive around a few of the newer areas to get an idea of how the place feels?"

"Sounds good," Christine said.

And that's what we did.

We drove to Miami Waters and saw a lot of older houses that didn't much appeal to us even though they were on a canal.

We had thought we would like something on a canal, but that turned out to be too optimistic. Houses on canals were a lot more expensive than we could afford. Like Williamstown, we could buy one, but would have nothing left over to live on.

Although we enjoyed driving through several canal estates, we ended up looking at a new area called Robina Waters. Again, houses on canals, very new ones, were way above what we could realistically afford, so we drove into the areas nearby that were not on canals or waterways. Gradually our ideas of where we could live compared to where we thought we could live began to change.

We finished visiting a real estate agent in Robina Village not far from a well-established area called Robina Woods. It had been developed ten years earlier whereas the newer area, was still being developed and had streets named after Melbourne suburbs, like Yarraville. Robina Woods had streets named after Sydney suburbs like Manly.

Not far from both areas was a huge shopping complex under construction, the Robina Town Centre.

"Once that's finished, house prices in this area will skyrocket, so you've arrived at the right time," the agent said.

We got a list of houses in the Robina Woods area and visited them. There were some nice ones, but they seemed humid and dark, being in small *cul-de-sacs* that had buildings on land higher up surrounding them. There was a large golf course, that the houses we looked at surrounded, a nice park along a creek, and lots of walkways linking small streets together. It was a lovely area, and we did find one house on a rise at the start of a small street, Firestone Court, that Monica liked the moment she walked inside it.

We went back and thanked the agent. We told her we had seen one house we liked and that, if possible, could we come back the next day for another look, to see if we still felt the same.

She was happy for us to do that. So off we went back to Christine's place at Tanah Mera where we sat and discussed the pros and cons of the various houses we'd seen and the price range we were willing to pay.

A snap decision?

The next day, Monica and I went back to have another look at the house she liked. Walking inside it has a nice feeling about it. It was bright and airy with large sliding doors that opened into a big back yard. The land area was 810 square metres, quite large compared to many blocks in newer areas that were lucky to get to 600 square metres. Christine's block where she built the house at Tanah Mera was only 450 square metres, the usual size in most newly developing areas.

This house was high enough above nearby houses to get fresh sea breezes and the main living areas faced north towards the sunshine. The living areas were at the front while the four bedrooms were at the rear. It was a layout that we both liked, although I wasn't too keen on the colour

scheme inside, it was mostly pale shades of pink. However, Monica fell in love with it.

"It would be nice to live in an ordinary house instead of rooms on top of an old shop," Monica said as we walked through the empty house.

There was no furniture inside because the owners had moved out months before, but even empty, there was warm feeling about the house. The living space was open, giving a spaciousness that blended with the outdoors through large glass doors. It was pleasantly cool inside whereas outside it was quite hot, and this was a surprise to find knowing that the house had been locked up and the curtains drawn. One would have expected it to be very hot inside. The carpet in one room had a large stain on it, but it was an old carpet anyway and if we moved in that would be the first thing to be replaced. There was a paved courtyard outside the lounge room area which adjoined the kitchen and a path beside the bedrooms to the rear. The rest of the yard was grass, neatly cut. Down the back there were a couple of small orange trees and one raggedy looking custard apple tree. It was a big back yard which I liked because that meant we wouldn't be too close to our neighbours, especially if they were

Our Tarago parked on the driveway while we look around inside.

noisy. I disliked neighbours being too close, because even if you couldn't see them, there was often little privacy, and that was a problem with most new estates where the houses sit on 400 to 500 square metres and the space between houses in only a metre or two. You might as well live in a block of flats as being in one of these free-standing housing estates. The main bedroom at the rear of the house was large with an en-suite, whereas the other bedrooms were a standard size. The master bedroom also had sliding glass doors opening into the yard as did the living room by the kitchen, the lounge room, and one of the other three bedrooms.

We sat by a nearby lake and talked about it. Subconsciously I think we had already decided that we would buy it.

When I asked her what she really thought about it she said, "I love it."

"In that case, should we make an offer?"

Was that a snap decision?

Was it like I often did, decide to do something on the spur of the moment, to grab it (an idea or an unexpected decision) and run with it?

Were we caught up with the idea of having freedom from work, and the ability to live wherever we wanted that made us decide so quickly?

I don't really know.

Sometimes you get a gut feeling that tells you something is just right. When that happens, you shouldn't ignore it. I had that feeling about this place, and because Monica seemed so keen on it, we decided to go to the estate agent to make an offer.

We went to the agent and offered $180,000.

Standing in the lounge room by the sliding glass door looking into the backyard. On the right is the window looking out from the kitchen, and we can see the paved area along the side where each room has a sliding glass door opening into the yard, which made the house light and airy.

The vendors wanted $210,000, and so we haggled a bit until we arrived at a final figure of $198,000. We paid an immediate deposit, and signed a contract. When we settled the balance, it would be ours. We explained to the agent that we had to sell our place in Melbourne before we could move and, if possible, could we get three months before final settlement. That would give us time to market and sell our place in Williamstown. The agent said it was unusual, most contracts up here are settled in one month, but she spoke to the owners, and they agreed. They had already moved out and were living in Brisbane, so it didn't matter to them if it took three instead of one month for settlement. The 25th of November was the date we agreed to pay the settlement for possession of the house.

To us it seemed abnormally fast to settle in one month, but that's what they did up here in Queensland. It always took two or three months in Melbourne. At least it did in 1995.

We were happy with the result of our decision. We were excited about going home and selling up, packing and moving, starting anew in a new place. We couldn't wait to get back to Melbourne so we could begin organizing everything.

Monica walking up the driveway to have another look before going back to the agent to make an offer. Below: Sold. Monica posing in front of the sold sign by the letterbox... Feeling happy, feeling relaxed, now that a decision had been made and we were the new owners of the house (in 3 more months anyway).

Feeling happy after paying the deposit to buy the house.

Preparing to sell

We put our place up for auction and the estate agents did considerable advertising in newspapers and magazines which generated good interest. Not being familiar with how buying and selling works, and the best way to go about it to maximize what we could get, we heeded the advice from the estate agents.

Our property existed on two main titles, an old law title for the buildings located on 159-161 Douglas Parade. This was on the corner of Princes Street. Behind the buildings and a section of back yard was another smaller block, 1 Princes Street, which had been used as a car park for customers at the licenced grocery that occupied the front part of the building's ground floor but was now an extension of our back yard. This was on a modern-day title.

The estate agents assured us we could get a better price if we amalgamated the two titles and sold everything as a single property for possible re-development, rather than selling both sections separately. Even with heritage listed conditions regarding the old buildings, there was still room for considerable development. It was costly and complicated to legally amalgamate the two titles, so we decided to leave this for the future owner to do. However, we actioned the two titles together as if they were one.

We shouldn't have done that and should have sold the titles separately. But hindsight is not going to rectify this mistake. We discovered a year later that the people who bought our properties sold the back block separately for a good sum and kept the front part for a few years before selling that again at double the price they paid us for the whole lot together. They did much better out of that property than we did.

The day of the auction

The two agents who worked together were sitting at the table in the eating area beside the kitchen explaining to us how it would likely happen. One of them suggested that we get a friend or someone we know to make the first couple of bids to help get the likely buyers started. My brother Paul and his wife Lynne were there, as were a couple of friends who worked with Fred at the abalone processing factory. One of them said he would start the bidding, and once it got going would drop out and let the genuine buyers go at it themselves.

As the building appeared the morning of the auction. Potential buyers and onlookers lined up against the wooden fence of the house on the other side of the street.

— Changing States —

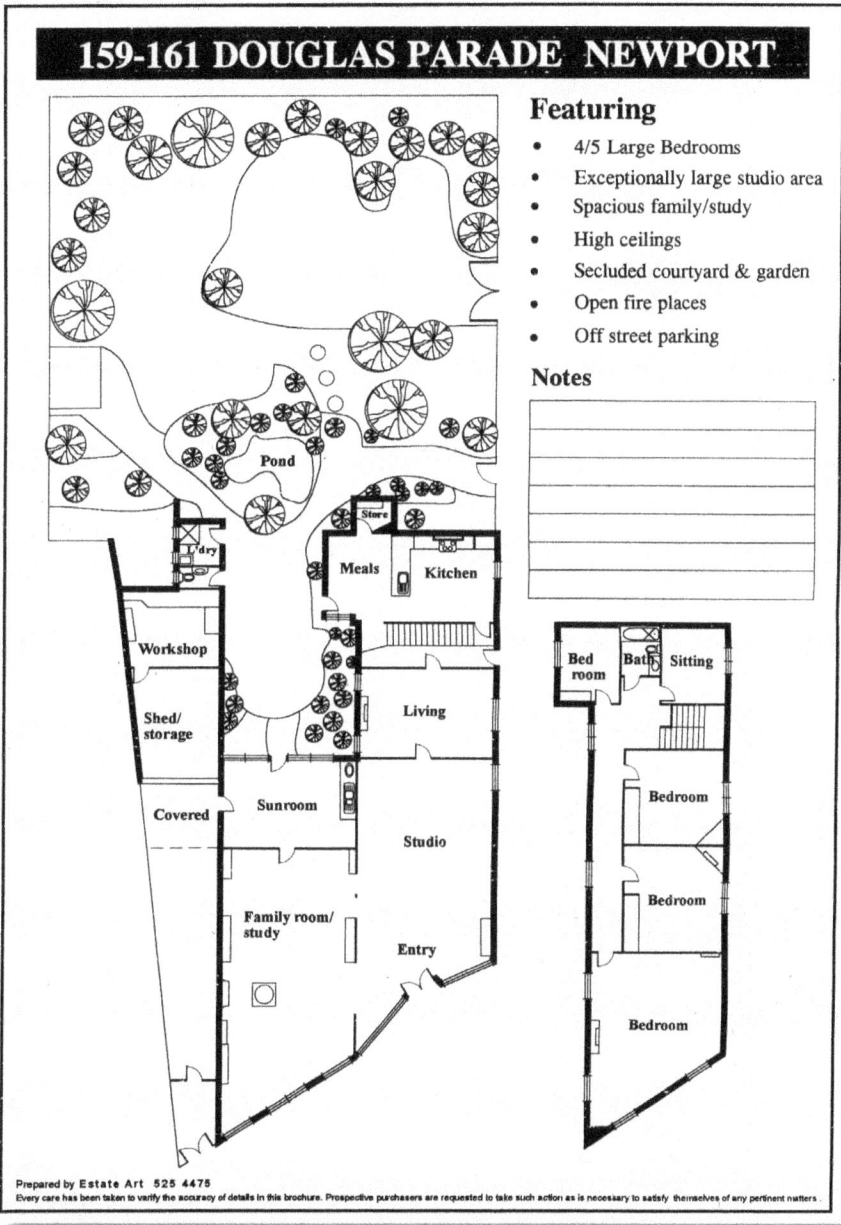

Signage and advertising pamphlet from the estate agent.

A reserve price was set, and if it didn't get to that price it would be passed in, and we could negotiate with the highest bidder to see if we could get the price up to or above the set reserve.

Earlier, the property had been open for visitors and potential buyers to wander through and have a look at everything, while we did our best to stay out of the way. The cats had disappeared somewhere in the yard to hide from the strangers wandering about. But most of the people who had been in for a look around were now outside in the street waiting for the proceedings to begin.

It was about fifteen minutes before the listed time, already a bigger crowd had gathered on the footpath beside the house opposite us in Princes Street. How many of them were neighbours there to have a look from surrounding streets was unknown but there were a lot more outside than those who had been inside for a look. Probably most there were onlookers curious to see how much we would get at auction. There were only two bidders who took a while to get started even after the fake bidder made the first offer at a low price that would obviously be ignored. But someone had to start to get any genuine buyers going.

I sneaked out the front to take some photos of what was happening while Monica, as nervous as hell, stayed inside with Lynne in the lounge room from where they could hear the auction going on just outside the window.

The crowd beginning to gather as the auction is about to start. They are all on the footpath opposite the main entrance to the building in Princes Street.

— Changing States —

It started with one of the agents ringing a loud bell which silenced the onlookers. He then read out the conditions of the auction so everyone understood the legal requirements. After that he talked briefly about the quality of the building, its history, and future usage possibilities. Once that was done, he asked for a bid to get started.

Silence.

Everyone stood still, waiting for someone else to start.

"Is someone going to start with a bid?" He asked. "Surely you aren't all here just to see what someone else does."

More silence.

Monica trying to distract herself from the auction going on outside the window behind her. Lynne with her son Matthew keeping Monica company in the lounge room.

By this time, I had moved back inside and was waiting in the dining room with Monica, Paul and Lynne.

Our friend called out his dummy bid.

"There you go," the auctioneer said. People started stirring, looking at each other, wondering who had made the first bid.

"I'm afraid you'll need to do better than that," the auctioneer stated. "Do I hear anther 20?"

Finally real bidding started, and I stopped listening as the auctioneer cajoled the bidders and tried to convince them to bid more. We had set the reserve at $350,000 and the agents struggled to get the bidding much above $300,000. They called a pause and came inside to discuss it with us, but I told them they would have to get closer to the reserve or we wouldn't sell. They went back out and started again and managed to get it a bit higher when the bidding stalled again, and they passed it in.

All done! Time to negotiate with the highest bidder.

They came inside with the person who had made the highest bid and we negotiated through the agents with this bidder and managed to get the price they were willing to pay up to $348,000 which was just under the reserve.

I knew, it was going to be hard to sell with interest rates at an all-time high of 17%, and money hard to get. We shouldn't have sold, but we'd made up our minds and once we'd done that we just wanted to sell and move on rather than drag out the process over months or perhaps a couple of years until we could get a sale, and there was no guarantee anything would be better in another 6 months or a year.

We settled on the price given to us which was as close as we could get to the reserve and signed the papers. The new buyers wrote the deposit cheque there in the lounge room and the deal was done. It was September 25. They could move into the place in November 25. It was a 90-day contract. They were happy with that, and it suited us too.

Too late for regrets

"You should have sold the back block separately," Phillip said, when I went to the shop and told him how it had gone. "You would have got $80,00 for that alone, and still would have got close to your reserve without that included. You'd have been at least $60,000 better off."

He was right. I had sort of rushed into it, without thinking about possible options other than what the agents suggested. They didn't care, they made money from the sale whatever way we did it. I presume they thought that if we sold the two together we would get a faster sale, and that's all they worried about, getting it over and done as quickly as possible so they could move on to another one.

But what was done, was done, and we would have to live with that decision.

Afterwards

Over the next month or so, house sales across the country dropped and we considered ourselves lucky that we had managed to sell our place, no matter how we did it. Australia was in a recession and one of the first things to suffer was the housing market. People couldn't afford the money to buy a house, and those who couldn't pay their mortgages couldn't even sell their houses. It was a desperate situation for a while.

There was a feeling of relief once the deal had been done. We could relax and wouldn't have to think about packing and getting ready to move for at least a couple of months. We did however book a removalist to come and take our stuff and transport it to Queensland so it would arrive at the new house on the morning of the 25th November. It was a two-day trip so we would have to get everything ready to go by the 22nd to be collected on the 23rd. These guys were booked out months in advance, so the sooner we arranged for our stuff to be picked up and delivered to the new location the better. I would get cardboard boxes and over the next two months we would go through everything and pack it ready for transport. The packed cartons and boxes could sit in the empty shop at the front as we proceeded. It would be easy to load them from there into the removalist truck when needed.

A lot of what we had in this place would not be suitable for moving to the new place. I called one of the two second hand furniture places in Williamstown and asked the owner of he wanted to buy our lounge chairs, glass dining room table and chairs, drinks cabinet, and he agreed after inspecting them. He would take them a couple of weeks before we were due to leave, so at least we had the use of them while still living there. With that done, that only left the clothes, books, records, drums, speakers, HiFi system and stuff I wanted to take with us. I had too many books, probably 6000 of them so I started giving them away to a local second-hand bookshop, sold some to other second hand shops in Carlton and finished up with around 2000 which I packed into boxes. The house we were going to move into was far too small to accommodate everything Monica and I had collected over the years. Our intention was to buy new furniture suitable for the house once we got there. Our queen size bed went with us which was the only furniture we took apart from four kitchen chairs and a small table. Brian's bed had already been moved to the flat he had started to live in over in Sunshine.

Of course, with all this packing and getting rid of stuff, our two cats were extremely nervous. They had no idea what was happening.

When the truck had come and all the packed items were loaded, the place was twice as huge as we remembered, its size seemingly exaggerated by the lack of anything in any of the rooms. The cats looked miserable. It was time for Monica to fly up to Queensland with them. I had already booked the flight. Sunny, we managed to give him the tablet the Vet had suggested which would make him sleepy so he wouldn't notice what was happening while he was being transported to Queensland in his special box. Shady on the other hand was scratching and fighting us and we couldn't get her to swallow the tablet no matter how we tried. We barely were able to get her into her travelling box. She would be wide awake and no doubt terrified when she was taken to the airport and loaded into the belly of the plane. Monica would also be on the same flight.

I drove Monica and the cats to Tullamarine to catch the plane. Christine would collect her and the cats at the Brisbane airport and they would stay with her for the couple of days before going down to the Gold Coast on the day of the settlement to take possession of the house and to let the truck driver unload our stuff.

I remembered there had been a phone in the house, but it had been disconnected at the exchange. I rang *Telstra* and organized them to reconnect the phone line at the exchange and to give us a new number. I was surprised at how quickly they did this. In less than half an hour the phone was operational, and we still hadn't moved in. I kept our phone in Williamstown connected until the hour before I left when I rang them and got them to disconnect it and transfer our account to the new number in Queensland.

With Monica and the cats gone, the house was enormous and empty. All that was there was a mattress, a pillow and a couple of sheets and a blanket that I used for a couple of days to sleep on the floor until it was time to leave. Things like my drums and my CD collection I had packed in the van ready to drive up to Queensland once settlement for our place had finalized. I didn't trust sending the drums in the removalist truck. I'd had drums broken in Europe years before, having them transported from Spain to Germany as unaccompanied luggage. I wasn't going to have that happen again.

The people who had bought our place, lived a couple of streets away and they asked if they could bring some of their stuff around to store in the empty shop, so I said yes, and they wasted no time in bringing a truckload of cardboard boxes packed with stuff. Nothing large, just boxes of small things. Their furniture would be brought in after they'd finished selling their place and could effect settlement.

On my last day there, I rang our solicitor (lawyer) and gave him the Williamstown Dry Cleaner's number after telling him that our original number at the house was to be canceled. I shoved the mattress, pillow and sheets into the back of the van with the drums and CDs and went around to the shop and waited there for the solicitor to ring me and tell me when settlement had been finalized, and I could let the new owners into the house.

I was having a coffee with Phillip when he rang and said, "Don't let them take anything into the house. Don't let them in yet."

"Why?"

"Their settlement hasn't come through."

"Shit."

Settlement confusion

Meanwhile, in Queensland, Monica and Christine and the cats in their boxes were in Christine's car in front of the house in Firestone Court Robina waiting for the estate agent to let them in and give them the keys. Also sitting there in the driveway in his truck was the removalist waiting to be allowed to unload our stuff. The agent wouldn't let them in, because our settlement hadn't been paid by our solicitor. It hadn't been paid because he was still waiting for the buyers of our Williamstown place to finalize their settlement, and they were waiting for the buyers of the place they had lived in also to settle. Presumably that person was waiting for a settlement further down the chain… a chain, that if broken by someone not being able to pay on time, would stuff up everybody.

I jumped into the van and drove around to our buyer's house. They were busy loading a removalist truck with their furniture in preparation to shift it around to 161 Douglas Parade. They had auctioned off their place two months earlier. Also parked in the street was another removalist truck with the furniture of the people who had bought their place waiting to move in when they moved out.

"I can't let you into my place yet," I told her.

"What's going on?"

"According to my solicitor, your settlement hasn't been paid yet. Can you ring your solicitor and find out what is going on?"

She was visibly upset, with me telling her I wouldn't let her in. I'd already let her take a lot of small stuff around, and now it was the heavy furniture they were preparing to shift.

"My solicitor is here right now. I'll go in and talk to him."

She came out a few moments later with someone I hadn't met before. She introduced us.

I explained that the settlement due for my place hadn't come through and that I was not allowed to let anyone move in yet. "Can you find out what has happened?"

While he went back inside the house to make some phone calls, the removalists continued to bring her furniture out of the place to load into their truck.

Her solicitor came back out fifteen minutes later and said everything was proceeding as it should.

"I'll go back to the factory and wait for my solicitor to call me when it's done," I said. "And when it's all sorted, I'll come up to the place with the keys to let you in."

Back at the factory I rang the new number Telstra had given me and Monica answered the phone. She told me the agent had let her in, but she still hadn't let the Removalist unload his truck. I explained what had happened down here, and that I would call the moment everything was fixed.

About half an hour later I got the call from my solicitor. He told me it was all done, the settlement had come through, and he had forwarded our settlement for the house in Queensland to the seller's solicitors. The balance left would be transferred to my bank account.

I rang Monica to tell her, and she said the agent had come back and said it was all done. "The driver is unloading our stuff and putting it in the garage right now. He's already put the bed together in the bedroom which was nice of him. I've got somewhere to sleep tonight."

"What about the cats?"

"We let them loose and they found a spot to hide in, the linen press. I don't think they'll come out until things quieten down a bit."

"It took a lot longer than I expected, so I won't be able to get far today. I was hoping to have left around eleven or so, but with all the delays it looks like it'll be closer to 3 o'clock before I can start the drive up there."

"Christine's gone home so it's just me and the cats.'

"I'll have to make one stop overnight. Depending on how far I can get this afternoon, hopefully I will arrive late tomorrow afternoon or early evening. Can't wait to get there."

A brief goodbye

I had already said goodbye to the rest of the family. I had been over to Sunshine to see Brian and say goodbye and he seemed somewhat indifferent.

I left our new phone number with him in case he needed to contact us. He seemed okay in the flat, so I didn't worry. It would all work out. That was yesterday, today was the last day I would be in Melbourne, for a while at least.

I said goodbye to Phillip and headed back up to our old place to hand over the keys to the people who were waiting to get inside. Their removalist truck was parked by the side of the building in Princes Street with the driver impatient to start unloading. With that done, I was free to leave.

No regrets

It felt odd this time driving through the western suburbs towards the highway north out of Melbourne, knowing I was leaving everything behind.

I had done it many times, we had done it together many times over the years, but this time it was different, this time I was not coming back, coming home, because home was no longer here. It would be in Robina, Queensland from now on, almost 2000 kilometres north, and Monica was already there waiting for me to arrive.

I also felt excited with the prospect of starting in a new place. The house was only seven years old. The suburb of Robina was rapidly developing with the prospect of being a major business centre in years to come. Not far from our place they were building a huge shopping centre (*Robina Town Centre*) and once that was completed it would attract lots of future housing and residential as well as business development to the area. We were in a part that was beside the *Robina Woods Golf Course,* an older well established leafy green suburb, a beautiful spot ten minutes by car from the new Town Centre being constructed.

Well, for better or worse, we had started a new journey into the future and only time would tell how it would turn out.

The main part of the yard, all grass. The hoses on the lawn are marking the shape of the pool we decided to have put in.
These pictures were taken the second week we were there.
The few small trees that aren't in pots were already there when we moved in.

The yard at the back of the house, all grass sloping down to the rear fence. We had to replace it a couple of years later because the wood was full of termites. We replaced it with a painted corrugated steel fence.

Looking at the north facing side of the house where the only paving was under the pergola in front of the lounge room and kitchen and alongside the two main bedrooms. The plants in pots are some we bought to put into the garden once a layout had been determined.

December, a chaotic month

The cats found several places to hide and keep out of the way until they got used to the new place. At first, we kept them indoors for a few days, fearing that if we let them outside, they could wander off and get lost because they weren't familiar with the area. We thought that once they were comfortable inside, we could let them out into the yard. Sunny would be disappointed because there were no trees he could climb, only a few saplings planted by the previous owners, and a small bit of garden along a path under a pergola and beside the bedroom doors facing the back yard. The rest was all grass, all the way around. The first time I cut the grass it took forty-five minutes.

The weather was variable, alternating between hot and windy to hot and humid and heavy with huge masses of clouds building up. There were often thunderstorms and when the rain came down it came down in buckets, pounding everything, instantly filling gutters to overflowing. It was the beginning of the wet season, and we were to have three months of this kind of weather. Before the much more comfortable dry season began.

Whenever there was lightning and thunder, shady would race into our bedroom and hide under the bed. It didn't seem to bother Sunny too much; he would just curl up in a corner and go to sleep.

Since the only furniture we had was a couple of cane chairs, which we brought with us only because the cats were used to them, and I thought they wouldn't be too upset if there was something familiar they could see and sit on. There was our bed, plus the kitchen table and chairs, and that was it. The first thing we did was to go to Harvey Norman, there was a huge store not far away, where we bought a lounge suite and two leather chairs, one for each of us, to sit in by the window where we could read.

With that done, we also decided to rip up the existing brownish-pink carpet and replace it with something more neutral and practical. They agreed to do this in a couple of weeks so we would have the carpet down before Christmas.

While we waited for the lounge suite to be delivered, we also explored the local area. We found paths connecting the ends of one street to another that went through little parks and gardens, so you could walk parallel to the street that the smaller streets connected to without having to walk along the busier street. This was great because there were no footpaths along the main road or the smaller side roads, and you had to walk along the street itself which we thought could be dangerous when it was busy.

We also explored the local shopping centres and at Robina Quays we found a swimming pool and the man whose company built it. It was his display centre with a lovely pool, and we discussed with him the cost of putting one into our huge yard. It was quite reasonable, so we contracted with him to build it. He would do all the arrangements with the council regarding permits before commencing.

He told us they could start within a couple of weeks, but that it would have to be finished after Christmas and the holiday break. That was okay with us, so we signed the contract.

Monica started going for regular walks along the different pathways between streets. She would walk every day. I went with her a couple of times but walking for exercise wasn't something I liked much. I didn't need that exercise since I went to Aikido training four times a week at the dojo in West Burleigh. Each time it was two hours of intensive training, loosening up, stretching, rolling and falling, throwing and being thrown; the training was full-on and intense, so I didn't really need to go walking.

About mid-December, on a Saturday morning, the street filled with cars early because the people next door to us were having a garage sale. There were people coming and going from very early (*the sun rises around 4:30 am during the summer and everyone is up and about early*), walking up the driveway next door to see what was offered for sale, bargaining and buying things. This activity started to diminish by around 8 am and that's when the swimming pool guys arrived with a small truck towing a trailer on which was a digging machine.

They quickly unloaded this and the guy in charge, Dennis, told me they would have to tear down the side wall between our house and the fence so he could get his machine inside to start digging. They also need to get their small truck up the sideway thus opened by removing the fence, so the dirt dug out of the ground could be taken away.

With Dennis supervising, the digging machine makes its way up to the side where the rendered brick wall had to be pulled down to gain access into the back yard.

A frangipani bush was ripped out and the wall toppled in no time at all. The wall was broken into pieces and loaded onto a small tip truck and taken away. It took no longer than twenty minutes.

They had barely ripped down the side brick fence when another truck arrived and parked in the driveway. It was the carpet laying people with the new carpet. They piled out of the truck and came inside and started to rip up the old horrible carpet, by which stage the guys from the swimming pool company (Robina Pools) were beginning to dig the hole for the pool. I had marked out the shape of it earlier using hoses to delineate the edge, Dennis used spray paint to mark the shape on the grass.

"This is a busy bloody street," he said, as he sprayed the paint.

"I had no idea the guys next door were going to have a garage sale, or that the carpet layers would come today as well. They never said when they would come, only that it would be before Christmas."

Half an hour later, the old carpet was rolled up and sitting on the front lawn. The original underlay was good, so the carpet layers decided to leave it and put the new carpet on top.

"It's better than the one we were going to use, so you might as well leave it there," they told me.

Whatever…

Dennis came up to me when I went back outside and asked, "Do you mind if I take away some of that carpet?"

"It's only going to be taken away and dumped. I'm sure they won't mind if you take some of it."

"Great. My nephew is building a holiday cottage and that carpet would save him a bit of money."

Before the first truckload of dirt from the hole in the yard was taken away, they had to take away the brick and cement rendered wall they'd knocked down.

"They're not taking concrete and bricks anymore at the tip," Dennis said before they started loading it. "But I know the guy who checks the loads coming in, and I'm sure if we gave him a bottle of whiskey or something like that, he would turn a blind eye and we can dump the bricks and cement."

"All right." I went inside and got a bottle of high-class whiskey that I'd been given as a present and because I don't like whiskey much, I'd not used any of it. The bottle was intact, unopened. I handed it to Dennis. "Would that do?"

"That's terrific. I'm sure we'll get it dumped after I give him that."

The cats had vanished. I found them hiding in the bathroom.

The carpet guys were thumping away with a device used to stretch the carpet which would have terrified them. They didn't like strangers, anyway, let alone a bunch of guys tearing the place apart and making huge noises.

With the old carpet taken out and rolled up to take to the tip, they are about to unload the new carpet seen in the back of the van. Dennis is there loading onto his truck the rolls of used carpet he wanted for his nephew.

When they'd finished the bedrooms and the passage they wanted to know if I wanted the carpet to extend into the living room as it had before. I told them no, to finish at the end of the passage. I would get the tiles extended to cover the part that had once been carpeted.

Outside the hole in the yard was getting deeper.

With the back half of the house newly carpeted, they moved into the lounge room area at the front of the house and got to work there. We were lucky that we had no furniture that had to be moved out of the way anywhere in the house other than in the bedroom we used. It made the job quick and easy. In fact, I was amazed at how quickly they had ripped up the old carpet and replaced it with the new one. A bit under three hours and they were gone, job done.

Next door the guy having the garage sale was a bit pissed off with us because he thought we'd blocked the street with the trucks and machinery and passers-by wouldn't be able to see he was having a garage sale. But the reality was that those interested in the sale had already been early, before our guys started their various jobs. Anyone else coming would be a straggler. Besides, he'd sold almost everything he'd had outside on the driveway and in his garage. I took no notice of him. Maybe he was one of those who always complained about something. I never got to know him because he and his wife moved a couple of months later. They'd only been renting the place.

Meanwhile the hole in the yard got bigger and bigger.

The small tip truck taking away another load of dirt out of the back yard. I don't know how may loads they took away, but it was a lot.

By mid-afternoon, it was done. It was as deep as they' were going to make it. It looked a mess. They took their digging machine away.

"We'll be back on Monday," Dennis said as he was leaving. "I've put a plastic barrier across the sideway, so people know not to enter. We don't want anyone falling into the hole, do we?"

Spreading the crushed rock across the bottom before putting in the reinforcing rods to give the pool the shape needed before pouring and praying the concrete.

It rained once the crushed rock was in and everything got soggy and muddy.

— Changing States —

After the last load of dirt was taken away the truck came back with a load of crushed rock which went into line the bottom of the hole.

On Sunday it rained intermittently and quite a bit of water filled the lower part of the hole.

Reinforcing steel rods had been delivered and dumped on the front lawn when they arrived on Saturday, and this was dragged in when they returned on Monday and they started cutting and shaping it to put into the pool to create the shape and to reinforce the concrete they were going to pour. A smaller digging machine was used to dig the trenches in which the plumbing was to go.

— Changing States —

Once the shape of the pool was delineated the next day the concrete was delivered. It came with a large pump because it was to be sprayed into the shape needed. This took several hours with quite a few trucks arriving one after the other. The whole pool had to be sprayed and shaped in one go so it would dry evenly without joins that would crack later. There were half a dozen guys going flat out doing this. I thought it was most impressive.

More chaos in the street as a series of trucks came in one after the other to pump the fast drying concrete through a very long hose into the pool where the guys sprayed it continuously to create the shape of the pool in one go. It had to be done without stopping so there were no gaps otherwise it could leak..

Once the pool was shaped and finished to this stage, Dennis explained that they had to leave it for seven days to harden before they could do anything else. They would in fact take a couple of weeks because Christmas would occur, and everyone was off for those weeks. What he wanted us to do was to spray the pool with water every day to keep the surface from drying too quick compared to the inside. The concrete was very thick and would take a while to dry all the way through. Spraying it with the garden hose would prevent small cracks forming on the surface as it dried.

Every day Monica went out in the afternoon and hosed the concrete so the surface wouldn't dry too fast and develop cracks.

We also contacted a pool fencing company and had them come out and measure the length of the fence required by law. They measured and went back and constructed the fence segments, some of which had to be curved, and within a few days they came and built a fence around the pool.

The lounge room suite arrived the week before Christmas, but our leather reading chairs would have to be made in Perth and wouldn't be delivered until mid-January.

We went to a tiling place to select tiles as close as possible to the ones previously used. There was no way would get the same tiles years later, so something similar with a similar colour had to be selected. The tiling place also recommended a tiler whom we contacted, and he turned up on a Friday morning to lay the tiles over the exposed part of the living room area. That day turned out to be the hottest day for years. It hit 35 C with a very high humidity. The tiler had another job on the go at the same time in Nerang, about twenty minutes' drive away, and when he finished laying the tiles, he went to that job. He said he would be back later when the glue had dried to grout and finish our job.

It was even hotter in Nerang, and when he came back two hours later to do the grouting, he didn't look well at all. In fact, he was dehydrated and got sick, but he finished the job.

A snap storm and a frantic search

Then it was Christmas and Christine came down from Brisbane to have a small dinner with us.

The cats were outside in the yard when a sudden squall blew over. There was thunder so loud it rattled the roof, and lightning that made the air sizzle and the hairs on your arms stand up. It sounded almost like the small glass window in the garage had shattered. I was sure lightning had hit the house.

Sunny came racing inside and hid in the linen press as the storm pounded us. Shady did not appear. I was worried about her and went outside to look for her. I couldn't see her anywhere. I knew she was terrified of lightning and thunder, so she would have run off to find somewhere to hide. She must have run out into the street and got lost, I thought.

Withing minutes the storm moved past us and things quietened down. The three of us went looking for her. Though the storm had moved on the humidity started to rise once again even though it was late afternoon, and the sun was about to set. We walked along the nearby streets looking into the hiding places we thought she could have found. We even asked a couple of people we saw out walking if they'd seen a small black cat anywhere, but no one had. Feeling very disappointed and upset we eventually made our way back home.

Not knowing what else to do, I looked around outside the house since the storm had passed and it was quieter. The sun had just set, and it would be dark soon. As I walked along the other side of the house, I passed the hot water system which sat in a corner beside a bedroom and the toilet and bathroom. I heard a faint meow. "Shady?"

As soon as I'd spoken, she started meowing, frantic and loud.

She was trapped in the small gape in the corner behind the hot water system. Since it was round and sat in a corner, there was a gap at the back, but no way shady could have got out because the tank was flush against the wall on both sides. There was no way she could climb out either. The tank was too smooth to get a grip on and she was squashed into an awkward shape unable to move her legs. She must have jumped up onto the water tank when the storm blew in and huddling back against the corner to avoid the rain lashing the house, she'd slipped down the gap and got trapped.

"She's out here," I called out to Monica and Christine who were inside having a cup of tea.

The raced out to see, and on hearing us all there Shady started meowing even more desperately.

I grabbed a spanner and after turning off the water, undid the connection to the house at the bottom for the cold water to come in and at the top where the hot water left the tank to enter the house. Stupidly, I thought I would then move the tank away enough to create a gap Shady could use to get out. There was no way I could move that 200 litre tank full of hot water. That amount of water is far too heavy for anyone to move. It's incredible how heavy water is. I would have to drain the tank before it could be moved.

It seemed to take forever once I'd undone the valve to release the water. It drained out and ran down across the grass ever so slowly and all the time we tried to comfort shady by talking to her. She must have realized we were trying to get her out and she calmed down, hardly meowing at all except for a few soft noises. It probably took around forty-five minutes for the tank to drain out enough for me to be able to move it away from the wall. As soon as there a gap wide enough, Shady shot out and raced through the laundry into the house where she hid inside the bottom of the linen press.

Christine took off then to go back home. By this time, it was dark. I moved the tank back into position, reconnected the pipes in and out, and turned the water back on. It would take a while for the tank to refill, and of course to heat up would have to wait until the night rate electricity switched on. There would be no hot water that night until very early in the morning. But that didn't matter, Shady was found and she was safe inside the house. When I went back inside after reinstalling the hot water system, she was eating some dry cat food in the laundry and seemed content.

The storm had passed, and we were all safe.

Finishing touches

In mid-January 1996 Dennis and his team came back and finished the pool with a blue pebble render after a few rows of tiles where the water level would be were cemented on. The coping around the edge was done with special paving bricks.

With that done, we could start filling it with water, which took all day using the garden hose. Fifteen 20 kilo bags of salt were added to make the water slightly salty. I was given a kit to measure the Ph levels and explained how to use it. But the best suggestion was to take a water sample periodically around to the nearest pool shop and they would test the water and tell me exactly what was needed to keep it clean and crystal clear, with the correct Ph levels.

The pool had partially filled with rainwater while it had been curing and this water would be pumped out before the blue pebble mix render would be done.

*Finished! And looking lovely as it started to fill up from the garden hose...
They left it raised enough above ground level for me to lay concrete and pave it with sandstone as I intended to do all around as well as under the pergola and along the side of the house facing the pool.*

My first dip in the pool. The paving would have to wait. I just had to try out the water and see how good it was.

Out and about

In that first year, Christine visited us a few times. We were her only close relatives nearby, with the rest of the family in Melbourne. We went to the newly opened Runaway Bay estate and had a lovely afternoon wandering about looking at hundreds of motor yachts and being serenaded by a trio of street musicians who wandered around singing and playing romantic Latin American songs and calypsos.

They had a Dominican Steel Drum, a guitar, and a small batá drum (*Itotele*) with a tiny cymbal and a miniature tambourine, a cowbell and wood block, attached to it. They were quite good, and I was interested to see how the *Itotele*, the smallest in the set of three batá drums, was used in a secular way.

She came with us to Jupiter's Casino to see the magic show Mystique in the Casino's International Showroom. This was interesting because no sooner had we sat down than one of the staff approached us and asked me if I'd like to appear in the show. This had never happened to me before, so I said yes. There weren't too many people in the theatre at this moment, so I followed the guy. We went backstage where he introduced me to the magician who was the featured performer. He explained that he would like to do a trick where he magically rips my shirt off while I'm still wearing a jacket.

"Wow that sounds great, only I don't have a jacket on."

I was only wearing shirt and trousers.

You can use this jacket," he said and handed me one an assistant gave him. "And this shirt too. Put this on over your own shirt and then the jacket goes on top."

I put on the shirt and jacket, and he demonstrated to me so I knew what to expect, how he would take it off without me having to remove the jacket.

He explained that he would do some simple tricks at first then call for someone from the audience and to select someone at random he would send an assistant down into the audience to pick someone. "She will wander about at random and finally stop in front of you and ask if you would like to come up and assist. You of course will agree and follow

I'm wearing the jacket and shirt given to me backstage before the show started.

her onto the stage. Once on stage I will get you to sit in a chair and will do a couple of sleight-of-hand tricks in front of you, and then when you stand up, I will tell everyone I am going to remove your shirt without you having to take off your jacket. Once I've taken the shirt off you will be free to return to your seat."

"And the jacket?"

"You can leave that on the seat where you are as you leave. Someone will collect it later."

"Well, it all sounds interesting."

"It'll be a bit of fun."

When I got back to the table, I told Monica and Christine what was going to happen. At that moment a photographer stopped and asked if we wanted a photo taken. Yes, of course we did. The photo he took shows me wearing the jacket and the 'special' shirt given to me to put on backstage.

The show started with a group of showgirls doing a dance number.

"This is just like the Lido," Christine said. She had been a showgirl in a couple of shows at the Lido in Melbourne, back in the 1960s, while Zara had been one of the dancers. Both had appeared in the show Tropicana, (in 1966) where I was featured on stage playing conga drums, but that was a long time ago.

We had a couple of drinks, and then the moment arrived. The magician's assistant wandered along a couple of rows and finished up standing in front of me. That was my cue to stand up and follow her onstage.

I must say, seeing the magician up close doing tricks right in front of me was still baffling. He was so smooth I couldn't see how he did them, but I was just as astounded as the audience watching. Then came the piece de resistance, removing my shirt without me taking off the jacket. I stood up. He walked around me, talking to the audience all the while, explaining what he was attempting to do, touching the jacket in various places he finally finished standing in front of me and casually took the lapels of the shirt in both hands and suddenly stepped back away, and *voila!* he had the shirt in his hands. He waved it in circles above his head while the audience clapped and made lots of appreciative noises, then he thanked me and said I could go back to my seat.

A couple of people near to us wanted to know how he did it, but I told them I had no idea, it all happened so fast. There was no way I was going to tell them it had been set up earlier. You just didn't do that. They didn't believe me, but then I didn't care anyway.

Someone said to me as we were leaving, "You're wearing a different shirt now."

"So?"

"What happened to your jacket?"

"I left it there." I said and before he could say anything else a surge of people leaving the theatre separated us and I didn't see that person again.

It had been an enjoyable night out.

A big job

A big job for me was to pave the area around the pool and under the pergola with sandstone. I started with the pool surrounds because the other area had cement brick paving already there so that could wait. I started with mixing concrete by hand in a wheelbarrow and day by day I managed to cover the area around the pool leaving space for garden beds. The rough-cut paving pieces were stacked all around for easy access. It was like a jigsaw puzzle, except I wasn't trying to make a picture, but to

fit pieces together so there was a minimal amount of cutting or braking pieces to fit, although I had to do that to fill small gapes here and there. Like the concrete, I would do one or two square metres a day which didn't seem much at first, but after a week or two it progressed rapidly. I used regular mortar mix to bed the paving and after it was dry I then filled the gaps with a white cement mix. As soon as the pool surrounds were done, I moved onto the patio and the path along the side by the bedrooms. I laid the sandstone over the top of the existing cement brick path which saved me having to mix more concrete for a base.

It took 3 months to do the paving, a bit over 60 square metres of it. The final touch was to coat it with a sealant to stop dust penetrating, although over time that didn't help much, but it did look good at the start.

Whenever I was doing anything in the yard, Shady would keep me company and follow me around. She also followed Monica about in the yard when she sometimes did yoga exercises. Monica said that Shady also tried to copy her when she did some of the stretching. Sunny never did anything like that.

Christine visited frequently and because it was usually hot she would join Monica in the pool for a splash. Monica couldn't swim and she usually stayed close to the edge where she could hang on and walk around.

— *Changing States* —

We didn't lose contact with my brothers and sisters in Victoria just because we'd moved to Queensland. At the end of January, two months after we'd moved, Monica flew down to Melbourne to spend a weekend with Paul and Lynne to celebrate the first birthday of their son Matthew, while I continued to work on the paving around the pool which had just been finished and was full of water.

A couple of months later Zara came up to visit Christine and naturally she brought her down to see us. We had afternoon tea and I showed Zara the renovations I'd made to the garden and the pool area, none of which she'd seen. In fact, it was the first time she'd seen the house since we moved from Melbourne. I think she was impressed by the swimming pool. I was proud of the paving job I'd done around it and under the pergola and the side path by the bedrooms. It had taken three months to do.

A year later Paul and Lynne came up with Matthew who was just on two years old and stayed with Christine for a few days. She brought them down to visit us and we all went to the beach at Burleigh Heads. So in those first couple of years there was a lot of back and forth between Melbourne and the Gold Coast, which meant that we didn't feel at all isolated or too far away from the rest of the family.

My two sisters, Christine and Zara with Monica and me, standing by the completed pool

Christine, Zara and Monica.

— Changing States —

With Paul, Lynne and Matthew at Burleigh Heads beach. And later back home where for a few moments Matthew doesn't seem too happy. They came up for the September holidays in 1997, and the weather was cool but lovely and sunny. Even so, it was much warmer than down in Melbourne.

— Changing States —

Parallel moments

Right from the second week we'd moved here, I continued with my Aikido training at the principal *Aiki Kai* dojo in Queensland, which fortunately was not far from us in Burleigh West. There were thirty or more people training there three times a week while on the other days the classes had around eight to ten people. Half of those training on the busy days came down from Brisbane.

The busiest classes were those taken by Graham Morris Sensei who was quite dynamic and much more martial orientated than some of those I'd studied and trained with in Melbourne. Graham Sensei had trained under Chiba Sensei and his senior teachers in England before coming to Australia and he was quite different from those I trained with in Melbourne. He reminded me of Jorge Rojo Sensi in Santiago, Chile, with whom I first started in Aikido, not in appearance, but in attitude towards the seriousness of the training.

Although I didn't know anyone else in Queensland, other than my sister Christine, some of those training in Graham Sensei's classes were familiar to me because I'd seen them and even trained with a few of them down in Melbourne during summer schools, which always took place in January, with students from all around the country attending.

Straight away I felt at home here, which was a good feeling. And barely a month after I'd started training at the Burleigh West dojo a young chap I knew from Melbourne who had been training at Frankston, and with whom I seen at gradings and special days at the head dojo in Clifton Hill, moved to the Gold Coast and started practicing at Burleigh West. We were happy to see each other because it's always nice to have someone familiar there when you start training new in a new place.

And for the next few years I would drive down to Melbourne (so I would have transport while there, also because I liked driving in the country) or sometimes I would fly down, for summer schools and to catch up with Zara and Fred and Paul and Lynne, and with Phillip, who was still working the drycleaning factory and shop. He was on his own though and starting to look worn-out. It was a bit much to do on your own, eleven-hour days, six days a week without taking any holidays.

Three years after we'd moved, he had to get a hernia operation and I flew down and stayed at the family home now owned by Paul and Lynne while I worked for a week at the drycleaning business to keep it operating as Phillip recovered from his operation. It was the same week that a prospective buyer of the business was to spend time learning the ropes and instead of Phillip teaching him, I had to do it. The following week, Phillip was back, and I could return to Queensland. A few months later he sold the business but rented the property to the man I'd met that week, and partially retired. He would come down from Bacchus Marsh, (and later Portarlington where he'd built a house by the beach), to help this new owner on Saturday mornings.

It took a while for him to fully retire because he would contract to work a drycleaning business for a month at a time a couple of times during the year to enable owners of these small drycleaning businesses to take a holiday. He knew that working six days a week year after year would inexorably wear you down, making life miserable. Perhaps having to get me to come down to run the business while he recovered from his operation gave him a premonition of how hard it could be to keep going on his own as he got older. We had been lucky that there were two of us and we could alternate working each a week in turn. But once I'd left to move to Queensland and Phillip was on his own with no time off, it became too much after a few years and he decided to sell out and retire or partially retire. By then he was living in Portarlington instead of Bacchus Marsh.

Winter School on the Gold Coast in July 1996 was the first big event I attended up here. In fact I was roped in to help with registrations and other matters relating to that like banking the money paid, and paying the bills, making sure everyone knew where their accommodation was, and working up a roster for cleaning the mats.

It was the first time a Winter training even was held in Queensland by Aiki Kai Australia, so we wanted to make sure it was a success. Everyone from the dojo helped in whatever way they could.

Our luck was that lots of people from around Australia wanted to come to the Gold Coast for the Winter School, and this guaranteed it would be a success. We had double the numbers attending compared the times the Winter School, was held in Sydney. I'm sure it had something to do with the lovely weather we have in July, the close proximity to surf beaches, and the fact that the accommodation and training was right on the beach on the other side of the Tallebudgera Creek at Burleigh Heads in the Tallebudgera Recreation camp and Centre, with access to the Gold Coast Highway, and public transport right at the entrance. A perfect spot. There was also camping and a caravan park on the opposite side of the highway along the shores of the Tallebudgera Creek for those who wanted less crowded accommodation or who brought their family with them for a holiday while they went and trained.

There was a great feeling of excitement, and camaraderie as the even progressed.

At the registration desk on the first day, One of my main teachers from in Melbourne came up to me and said, "I was wondering where you were. I haven't seen you at Clifton Hill for some time."

He was one of the most senior teachers and a member of the technical teaching committee and had been one of those members who graded me at Clifton Hill for my third, second and first *kyu* tests, so he knew my ability well.

"You're due to be tested for *Shodan (the first black belt level)*. Do you want me to put you on the list to be graded?"

"Well, that would be great, but I haven't prepared for it, what with packing up and moving up here last November."

I thought about it for a moment and then said, "Since I'm now part of the Queensland group I should wait until next January and have Graham Morris Sensei evaluate and recommend me for Shodan. I think that's the right thing to do since he is now my head instructor."

"You could do it now, but if you want to wait another six months, that's fine by all means. I'll have a chat with Graham," he said as he wandered off.

I felt more comfortable now knowing it would happen in another six months. It would allow me time to mentally prepare myself. I knew the techniques and what was required, and was confident I could do it, but I didn't want to go behind Graham Sensei's back. I would rather wait and have him recommend me for the test to be taken next Summer School in January 1997.

Sugano Shihan gave me permission to take photos during his teaching sessions and I managed to get a few good ones. Unfortunately on the last day when I was in a position to get some great shots, the battery went flat and I couldn't shoot anything. It was embarrassing, but I didn't tell anyone. I wrote a report for the national Newsletter and sent a couple of photos with it and they published it in the following issue of the quarterly newsletter. It was published and distributed from Tasmania. Before leaving Melbourne I had written a story about how I began training in Chile and sent it to an Aikido magazine in the USA called **Aikido Today**, and they published it.

I took photos throughout 1997 and 1998 of all special training days and technical teaching events that we held in the dojo at West Burleigh. Some would be used in articles and reports I sent to the national newsletter, others would become references for my own training. Those and later sessions from subsequent years I have collated into two 100 + pages PDF files which have never been published but are my own personal records of my early years of training on the Gold Coast. By this time I was using a digital camera and not a motor driven analogue one as I had up until 1997.

Some people were surprised that Sensei allowed me to take so many photos over time, as they were sure he didn't want applications and techniques to be fixed, but I explained that there were so many different instructors who claimed that what they were teaching was what Sugano Shihan taught them and that we should do it that way, that it was confusing. I reminded them that each one who claimed that, did it differently, which obviously reflected their own interpretation and experience. What I wanted to do was have a record of how things were done at a particular moment in time which could be used as a reference to look back on if there was disagreement later in how something was to be done. It would also be interesting over time to compare Sugano Sensei's approach to the same technique after several years had passed to see if there was a difference from what he did earlier.

He told me that it might look the same externally, but internally he was always evolving and so it felt different to him each time he did it. That was interesting because I do have photos of him doing *Iriminage* from different periods in his life and basically what he appears to be doing was much the same from an external viewpoint, but who knows how it felt internally as he was doing it. That you can't tell from a photo or even a video. Still, the PDF files of the sessions at Burleigh West dojo and the shots I took at subsequent summer schools in Melbourne over the years are still a valuable reference.

Writing and publishing

Fragments from a Life is the title I gave the small book I produced about Dad's life and experiences as a young person, in Northern Greece, (Epirus) and how he was affected when the part of Greece he lived in was annexed to become a part of Albania. It also covered his immigration to America, his return to North Epirus after 7 years, and his eventual immigration to Australia in 1924 where he started a new life. I went through the notes he left in three small notebooks, and filled in the gaps by discussing with everyone else in the family what they remembered regarding the stories he'd told us over the years.

I did this during 1996, our first year up here.

What I had was an incomplete narrative written in the first person, by Dad. Added to that I had the bits and pieces we collectively remembered, (a third person point of view) and to add verisimilitude to give it a context within a historical period, I also added a few general pieces of information regarding those early years at the beginning of the 1900s.

It was an experiment. With lots of short pieces, some not more than a paragraph long, a conventional linear narrative wouldn't work.

I imagined if I thought of each short segment in the way you think of a photograph, and photos in an album, that may not be in chronological order, flipping though that album and looking at the photos gives a context in which a story evolves. You can look through the album at random, or page by page, and still the story inherent in the photos emerges.

I did this with the book. Each segment was the equivalent of a photo. Each segment was not always in chronological order, but in the order in which Dad remembered as he wrote his original notes. By interspersing our collective memories, as well as snippets of historical data, I had an interesting book, but it needed a beginning to draw in the reader, as well as to provide the link from the present back into the different times in the past. So I invented a scene in which an old man has returned after 50 years to the village in which he was born and spent the first years of his childhood, and becomes distraught because the town appears dead, mostly abandoned and falling into ruins, but mostly because can't find or recognize the house where he was born and where he used to live.

That scene was invented, and didn't happen, even though at the age of 75, Dad with Mum did go to visit the relatives we still have in what is now Albania but used to be a part of Greece and was stunned to find how little had changed yet simultaneously how much it was different from what he remembered. Whether he went to find the house he was born in and lived in as a child, I can't be sure, but creating that opening scene was the key to linking the fragmented segments of his story together.

The story is therefore a memoir and not a biography, and reads, I hope, more like a novella than an historical document.

I printed 12 copies and added a photo at the beginning of him when he first came to Australia in 1924. He would have been 26 years old at least that year. At the end of the book, I put a copy of the last photo taken of him at the age of 91 or maybe a year or two older, which I took at home in Yarraville four weeks before he died.

I took the twelve copies to a bookbinder at Broadbeach and had them bound in leather with a gold embossed title. I gave a copy to each of my brothers and sisters as well as to a couple of close nephews. Ten years later I gave a copy of this book to a writer I met when I joined the Gold Coast Writers' Association. He was a Greek Egyptian and had also experienced dislocation and disruption before migrating to Australia years ago. His name was Chris Andalis and we hit it off and became friends.

Chris Andalis was in his late 70s. He had been a teacher in Adelaide, before retiring and moving to the Gold Coast. He wrote a regular column for the Greek newspaper in Melbourne **Neos Kosmos**, and was part of a group of Greek Australian writers in Melbourne. He wrote poetry in English, Greek, and Arabic, and had published a chapbook of his poetry. I told him about Dad and the notes he'd left and about the book I'd written and printed as a limited edition strictly for the family. He expressed interest in seeing it so I gave him a copy. He thought the book **Fragments from a Life**, was fascinating and insisted on translating it into Greek for me. "It brought tears to me eyes," he said.

I couldn't read Greek so I didn't see much point in having it translated. I was reluctant at first, but he convinced me that he really wanted to do it, because Dad's story reminded him of his own experiences, which he had not written about, and similar experiences that many other Greek immigrants had gone though, most of which have gone unrecorded.

"This has to be translated," he told me.

I was happy to let him do it.

He began by translating one segment **The Day of Arrival**, which I had published as a short story long before completing the book as a whole, in a magazine called *Australian Writer,* (Oct Nov 1994). He then went on to translate the whole book.

He refused to accept any payment whatsoever, no matter how much I insisted. Translating is not easy, but he said he did it because he loved the story.

We fiddled around with the layout of the manuscript together and it did match my original layout in the limited edition. He then suggested, once I'd printed the manuscript in Greek, and which I couldn't read, that I should enter it into an annual competition for Greek Australian writers run by the *Agelidis Foundation* in Melbourne. I did that, and heard nothing about it for some time. Then one day Chris rang me and said my story had won the first prize for that year (2008). He came over to visit me and gave me the cheque and a small certificate they had sent to him for winning the first prize. The cheque was for $200.

"You should keep the money, " I said, "for all your work in translating."

"No way," he insisted. "It's your money. You wrote the story."

No amount of arguing would convince him to keep the money, and so I had no choice but to accept it.

"One of the judges wants to talk to you about publishing it," he said. He gave me her telephone number,and since I was planning on being in Melbourne for Summer School training in a few weeks, I called her and made an appointment to meet her while I was down there.

We met in Lygon Street Carlton at a well known Italian restaurant for afternoon coffee and cakes. She was a professor of Greek literature at Melbourne University, but she also had a small publishing firm and she wanted to publish the book, in Greek of course, since that is what she did. She had a couple of her own books apart from several others already published.

But when she started talking about it needing to be 'properly translated' because the language Chris had used was not 'academic' enough, and how much she charged to re-translate it from English I was put off.

I thought, if it was that bad, then why did you as one of the judges with the *Agelidis Foundation*, award it the first prize for that year?

I didn't ask her. She kept going on about how she could distribute it through the University's Greek language department, and what it would cost to publish it. I became less interested the more she tried to convince me. (*She wanted $3000 to translate it, plus extra for publishing and printing.*)

"I'll think about it," I said. She gave me her contact details, and then we parted.

I spoke to Chris when I returned to the Gold Coast and he just shook his head. "There's nothing wrong with the translation. She's a scammer out to make money off anyone gullible enough to believe her about writing and publishing."

He obviously knew her from his association with Greek Australian writers in Melbourne and the *Australasian Hellenic Education Progressive Association* or A.H.E.P.A.

"I'm going to set it up in both languages and I'll publish it and get *Digital Print Australia* in Adelaide to print it." I told Chris. They printed my book of novellas and short stories **Convergence - Aspects of the Change,** (*Zeus Publications*) which I had done with four previously published short stories, two of which had been expanded into novelettes.

Once the two books were ready I converted both to PDF files and emailed them to *Digital Print Australia*, and in a few weeks I had fifty copies of **Fragments from a Life** in English and in Greek.

Chris was over the moon with his copies, and insisted that we should do a book launch in Melbourne. He would call the Greek Australian Writers group and see what they could arrange. A day or two later they contacted me and we made an arrangement for the event to be held at a small hall in Bell Street, Coburg, on a Sunday afternoon.

I flew down to Melbourne in the morning and Paul picked me up at the airport, and after lunch, he and Lynne and Matthew took me to the venue. It was crowded when we got there. Chris and his wife, who had been holidaying in Adelaide were there, as were about fifty other people, most of whom were unknown to me, although when a couple introduced themselves to me I did recognize their names. There was a board with photos of the cover and a couple of photos from the interior of the book on display along with a newspaper article in Greek. I was surprised at how well it had been set up. Apparently we were late because we'd got the time wrong.

Almost the moment we arrived they started with the organizer making a long speech in Greek before introducing me. I then got up and spoke in English, since I don't speak Greek, and that was fine because everyone there was bi-lingual. I was presented with a book in Greek about all the immigrants who had arrived from Epirus going back to the beginning of the century. An article about Dad, and his brother, our Uncle George, was in the book along with a photo I had taken of him, which I have no idea how he obtained it. They spoke about Chis Andalis the translator, about his work and asked if I would read one of his poems from his chapbook. I also read the opening scene from my own book.

After that we sat at a table with the books in both languages stacked up while people from the audience lined up to purchase a signed copy in either language. Some actually bought copies in both languages as they explained when handing over the money, "In Greek for us, but in English for our Children."

Almost everyone commented on how happy they were that I had written a story that was so much like their own. It turned out I was the first of the second generation amongst the Epirotic Greeks in Melbourne to have written a story of the experiences of their parents. Apart from two copies in Greek and English that were donated to the Association's library, every other copy I had brought with me was sold. I even had to take some orders for people who paid up front so I could send them copies later.

Paul drove me to the airport and I flew back with an empty suitcase and a pocket full of money. It had been a very successful day.

A couple of weeks later, Chris arranged for a book launch at the Greek Club in Brisbane. We were amongst a group of five Australian Greek or Greek Australian authors to present books they had written. It was held as a special function at the Greek club and there would have been a couple of hundred people there. After dinner each author spoke in turn about their book, how it had been written and matters relating to that, after which people lined up to buy copies. Again I sold all the copies I had just had reprinted, forty of them in Greek and in English. The four other authors also sold as many if not more copies than I had.

I will always be indebted to Chris for translating Dad's story and the successes we had with it. We lost contact after a couple of years because his wife left him and he started to be affected by age and illness. He was almost twenty years older than me. His son arranged for him to be sent to a nursing home, and I have no idea what happened after that.

In 2013 I reset the English version and added quite a few old photos that had come to light over the intervening years. I redesigned the book with the addition of the photos that didn't appear in the original version. It also has a more attractive cover this second time around and is now available on Amazon and similar places whereas before, it wasn't.

I would have to say, it was my second most successful book.

The covers from the two editions. The sepia cover was th same on the Greek edition only the text was in Greek instead of English. When I revised the book and added photos that didn't appear in the first edition I also redesigned the cover which I think produced a better looking book. The image of Dad and Mum walking along a city street in Melbourne that graced the first edition now appears inside in the second edition. The sepia image of Dad as a young man in his late 20's was a formal portrait he had taken in Melbourne while the colour image of his older self was one of those I took at home a few weeks before he passed away, and as such, represent the beginning and the end of his life in Australia. The ship is the Re' D'Italia or the Red Italia as he called it. It was the ship in which he and his friends travelled to Australia in 1924, arriving in Melbourne in December of that year.

The display with photos from the book advertising the event.

Reading the opening scene.
Signing copies for buyers.

With my friend and translator Chris Andalis enjoying the 'limelight' at the book launch organized by AHEPA. These photos were taken by my brother Paul.

— *Changing States* —

My brother Paul speaking to one of the organizers of the event. Lynne and Matthew were also there.

Aikido — from newsletters to books

My most successful book is my Aikido book, ***Aikido — Basic and Intermediate Studies.***

The first edition of this book has 274 pages with over 1000 photos converted into drawings plus several hundred small sketches indicating movement and direction. It covers all aspects of basic Aikido training as the title suggests, from beginner level to Shodan level (first black belt) and was a long time in gestation.

The rear and front covers of the first edition of my Aikido book.

It began mid-1999 at a Winter School on the Gold Coast when Graham Morris Sensei said to me that *Aiki Kai Australia* was looking for someone to edit their newsletter. The man in Tasmania who had been doing it could no longer do it and they needed someone who knew about writing and editing who was willing to take it on. I had given Graham Sensei a copy of ***Fragments from a Life*** to have a look at and he obviously thought I might be a good candidate. He had also seen the article I'd had published in ***Aikido Today*** Magazine in the USA about how I began Aikido training in Chile.

"You'd be perfect," he said. "I've already suggested you to them so someone should be contacting you about it soon."

I thought about it for a few moments and then decided if they contacted me I would agree to become the new editor. I thought the experience of putting together a newsletter with photos and articles contributed by the members of *Aiki Kai Australia* from around the country would be interesting to say the least. It would also be a learning process and give me a place to publish articles I could write about Aikido. Since I was by this time a *Nidan*, (Second Dan black belt) at least I would know what the contributors would be talking about.

Shortly after telling Graham Sensei that I would do it, I was contacted by the National Area Representative (and Vice President) on the association who explained about templates and what the Technical teaching Committee expected to newsletter to be like. I already knew what it looked like because I had been receiving copies regularly in the mail every six months since I was a member of *Aiki Kai Australia*. Every one in the association received the newsletter.

Since it came out intermittently, sometimes three times in a year but often just twice, after summer and winter, it wasn't really newsy but usually had reports of activities that went on within the association across Australia.

I was sent files with templates for the layout which simply had to have the articles and photos and reports inserted. The problem was everything had previously been done and designed on a Mac computer, and I used an IBM. I couldn't use the templates sent to me and had to design new ones so I could use Word instead of *Quark Express* which had previously been used. The text files they sent with illustrations and photos were okay. It was quite a challenge since word wasn't really suitable, but I managed. I also had to organize to have it printed and this meant that I had to use an agency that could convert the files into Quark and create the sheet film from which the newsletter was printed. Everyone used *Macs* and it took a while before I found the only person who could convert the files from IBM and make the film sheets from which the printer could produce the newsletter. I would do the layout in Word, placing the scanned photo images where they needed to go, but when he produced the film sheets he rescanned the images and put them in the appropriate places. The printer I used was one he recommended, and I used this sprinter for the first two years.

Printing was offset, so they printed from film sheets which contained four pages of the newsletter. Since we only did eight pages that meant two sheets of film A3 size. It was like a giant negative of the pages. We got 1000 copies sprinted and the printer would call me when they were ready to be picked up. It was up to me then to fold and post individual copies out to the members on the mailing list. This meant opening an account with *Australia Post* for bulk billing. We would fold the issues at the dojo with a few people helping which made it a bit easier.

As I was preparing my first issue as editor, we received the news that *Doshu, Kisshomaru Ueshiba*, The head of AikiKai worldwide, had passed away, so my very first issue actually featured news that was current.

The second issue was prepared early so that news of Tamura Shihan being invited by Sugano Shihan as a special guest teacher at Summer School in January 2000 in Melbourne could be posted to all members before the end of the year to encourage them to participate at this event.

The front page of my first newsletter for Aiki Kai Australia, published well past the end of winter.

I followed their design with three columns per page, and for the first few issues over the subsequent couple of years I used the same layout but each time modified it slightly, so over time the publication evolved and began to look a little different from how it had looked before I started editing and designing it. I didn't want to do too much at first; it was a learning process for me, but in time as I increased page numbers from eight to sixteen, and then to twenty-four, it no longer was a newsletter although that was still part of its official title, it had become a bi-annual magazine that featured articles by newcomers as well as by senior students, and some members of the Technical Teaching Committee. And of course photos, many of which were taken by me. I was also by this time regularly contributing editorial comments, reports and articles.

It became much easier when the man who produced the film for the offset printer told me his son had set up his own printing business and that I should give him a go. I went and saw him and discovered he was using a new digital printing process and that all I needed to do was create a print ready PDF file of the newsletter and he would print from that. I was still using word, but I could convert those files into a PDF, which made things a lot easier with no need for a middleman or agency to produce film for offset printing. In time I bought *InDesign 2,* which was a layout and design program designed to work with *windows* computers for preparing publications for printing. It gave me better control over the layout and design and had a built in PDF converter as well. It made producing the newsletter so much easier, as well as enabling me to prepare books.

I would never have considered doing an Aikido book if it hadn't been for one of our students who had his son training in the Children's class. A new school had opened up in Upper Coomera and that's where they lived. He suggested we might like to teach a class once or twice a week to students in the school as part of their *physical education* program.

At this point in time (2002) I was teaching a regular class on Wednesday night, as well as attending Graham's classes on Monday, Thursday and Sunday morning. I was also acting as secretary for Qld Aiki Kai. Both Graham and I went to the new school in Upper Coomera and spoke to the teachers and they seemed enthusiastic about the idea. They liked that it was a martial art that didn't have competitions and that its principle concepts involved harmonizing with another person in order to reduce or negate conflict. They also liked that much of the terminology was in Japanese and suggested that we could look at it as part of their cultural studies. But what they would need was for us to structure the teaching to cover the length of each term, and that they wanted written material regarding each lesson taught, so it could be discussed in other cultural classes aside from the physical activity of the training.

Wow, that was going to be more complex than we had envisioned.

I sat down and designed a ten week course that covered the very basics; movement, balance, exercises to control and break balance, learning how to fall safely to avoid injuries, awareness of surrounding space, and basic application of simple principles that beginners need to learn.

Once we had a 10 week plan, I then had to prepare written and illustrative pages covering each lesson for the ten weeks. Together with Graham, I started to take photos of movements and techniques. These we took on Sundays after the regular class had finished. Once I had the photos that matched the content of the class plan I would spend the following week working on converting the photos to computer drawings which I thought made it simpler and easier to understand. Designing a layout that covered a two page spread, I put together 10 four page documents each one covering what would be taught during each lesson.

Above is an example of the type of illustration used created from a series of photos taken and then converted to a drawing. I also remove d the background so there was nothing to distract from the actual exercise, which in this case a stretching exercise called **Hai Shin Undo.** *Most of the exercised depicted in the illustrations for the ten week course were with Graham Sensei and myself.*

We went back to the school and showed them what we had produced and they were even more enthusiastic. I was going to be the teacher because Graham was working full time and couldn't do it, whereas I was retired and had plenty of time. As the year came to a close, we started working on the second ten week course and this became more interesting because there were more technical applications to various attacks and defenses while standing, (*Tachi Waza*) plus attacks and defenses while one is standing and the other seated (*Hanmi Handachi*), and attacks and defenses while both are sitting in *seiza*. (*Suwari Waza*.)

Every Sunday Graham and I would take digital photos of the techniques I was to be teaching, and during the week following I would convert them into the drawn images as well as compose the accompanying text to explain the technique. I had quite a lot of pages done over a six month period leading up to the end of the year, enough to cover two ten week courses.

The end of the year arrived and the school closed for the summer holidays, but Graham and I continued taking photos of what I thought should be a third ten week course. It became a regular routine. We would stay back at the end of the Sunday morning class and spend 30 to 45 minutes shooting one or two techniques in short sequences. I was using a digital camera, but there was slight lag between when the shutter was pressed and the camera took the photo, so we couldn't do the techniques as a continuous movement, but had to pause at various points so the photo could be taken. Later, as digital cameras improved and I got a new one that could shoot up to five frames per second, I could shoot a whole sequence of shots as a technique was done without having to pause for the photo. I would later select appropriate photos from the sequence taken to illustrate the high-points of the technique and convert those ones into drawings using *Photoshop*.

*This sequence of a hip throw (**Koshinage**) was also shot as four separate images and was part of the third ten week course where more advanced applications were considered.*

Those early sequences were shot without us wearing the traditional hakama normally used by black belt holders so the positions of the feet could be seen which would make the technique easier to understand.

As the new year started we were ready with the courses designed and reading and discussion material prepared. Then the school contacted the dojo and told us they had decided not to proceed with Aikido classes.

It didn't bother Graham much, but I was disappointed. I had been looking forward to teaching the classes at the school, because it would have supplemented my meagre income in retirement, but it wasn't to be.

"We've done too much to let it drop like that," I said to Graham one Sunday shortly after we'd found out. "I'm going to turn it into a book. I've already got a hundred pages done, so if you're okay with it, we could keep taking photos to build up a more comprehensive series. I've done too much work on it to waste it."

Graham didn't mind, so we continued every Sunday for a short time after the morning class to shoot more photos. It was easier by then because I had a better digital camera and could shoot continuously while a technique was applied to an attack. And for these more comprehensive applications of aikido principles we both wore our hakama. As 2003 progressed I built up a large collection of technical photos and converted all of them to the same style of drawing to match what had previously been done. By this time the idea was to cover all that is generally taught from beginner to first black belt or Shodan level in one comprehensive book.

I had many aikido books in my personal collection and most of them barely covered more than a small portion of what you learn over the time needed to go from a beginner to a black belt. I wanted my book to be as comprehensive as possible.

During 2004 I completed the 274 page book and found a publisher in Canada. It was to be self published but they used a program to prepare their books I'd never seen or heard of before. I didn't want them to do the book layout since there were too many images that could confuse them so I asked if they could send me the software and I would put the book together for them into a print ready file. I did this over several months and finally the book was ready to be released in 2005.

They sent me 30 copies for my own use, but it cost me heaps for import duty and transport from Canada to Australia. Initial sales were very good, but the royalty paid to me was often less than a dollar per copy sold in Canada and the US. Someone was making money on this book and it wasn't me. After a year or so with excellent sales, but virtually no gain for me, I decided to cancel my contract with them, wear the losses, and convert my original files to a print ready PDF which I then had printed in Australia (in Adelaide), copies of which I would sell at National Schools I attended. This was a much better arrangement for me.

Around 2010 I arranged with an international distributor who also printed books on demand, to print copies as needed and they made it available all over the world. I revised parts of the original book and I added extra material with another 30 or so pages so the new edition had a new ISBN and has continued to sell moderately to the present day. I usually get around $10 royalty per copy which is much better than when I published the first edition.

I also produced a book of Aikido articles that I had published in our newsletter and in other places such as websites and magazines. This came out a year after the revised *Basic and Intermediate Studies*. Both these books sell as print on demand books, and continue to do so the this day.

Back and front covers of my two best selling books.

A number of the articles in this second book have also appeared in foreign websites translated into Spanish, Portuguese, Flemish and Russian. Some were done with my permission, but the Portuguese translation of the title article I discovered accidentally after googling my name so see what would come up. I was never asked about that one. I would have given permission, but it would also have been nice if I was asked first.

— John Litchen —

— Changing States —

Once the swimming pool was completed, the carpet and extra tiling done, and we had some furniture, we finally started to settle down. I began Aikido training, and Monica would go for a walk in the afternoons when the temperature had cooled down a bit. She walked every day usually down Ron Penhaligon Drive as far as the roundabout and then returning via Glen Eagles Circuit which would bring her back to our street, Firestone Court. It was probably an eight kilometre walk. Sometimes I accompanied her, but not every day. Glen Eagles was steeply undulating which meant plenty of walking uphill and downhill, whereas Ron Penhaligon was a gentle downward slope to the roundabout with only a slight dip where it crossed a creek that went from a lake in the middle of a reserve on one side into the golf course on the other side and another smaller lake somewhere in there. These two lakes were always full of water birds, mostly ducks and water hens, as well as magpies, kookaburras, butcher birds, lorikeets, parrots, galahs, and white cockatoos. There were lots of other smaller birds that lived in the trees and bushes clumped in various parts of the reserve. There no doubt were snakes, lizards, goannas, possums and other native animals because sometimes I would encounter them in our yard which over time became quite overgrown and a bit wild. Since the golf course and the reserve surrounded the area where our street was located, it was no surprise to sometimes come across something that needed to be avoided as it travelled through our yard from one part of the reserve to another, like a goanna or a snake.

The reserve was part of a series or nature reserves that linked the Hinterland with the Coast, so they were often full of wildlife. There were tadpoles and frogs, yabbies and tortoises, and freshwater fish in the lakes and the creek which no doubt attracted many of the water birds. The nearby canals and the lakes connected to the canals had salt water in them since they were linked to the sea. They were very clean and were full of sea life including bull sharks which come into them in the summer months to breed. No sensible person swims in the canals because of the sharks. Fortunately, we are too far south to have crocodiles which are sometimes a problem further north.

Apart from the walking, we also took up Tai Chi and would practice once a week at a class in Burleigh Heads on a Thursday morning, after which we would have lunch at a local café near the beach before doing our weekly shopping at the New Robina Town Centre. Both Monica and I looked forward to the Tai Chi and the lunch and shopping afterward. It made for a lovely lazy day which we thoroughly enjoyed every time.

Lots of locals would be out walking everyday either early in the morning or late in the afternoon. They would greet each other in passing. Many walked with their dogs, and often Monica would find herself accompanied by a small dog from one of the houses she passed. It would stay beside her trotting along to keep up, and when she got home and started up our steep driveway, the little dog would head back to where it came from. It didn't take long before she knew most of the regular walkers and so she began to feel as if she was part of the community. Even though people didn't interact or stop for a conversation, the fact that they acknowledged each other meant they all knew who was a local and who wasn't, and greetings were always friendly.

The area had a pleasant feel to it and there was none of that frantic rush we used to see in Melbourne. I'm sure there was of traffic in the mornings and afternoons as people left for work or returned, but since we were retired as were a lot of those around us, there was none of that peak hour madness. Everything was laid-back and relatively quiet. We really liked it here.

A year or so later when we stopped doing Tai Chi, we lost interest when we had to change venues, we just went to the Robina Town Centre for lunch before doing the shopping. It was still a pleasant day out.

Robina was a long way from Surfers Paradise, and that was good. We had no reason nor desire to go into Surfers since whatever we needed, we could get at the Robina Town Centre or the nearby Pacific Fair shopping complex. The Robina Town Centre had just been completed, (at least the first stage) and it was very handy for us, so we tended to go there most of the time. They had cinemas as well so we could catch the latest movies without having to travel to older established cinemas

We were in a good location which I must say was a bit of luck for us. As the suburb grew with more houses built on the other side of the golf course and closer to Robina Town Centre, the suburb flourished, and the newer parts were considered fashionable. Values went up and have continued to rise over the years as more development occurs across the district. The town centre had also undergone several major renovations and is a huge complex now, completely unrecognizable to what was built and completed in the same year we moved here. It is now a major business centre for this part of the Gold Coast being close to the airport and right beside the major Highway to Brisbane.

Relaxing with Shady who didn't like being picked very often. If she decided to sit on your lap then it was okay, but if you picked her up to put on your lap, she would more than likely resist. Sunny was far more relaxed and less nervous than Shady.

— *Changing States* —

Very relaxed...

Constant change

In the first couple of years here, the development around us was phenomenal. Within twelve months the single one-lane-each-way, Robina Parkway morphed into a double lane divided road to carry always increasing amounts of traffic.

I watched in amazement as new houses, 6 at a time, would appear along one side of the now double lane Robina Parkway Road. Not long after the road was completed as I drove down towards the turn-off to the Robina Town Centre, I noticed 6 slabs had been laid in a row. A week later there were 6 housing frames already constructed. The following week the roofs were tiled while another 6 slabs had been laid down in preparation for the next group of houses. Another week later the first six had the external walls up while the roof tiles were being laid on the second six houses. At the same time, another 6 slabs had been laid down further along. I couldn't see what was going on the other side of this new row of 18 houses, but by the end of three months they were all completed, and trees had been planted to give the buildings some future shade. The whole area close to the newly built Robina Town Centre was being covered with houses at a phenomenal rate. There were in the late 1990s as many as 18,000 people moving to the Gold Coast each year. They had to live somewhere. Not only were houses going up all over the city area. There were also Highrise apartments buildings going up along the Surfers Paradise beach front as well as at Broadbeach and other beachside locations. The whole skyline was undergoing reconstruction and redevelopment. The Tallest residential building in the Southern Hemisphere was built and other equally as tall buildings altered the appearance of the skyline. The City of the Gold Coast was and still is the fastest growing city in Australia and is the sixth largest city in the country as well as being the largest regional city and Queensland's second largest city. The whole area from the Gold Coast up to Brisbane and on to the Sunshine Coast has seen an equally proportionate increase in population.

In 1995 the Gold Coast population stood at 314,000. In 1996 it was 229,000, and that included Monica and me. By 1997 it was at 348,000. In 2009 it passed the 500,000 mark and at the last census in 2021 there were officially 625,087 residents. If it keeps up at this rate, we'll have well over a million people here in another 20 years.

It makes you wonder where all the people come from. If they are leaving such cities as Melbourne and Sydney, how come their populations haven't decreased? Those cities too— as with all major cities throughout Australia —are rapidly increasing their populations.

Increasing traffic congestion reflects the rapid increase in population. It now takes as much as forty-five minutes to get to places that once took ten to fifteen minutes. God help you if you want to go further afield. There are more roundabouts here than anywhere else I've ever been, and many more traffic lights than there used to be all of which create delays increasing travel time. These days I don't go too far from home, so it doesn't bother me much, but it is noticeable, even over the short distance from where we live to the Robina Town Centre.

A view of the Robina Town Centre after the first stage had been completed. The car park was later built over with a completely new addition added a few years later. The lake was also repositioned as further extensions took place. This image was taken from the Balloon Walk.

— John Litchen —

Behind Monica is a huge area laid out with canals ready for houses to be built.
Within two years, all that area was covered in houses and no longer looks barren and empty.

The Balloon Walk was a helium filled balloon connected to a cable that allowed it to rise up around 250 metres. Under the balloon was a ten sided cage in which you could walk around to get a 360 degree view of this part of the Gold Coast. You could look down through the empty middle to the Town centre below. It turned out to be not so popular and after a year it disappeared.

— Changing States —

Monica looking down at the Town Centre below... Bottom: the view towards Burleigh Heads.

A writers' group

We also joined the Gold Coast Writer's Association, well I did, and Monica would come with me once each month on a Saturday afternoon, to the meetings. It gave her the opportunity to meet other women and to interact socially after the meeting with afternoon tea.

The meetings were held at Pacific Fair then, but a year or so later moved to a space above the Burleigh Heads Library. They were enjoyable meetings, and it was here that I met Chris Andalis who later offered to translate the book I'd written about Dad's life into Greek.

We looked forward to the monthly meetings mainly because of the socializing over a cup of tea or coffee with sandwiches or biscuits afterwards. The association put out a quarterly newsletter and I contributed a few short articles on writing to it. These articles and a few I'd had published in a Melbourne magazine, *Australian Writing* (which later became *Stet*) formed the basis of a small book on writing that I prepared thinking that the local writer's group would be interested.

Attributes a Writer Needs was self-published with copies initially printed by Digital Print, in South Australia. I later had it listed through *Lightning Source*, for distribution and printing worldwide.

I launched this book at one of the Gold Coast Writers' meetings, and although everyone expressed interest, only one person bought a copy. I was disappointed considering how well my earlier biography of Dad had sold at the two book launches it had.

What I realized after that event was that members of this writers' group generally were interested in selling copies of their own books and not so interested in buying copies of other member's books. None of the member's book launches I attended were much different from my own one. I wondered if it was the same with all such small writer's groups that were more like a club than anything else.

At the book launch with the writers' group.

Monica and Sonia

In 1998 after we'd settled into the new house, I thought Monica seemed lonely. She didn't know anyone up here. I had friends I'd made while training in Aikido, but Monica seemed more withdrawn, so I suggested she fly over to Perth to visit Sonia. Although they spoke on the phone a few times a year, it had been a long time since we'd driven across the Nullabor to Perth to visit them —in September 1981. Her daughter Fiona and Brian were about the same age, with Fiona a year older. Now they were adults, and Fiona was over in Europe in Brussels working for a shipping company. And we were getting old enough to become pensioners in the not-too-distant future. Monica was 58 in 1998 and Sonia was probably over 65 and already a pensioner. Both had been mothers late in life.

She flew over to Perth, leaving here at 5 am and after a five-hour flight arrived there still reasonably early in the morning. Perth is two hours behind us in time, being on the far western side of the continent. She caught up with the two friends she had travelled to Australia with in 1970, Laura and her sister Alicia, but the bulk of the time in Perth she spent with Sonia. I think she had much more in common with Sonia than she did with Laura and Alicia. After a couple of weeks there and an enjoyable time, she returned, feeling much better.

In 2003 we asked Sonia to visit us, and she flew from Perth to the Gold Coast and stayed with us for a week. We took her to the usual places one takes a visitor, like *Palazzo Versace* which was the first 5-star hotel complex on the coast.

Monica with Sonia in the plush marble foyer of Palazzo Versace.

I just had to have a picture taken with Sonia at the seaside entrance to Palazzo Versace. It was in May 2003 and summer was over. Temperatures were cool enough to wear warmer clothing. In Perth it would have been end of Autumn.

— Changing States —

Monica and Sonia enjoying each other's company on the beach

In Surfers Paradise beside the famous entrance arch to endless world famous beaches.

The two lovely ladies posing beside the pool. The plants in the background had grown considerably in the 10 years since the pool was completed, creating a pleasant oasis.

— Changing States —

We visited the world famous Gold Coast beaches where the two friends frolicked on the sand. They had a great time reminiscing and catching up on what they'd both been doing over the intervening years.

Although it was never mentioned I think both knew they probably would never see each other again; they were getting on in years, Monica at 63 and Sonia close to 70, and they lived on opposite sides of the country. As you get older you are less likely to be bothered travelling great distances, and when family and friends live vast distances away on opposite sides of the country, the possibility of seeing each other again often disappears. They spoke regularly on the phone, but that's not the same as seeing each other in person.

Monica was quite sad when Sonia had to fly back to Perth.
She even had tears in her eyes.

> Part Four
>
> Adventures and journeys
>
> Aikido and New Zealand

Summer school in Melbourne (January 2000)

In January 2000 Aiki Kai Australia had a special guest, Tamura Shihan, who was invited by Sugano Shihan to come and teach. Tamura was senior to Sugano although they were both uchideshi with O'Sensei back in the late 1950s early 1960s, before both went separate ways, Sugano Shihan to Australia and Tamura Shihan to France where the organization he heads has over 30,000 students training. This was to be the first and only time Tamura Shihan had come to Australia. Many aikido students from other countries took the opportunity to come to Australia for this National Summer School, among them a small contingent from New Zealand. One of the things I did as the newsletter editor was to interview these visitors for a report on the event that I would put into the next newsletter.

I had setup an interview with Tamura Shihan, which was to take place after the official dinner and during or after the party following the dinner towards the end of the week's training. It was a fun night with hundreds of people having a great time. A couple of our most senior members were to be at this interview, and I had a list of several questions I wanted to ask. Since Tamura Shihan's English was practically non-existent, I needed a translator. None of us could speak French which was our guest's second language (after 30 years in France). The interview would be conducted in English and Japanese. English for the questions asked which would be translated into Japanese by Machiko, (who used to be one of my teachers on Friday nights at Clifton Hill dojo) with the reverse for the answers; Machiko translating back into English. I would record the interview and transcribe the English parts for the newsletter.

Once the dinner was over and lots of people were dancing, I went looking for Tamura Shihan to remind him about the interview which he had agreed to, but on entering the dancing area I saw him surrounded by several female students all dancing together. He was obviously having a great time.

I looked at Machiko, and Tony Smibert Sensei, our Vice President (and most senior of Sugano Sensei's students) and asked, "Are we ready?"

"We have to wait," Smibert Sensei said.

"Why?"

"We can't disturb him while he's dancing."

"So, we wait until the dance is over, and then we do the interview."

"We might have to postpone it until tomorrow," Machiko suggested.

"He's very senior…" Smibert Sensei started but I interrupted him. "He agreed to do it tonight after dinner. I'll go and remind him."

"You can't do that."

"Just watch me." I said and started towards the group where Tamura Shihan was the centre of attention. I'm in favor of proper respect and understood their concern, but it was an informal event, not anything official in the dojo, and everybody was a bit tipsy and relaxed. I didn't see there would be a problem. Besides, Tamura Shihan had only a couple of hours earlier agreed to be interviewed so it wasn't something unexpected.

As I started towards them the music stopped and, in the pause, I went up to the group and said *"Perdonnez moi, Sensei,"* and as he turned to look at me, I added *"Je pense que se le temp por l'interview,"* which was the limit my broken French could manage.

"Ah, Oui," he said and grabbed my arm so I could lead him out of the group.

He'd had a few drinks and was quite merry. I could see Smibert Sensei and Machiko staring at us as we walked towards them.

"We should go downstairs to the dining room," Machiko suggested. "It's too noisy up here."

She said something to Tamura Shihan in Japanese, and he nodded enthusiastically.

We went downstairs and found a table where I set the recorder in the centre to record, and at this point Smibert Sensei started to ask questions which Machiko translated. The two of them conducted the interview which went for around forty minutes and only towards the end did I get a chance to ask a couple of the questions I had listed to ask. The interview had been hijacked, but there was nothing I could do because I was a junior student here.

With the interview over, we returned to the party to continue having a good time.

Back home a few days later I transcribed the English parts of the conversation and then gave a copy to the Japanese wife of one of our local students. I also gave her a copy of the taped interview so she could tell me if the translations of the questions and answers were accurate. They were, and the interview went into the next newsletter.

I sent a copy to Tamura Shihan in France, and he responded with a personal letter to me and some copies of his association's newsletter (in French).

Tamura Shihan   *Tamura Shihan demonstrating suwariwaza kokyuho*

A seminar in Christchurch

As a result of interviewing our New Zealand visitors at that summer school, I was invited to attend a spring seminar in Christchurch. I flew over to be looked after by Andrew Williamson and his wife who were the head instructors at the Christchurch dojo. It was there I met Kevin Allen, an Australian who worked for the Antarctic Division, based in Christchurch. He would regularly fly down to Antarctica on the supply planes and often sent me photos taken on the icy tarmac where the planes land. He had started his aikido training in Alice Springs before moving to New Zealand.

This spring seminar in Christchurch only went for a weekend in October, so it wasn't a long time away. It was here I met the head of (*Shinryukan*) Aikikai New Zealand, Takase Shihan, who invited me to attend their national Gasshuku in February 2001. They always held their summer school week in February or March after the on-season airfares dropped once the holiday season was over.

— Changing States —

During the Spring Seminar in Christchurch with Takase Shihan teaching. At the end of a day's training... Kevin Allen is in the right hand corner

Canberra (January 2001)

In 2001 for our summer school held in Canberra at the Australia National University, Takase Shihan had been invited as a special Guest. There was some controversy about this, as Sugano Shihan had not officially invited him, but it had been put around that Takase Shihan had been invited. Who did this, I have no idea, but the TTC felt they were under an obligation to make it official, so it was done. There were a number of senior students who refused to attend classes held by Takase Shihan, claiming they only trained under Sugano Shihan, which I thought was narrow minded, since they missed out on interesting aspects of techniques that were familiar but different in subtle ways.

I suspect one of the reasons was because Takase Shihan (6th Dan) was younger than them and had been training less years than them, yet he was a much higher rank, so perhaps there was some jealousy involved on a subconscious level, but there was certainly a lack of respect. They just used the excuse that they only trained under Sugano Shihan to justify sitting there and criticizing, when Sugano Shihan had often said it was good to train with other Shihan to gain a different perspective.

Takase Shihan made the point that aikido was different for each individual and that sometimes things worked and sometimes they didn't. Everyone would eventually find their own way of doing a particular technique, but whatever way worked for them the underlying principles should be the same; blending, moving from your centre, redirecting to unbalance to throw or pin, to control without hurting or damaging uke. He asked that they try his way to see if it could work for them. He never once said that this was the way to do it. Only that this was the way he did it, and it worked for him. He offered it as an example for students to experiment with.

Takase Shihan in Canberra demonstrating riotedori tenchinage

It was quite funny, the day Takase Shihan arrived, he was being escorted to where his accommodation was located. He was walking along accompanied by several very senior Australian Aikidoka, when he saw me sitting at a bench not far from the building. I had arrived the day before and was settled in. I was the first familiar face he'd seen since he arrived.

"John," he called out. And as I stood up, he started towards me, leaving his escort standing perplexed, wondering how was it that I knew Takase Shihan well enough for him to come over and greet me like a long-lost friend?

We shook hands and while the escort stared at us, he said, "Meet me after I've settled in, and we'll have a beer together."

"Sure, I'd love that. I'll wait here, okay?"

"I won't be long."

He re-joined the escort, and they disappeared around the corner of the building.

Five minutes later he was back, and we went to a bar on the campus where we joined a small group of students there for the summer school. He mixed in with us as if he was one of the boys. There was no aloofness, or expectation of being treated like he was someone special. It was very different from the way our senior students kept Sugano Shihan separated from having access to the general student body. But then he was a lot younger than Sugano Shihan, and me as well. I hadn't started doing aikido until I was 50 years old, and that was back in Santiago in Chile while Monica Brian and I were there on a long holiday twelve years earlier. Perhaps Takase treated me with respect because I was older than him, even though I had not been doing Aikido for as long as he had. To start this kind of training is very different when you are fifty compared to how it would be if you started in your twenties. Takase Shihan had started aikido when he was a student at university and had been doing it for 30 years or more. Some of our senior students had been doing it since Sugano Sensei started teaching in Australia almost forty years ago. (Aiki Kai Australia's 40th anniversary would be coming up in 2006).

After Takase Shihan's set of classes were over we sat down and over a beer or two I interviewed him for the upcoming newsletter. Takase Shihan spoke perfect English, well, he did have a kiwi accent, and he reminded me that he had invited me to attend their gasshuku the following month.

"It will be a big one with four special guests. You shouldn't miss it."

"I'll be there."

"Email me your time of arrival and I'll have someone pick you up."

With Takase Shihan in Canberra

Three weeks later at the Howick Sports Centre in Auckland, New Zealand.

Three weeks later at the beginning of February, I found myself being picked up at the Auckland International Airport by a rather large jovial man called Colin Pearson, who drove me into town to a restaurant beside where their central dojo was located and introduced me to several other senior New Zealand Aikidoka. Takase Shihan was there with them and seemed pleased to see me. There had been some delay both at the airport, as well as with heavy traffic on the way into the city centre. While driving Colin got a phone call which he briefly answered with "We're on our way, should be there in another fifteen minutes."

He turned to me and said, "That was Sensei, wanting to know where you were."

Takase Shihan knew when I was arriving because I had emailed him as he had requested. He sent Colin to collect me at the airport.

I was handed a beer the moment I sat down by a wiry gentleman called Billy Orr. He and Colin were great friends and Takase Shihan had directed them to look after me. They became terrific mates, and I stayed at Colin's place which was a fair way out of the city, not far from the Howick Sports Centre which was also not far from where Billy lived. Howick Sports Centre was the venue for the *Gasshuku* starting the next morning.

This was a remarkable summer training session with four very senior Japanese teachers invited to attend and teach. I can only remember three of their names now; Masuda Shihan — the most senior of them, Watanabe Shihan — Takase Shihan's teacher when he was at University , and Miyamoto Shihan. During the *Gasshuku* I attended a barbecue party at Takase Shihan's house along with Colin and Billy and other senior members of Aikikai New Zealand. Wherever Colin and Billy went, they took me with them.

Colin and I got on very well together. He was a superb photographer and had a large range of cameras and lenses. He was the official photographer who documented every major event Aikikai New Zealand held. Like Billy, he was a 5th Dan and a member of the committee that organized the events they had in Auckland. He also taught a class once a week at a local dojo. Billy took several classes a week at the Howick dojo. Naturally I attended those classes while I was there. Their knowledge of the technical aspects of aikido was outstanding.

I also got on very well with Watanabe Shihan, who couldn't speak a word of English, but could speak Spanish since he often went to Spain to teach. We conversed in Spanish. He was also a keen photographer as well as a sketch artist. Everywhere he went he had a small sketch pad in which he created watercolor impressions of the places he visited. Some of them he would turn into large watercolor paintings once he returned to Japan. I had a fantastic time with these very friendly aikidoka.

Above: at the barbecue at Takase Shihan's house.
Bottom: Lunch break with Takase Shihan ans Miyamoto Shihan during the gasshuku.

Enjoying a beer with Masuda Shihan and Watanabe Shihan

Practicing shihonage

Watanabe Shihan

— Changing States —

*Enjoying a joke with Billy Orr during a class at his Howick Dojo.
Riotedori tenchinage with Billy Orr.*

Gokyo Omote.

This time with Monica

I had already been to New Zealand three times in the first 2 years of the new millennium so I thought it only fair that the next time I went I should take Monica with me.

She never complained about me going off to do aikido over there or back down in Melbourne, which was really kind of her. She could have complained about me leaving her at home, but she never did. She knew it wasn't a holiday, it was training. She also knew how much I loved aikido training and that it was a major part of me. I considered myself very lucky to have found such a wonderful and understanding life partner.

In August 2002 Monica and I flew to Christchurch for a holiday during which I would attend their spring seminar. This would be the first time Monica actually went to New Zealand rather simply passing through (in transit) on her way to and from Chile.

— Changing States —

We flew over cloud covered mountains before coming down and landing in Christchurch. It reminded me of the time we flew from Argentina to Chile over the Andes. Only this time I managed to get two photos. We had gone over and past them before I could wind the film on for more shots. I was still using a *Moniolta SLR* analogue camera. Digital cameras had yet to be developed enough to compete with 35mm SLR type cameras.

It was hard to see the actual mountains because there was so much cloud cover. As far as we could see the whole mountain range was obscured by cloud and it was only as we started to descend after passing over the bulk of the range that I caught a glimpse of snow covered mountain tops.

Andrew Williamson picked us up at the airport and drove us into town and helped us to select a hotel in the middle of the city where we booked a room for the week we going to be there. I'm not sure now but I think it was The Wyndham Gardens hotel, which was a short walk from the Casino, which we never visited.

The hotel we had was right in the heart of the city with pubs and restaurants close by. The actual training was to take place in a scout hall temporarily converted to a dojo for the weekend spring seminar. The hotel was luxurious, and we made the most of it. They even supplied luscious thick toweling bathrobes to wear, a first for me. They had washing facilities down on the ground floor so I could wash my training Gi after the day's sessions. Andrew picked me up at the hotel to take me to the seminar dojo while Monica spent time doing some shopping.

In the afternoons and evenings after the day's training we would wander through the gardens and parks which were in bloom and stunning to look at. There are probably more parks and gardens here than in any other city of comparable size that I've seen. The population was a bit less than that of the Gold Coast when we arrived in 1995, being about 380,000. (The Gold Coast was around 450,000.) There were several delightfully old, restored trams that trundled from the Botanical Gardens through the major parts of the city and of course we took several tram rides so we could see what the place looked like without having to walk for kilometres. We also took a free shuttle bus ride to a business district some distance away from the centre of the city.

There were many restaurants withing as walking distance of our hotel, but we usually found ourselves in the outdoor area of a very English looking pub (*The Oxford*) built beside the narrow Avon River where you could take a ride in a punt. The meals were substantial and reasonably priced, and it was always packed, a sign that the food must be good.

What I liked about Christchurch was the feeling of calmness and relaxation. No one seemed to be in a hurry, and it was always pleasant to wander about looking at shops in old as well as new buildings.

— Changing States —

Beautiful flowers and a pine tree that normally grows in southern Chile in a park only a few hundred metres walk from our hotel.

Roundabouts full of flowers and old trams that reminded me of Melbourne when I was in my late teen years were a nostalgic sight.

Being a city of around 150 years old, much of it looked as I remember buildings in London had been when I was there in the 1960s. Interspersed between very solid British looking architecture were a few new buildings with modern glass facades. They stood out and to my mind's eye, looked out of place. The big square in the centre of town was dominated by a magnificent bluestone cathedral which has probably been there as long as the city has existed, around 150 years. There were always visitors by the cathedral.

What Monica liked about Christchurch was that it reminded her of a similar sized city in Chile where the ocean was on one side and not too far inland were the magnificent snow-covered Andes Mountains. These mountains always dominated the landscape. She compared it to Concepcion, which like Christchurch in recent years was partially destroyed by terrible earthquakes.

In Christchurch it wasn't the Andes, but the snow-covered Southern Alps which extended the length of the South Island were just as spectacular. The most famous, Mount Cook (*3724 metres high*) is the highest mountain in New Zealand and is located in the central part of the Southern Alps. It is a five and half hour bus ride from Christchurch which put us off visiting it. We didn't have enough time to go there and stay there overnight before coming back the next day, just to see a snow-covered mountain. I'm not that fond of snow anyway, after spending a couple of winters in Europe years ago. It's no fun if you have to live with it for months on end.

Even though it was sunny most of the time, the air was cold. Christchurch is quite far south and with winter having just passed and still with much snow on the Southern Alps not far away the sun didn't do much to warm us.

Once the seminar was finished Monica and I visited the beautiful gardens a short walk from the city centre, we took a couple of tram rides through different parts of the city, visited a couple of fabulous bookshops. We bought a few souvenirs at a stall in the city centre near the cathedral to take home.

This magnificent cathedral in the centre of Christchurch was later destroyed by a massive earthquake, in 2010 and 2011, as were the nearby buildings, but that was long after we'd been there.

Monica checking out the stalls before deciding which one to enter in search of a souvenir.

On our last day in Christchurch we took the daily shuttle bus to Akaroa, about 80 kilometres away on the Banks Peninsula where a coastal town that was a popular tourist place beckoned. It left at 10 am and was a two and a half hour drive. The driver took his time and explained what there was to see as we drove through pleasant rolling hills and rich agricultural lands. He even stopped at a railway crossing though there was no train in sight and the lights weren't flashing. "You have to stop at every railway crossing," he said, "to make sure there's no train coming. It's the law." We were stopped for almost a minute while he checked both ways, before trundling over the lines to continue our slow journey.

We stopped on the way to buy some wine and cheese at a gorgeous farm overlooking the Banks Peninsula and the ocean before continuing the last few kilometres into the French provincial looking town of Akaroa around 12:30. We had until 4:00 to look around before catching the same shuttle bus back to Christchurch.

The Banks Peninsula (named after Joseph Banks the botanist on Captain Cook's ship the Endeavour), was formed from two ancient volcanoes and both Akaroa Harbour and Lyttelton Harbour are what is left of

From the farm where we stopped to buy cheese and wine we got a superb view of the inlet formed from the volcanic calderas before we drove into Akaroa.

the calderas after the sea filled them. Unlike in Chile, none of these volcanoes are active, but that's not to say they are dead. New Zealand sits on the edge of a rising Pacific Plate and volcanoes along the edge of this plate could erupt at any time. In other parts of New Zealand, especially the North Island, there are thermal springs and bubbling lakes of mud so volcanic activity is happening there although there are no active volcanoes. Not far off the coast of the north island there are a couple of islands that are nothing more than semi active volcanoes with constant rumbling and small tremors. Tourists are taken out to see these, but it is not something I would consider. I'm not that interested is seeing a volcano active or otherwise up close. Across to the other side of the Pacific Ocean, there are plenty of active volcanoes as the Pacific Plate subducts beneath the American Continent (both North and South) forcing the mountain ranges all along the western side of the continent to rise slowly with periodic volcanic eruptions and earthquakes.

— *Changing States* —

We didn't have a lot of time to explore but there was time for a walk around this small town as well as for lunch before taking a two-hour Black Cat boat trip out into Akaroa harbour towards the ocean in the hope of seeing dolphins and perhaps a whale, but unfortunately, none of those appeared in any numbers. We did see a couple of dolphins. I was surprised how small they were compared to the dolphins we'd seen in Australian waters. These were a different species I was told. The boat trip itself was pleasant enough. We passed a section devoted to aquaculture, where Green-shell Mussels and Pacific Oysters were being cultured, as well as had a close look at Cathedral Cave which is part of an ancient volcano that formed one side of the Harbour.

The farmed mussels and oysters towards the harbour mouth are much sought after as they are richer and plumper than their wild counterparts, which promises much for the future of aquaculture. With wild stocks of shellfish and fish in general being depleted from overfishing by commercial fishers and poachers all over the world, aquaculture promises to be a logical solution, since stock can be strictly controlled for both quality and availability.

It seemed that when we got back to the jetty there was little time left to anything else but go straight to the bus stop to catch the shuttle back to Christchurch. It would have been nice to explore further afield, to see the rugged country to the south but we had a flight to catch the next day back home to the Gold Coast.

Monica walking along the beach front towards the pier where the 'black Cat' was waiting to take passengers on a trip around the harbour.

— Changing States —

On board the Black Cat for a trip around the harbour.

Below are the only two dolphins we saw over the two hour trip on the Black Cat. They didn't jump out of the water, but merely broke the surface periodically to breathe. A small species known as Hector's Dolphins. We didn't see any whales, penguins, or for that matter, hardly any seabirds, which was a minor disappointment.
The ride on the Black Cat catamaran was pleasant enough.

I did promise myself that we would come back for a better look at the South Island some time in the future, but it never happened.

— Changing States —

Rows of buoys supporting cables on which green shell muscles are seeded and grown. Aquaculture is a major industry in New Zealand, producing some of the finest mussels in the world.

Cathedral Cave, cut into the side of the caldera by the sea over time.

In New Zealand again with Monica

Barely seven months later, at the beginning of March 2002, Monica and I were again flying to New Zealand. This time we hoped to spend more time there so we would have a chance to see more of the country than we had when in Christchurch the year before.

The excuse for the trip was that I was attending another summer gasshuku held in Auckland with Masuda Shihan and Yamashima Shihan as the guest instructors. Masuda Shihan visits New Zealand regularly, usually around the time they hold their annual summer Gsshuku. This one would go over four days and after that we would hire a car for a week so we could go wherever we wanted before returning home. It would be a nice holiday.

Of course we wouldn't get far in a week, New Zealand's North Island is quite large, (as is the South Island) but we would see more of the country than we had been able to see when we were in Christchurch seven months earlier.

We arrived tired but Monica was excited to be here in Auckland.

Colin met us at the airport and we took off to head into town. I had booked a hotel room online with a boutique hotel in the heart of the city. I didn't want to hassle Colin by having both of us stay at his place.

He would have been happy to have us there, and if I was by myself I wouldn't have hesitated, but Monica preferred that we stay at a hotel where we could come and go as we pleased without depending on anyone for transport. Colin lived a long way out of the city which would have limited our ability to go and do what we wanted, and while I was training at the seminar, if we'd stayed with Colin, Monica would have been isolated and on her own. Or alternatively, she could come with us but would end up having to wander about the city all day while we were at the gasshuku. We would have to meet her afterwards in town somewhere, before returning to Colin's place way out in the suburbs. It simply wasn't practical. At a hotel in the heart of Auckland city she could come and go as she pleased, and be totally independent.

On our way into the city, Colin made a detour and took us to an extinct volcano that overlooks Auckland. Whether it is extinct is uncertain, it hasn't erupted for hundreds of years. New Zealand sits on the edge of a volcanic ridge extending across the Pacific and there are active volcanic sites all over the North Island. This volcano is dormant. One would hope it doesn't erupt in the near future, if at all because Auckland would be devastated if it did.

Auckland is enormous, with a population approaching two million. It extends over hills and around bays and inlets with small islands all of which are the remnants of 48 old volcanoes or not so old dormant ones. It is a beautiful city full of greenery and gardens in amidst tall buildings. It has the biggest marina I've ever seen where there must be a thousand boats moored. It's a spectacular modern city.

One of three 'extinct' volcanoes that are high enough to afford views of the city

The grassy crater at Maungawhau Reserve.

A view of Auckland from the crater rim.

The crater is much bigger than it looks in these photos. If you look carefully you can see people down inside the crater which gives an idea of its size. Colin took some pictures of us together, and Monica took one of Colin and me. After half an hour or so, we got back into his car and he took us to the hotel we'd booked, The Airedale Hotel. It was an eight story hotel opposite the Town Hall, just on the edge of the main city business area. A great location because it was a short walk to the dojo from there, as well as a reasonable walk to go down into the main part of the city all the way to the harbour.

— Changing States —

No matter when you go to this spot, it is always crowded with locals and visitors taking in the fabulous view of Auckland and its surroundings.

The Airedale Hotel. The entrance to the lobby is on the right, It connected to a lovely coffee shop restaurant with a separate entrance in front of the triangular part of the building. Our room was on the seventh floor on the side of the building facing the Town Hall which is where I was standing to take this photo.

The room was like a small suite. It had a microwave, a jug, glasses and plates and cutlery, so we could prepare snacks and eat them there. The sleeping area was separated from the lounge living area although it wasn't a separate room, but there were folding doors you could draw across to make it private so it seemed like an extra room. The view from the windows was towards the Town Hall and its clock tower.

The view from our window of the Town Hall.

After we'd checked in, Colin took us for a drive to a little restaurant down by the yacht club marina. This had to be the biggest marina I'd ever seen. There must have been at least a thousand boats there from millionaires luxury yachts and cruisers to runabouts and motor cruisers and everything in between. The view of central Auckland through a forest of masts and spars, ropes and rigging, with the late afternoon sun sparkling on the water and on the glass facades of the modern city buildings in the background was stunning. And I didn't have my camera with me!

Once we got back to the hotel, it was around four-thirty. Monica said she was tired and wanted a rest, so I grabbed my training gear and Colin took me to Howick dojo where Billy was taking a late afternoon class. I joined in and throughly enjoyed the training. It only went for an hour and afterwards the three of us went to the local pub for a beer. By then it was around six so Colin took me back to the hotel. Monica and I invited him to have dinner with us. There was a Japanese restaurant a short walk along Queen Street from the hotel so we went there. The food was okay but nothing remarkable. We enjoyed it though.

Colin left us after the dinner, and went to get his car to drive home. We wandered back to the Hotel and settled in for the night.

I was exhausted and looked forward to a good night's sleep.

I woke up suddenly with the clock alarm beeping loudly. It was 4 am. I hit the stop button and went back to sleep. Ten minutes later it went off again. Whoever had been using the room prior to us arriving must have left it set for an early start. Cursing loudly I looked for and found the power switch and turned off the bedside clock with its blasted alarm.

By this time I was wide awake, and it was hard to go back to sleep. Monica had woken up briefly but had no trouble going back to sleep. I lay there for a while and eventually dozed off.

Suddenly I was woken again, this time by a loud chiming of the bells in the clock tower of the Town Hall over the road from us. It played some kind of ridiculous melody, before it chimed five times, and then went silent. Five in the morning and we were both wide awake.

I looked out the window and saw that we were about the same level as the top of the clock tower. No bloody wonder it was loud! We both dozed off a bit and then again at six it started with the little insane melody followed by six very loud chimes.

Apparently, it did this every hour during the day from five in the morning until midnight, after which it was silent to give people in nearby hotels some respite. If we'd known that, we would have booked a hotel at the other end of the town, but we didn't know. It's not something that was mentioned on the hotel website or in any of its brochures. I suppose we would get used to it.

Since I was awake, I went downstairs looking for the laundry so I could wash and dry the gi I had used in Billy's class the day before. After breakfast we went out for a walk and found a huge bookshop, *Whitcouls*, which was on the other side of the road from the hotel and not more than 200 metres away. Several floors of books and CDs, and it was here I found some CDs featuring **Cachao**, (the greatest bass player and composer of *danzones* in Cuba), which I immediately bought.

The Sky Tower

The **Skytower** is New Zealand's tallest building, at 328 metres high, that's just over 1000 feet. That measurement is from the tip of the aerials on top of the building to the base. The main observation platform is one of several and sits just below a revolving restaurant. Above the restaurant is an outdoor deck with telescopes for observation, but we didn't go there. We stayed on the main observation deck which has glass panels in the floor around the entire circumference of the deck. You can look straight down to the ground beneath your feet at least 250 metres down. Monica was nervous about standing on the glass floor but a lot of people were doing it, so she did too. The highest viewing platform is the Skydeck which features seamless glass giving 360 degree views around the entire city, and absolutely spectacular it is. Between the restaurant and the open viewing platform above it, and the high viewing platform there are telecommunications arrays and other electronic monitoring systems. There is a spectacular display in the entrance on the ground floor with a huge series of screens displaying information about the tower and its construction. To get up to the observation platforms, the restaurant and the coffee shop you need to take lifts, which are glass fronted. They are incredibly fast and you feel your stomach sinking as they shoot up to the top.

They tell me the tower is earthquake proof, but who knows really?

If something above 8 on the Richter Scale occurs within 20 kilometres it's unlikely to remain standing. But then the whole of Auckland wouldn't remain standing either, so I guess it doesn't matter then. It is windproof for winds up to 200 kilometres an hour, something they say can occur once in a thousand years.

It seemed reasonably safe, so we took the lift up to the main observation deck to have look.

Monica tentatively walking along the glassed floor sections of the main observation deck. She only took a few steps and hung onto the rail while I took a photo, after which she quickly returned to the more solid looking floor towards the centre of the space. The tower extends another 50 or so metres above this deck.

While we were there, we saw people lining up to take a controlled *'bungee jump'* from the open platform above the revolving restaurant. They were dressed in blue and yellow jumpsuits and would be dropped using a cable that was controlled, so there would be no bouncing up and down or anything like that. The cable was lowered rapidly enough I imagined to give you that vertiginous feeling of falling, but it slowed as you reached the ground and came to a gentle stop. I caught a glimpse of someone falling down and managed to snap a quick photo before the person disappeared below.

"Would you want to do that?" Monica asked as she saw the person dropping rapidly down out of sight.

"Not in a million years. I would never have done anything like that even when I was younger. Even less likely now. Falling from a great height is not my idea of fun."

Yet there was a queue of people lined up to do it.

I'm sure it was perfectly safe, a lot safer than bungee jumping off a bridge into a chasm, but still, it's not something I would do.

Previous page: the view of our hotel and the Town Hall with its noisy bell tower seen from the Observation deck, and above: looking towards the yacht club and marina where we had lunch with Colin. Below: Freeways entering and leaving the city

Some streets in Auckland.

— Changing States —

Around six that evening I walked up the road to where the dojo was in Cross Street, I had a present for Takase Shihan, a fine bottle of old whiskey. Unfortunately he wasn't there, so I would have to present it to him later. I watched the class for a while before returning to the hotel.

The next three days, Monica was basically left to her own devices while I trained at the *Gasshuku*. She would get up and have breakfast with me before I left, then she would wander off to do some shopping. She took a bus a couple of times to a market on the outskirts of the city, which she liked. She loves markets because of the fresh fruit available as well as the odd hand made trinkets you can get as souvenirs.

With the gasshuku over we took a ferry ride across to a nearby Waiheke island where there is a small town, a bit like a country town, only it's a thirty-five minute ride on ferry to get there. Everything on the island has to come there or leave there by ferry. There were a lot of people on the ferry; the place was very popular with day visitors. The ferry landed at a small cove where trucks were waiting for goods to be unloaded. The passengers like us got off and took a waiting bus into the town which was only a few minutes drive from the ferry terminal.

We had lunch at a local pub, a busy place with spectacular views, walked around to take in the sights and views of narrow bays, and eventually caught the bus back to the terminal to take the ferry back to Auckland. A pleasant day's outing.

Not far from the terminal in Auckland, there was a car hire place so I hired a car for seven days. I would pick up the car the next morning.

This was the ferry, a super-cat, which we took across to Waiheke Island.

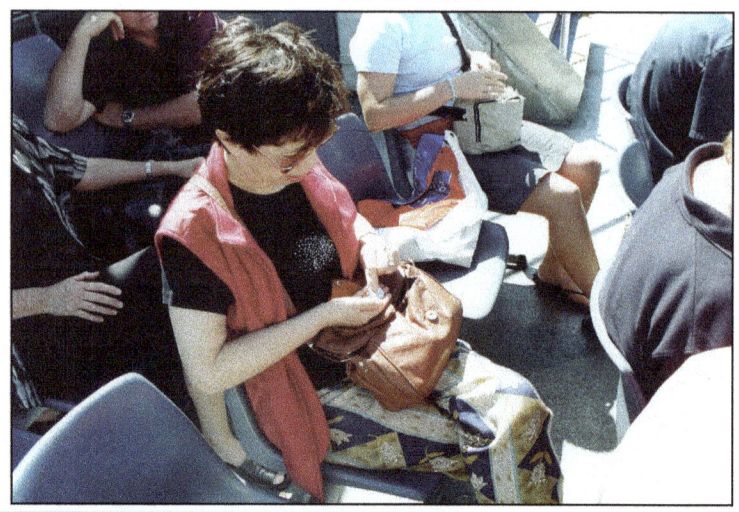

Above: Monica on the ferry to Waiheke Island. Middle: Shops and a general store.
Bottom: houses scattered around a harbour. Note, up in the top right hand corner there is a party taking place on an overhanging balcony shaded by umbrellas. A very laid-back, easy-going place.
Next page: Monica looking for fresh fruit. She always was on the lookout for something different, something local to try. We found orange apples and golden queen peaches. They also have olive groves and vineyards on Waiheke island. Local wines are highly sought after.
Street scenes showing the sub-tropical aspect of the island.

A drive in the country

We left around ten thirty after having a small breakfast in the room, packing the last few items and taking the luggage down to the car. I paid the bill and we took off. We left the city using the same freeway that we needed to get to Colin's place at Papakura. This was the Auckland Hamilton Motorway, highway One. Because it was past morning peak hour we trundled along at a good pace and soon left Auckland behind us.

Our aim was to go to Rotarua to see the bubbling mud and the thermal springs. After that we would take a leisurely drive up along the coast in a wide circle back to Auckland. Monica had never seen a bubbling mud volcano.

I remembered going there in 1964 when I was travelling to Europe on the Elenis, a Greek passenger liner. It had stopped for 24 hours in Auckland. A group of us had hired a car and we drove to Rotarua for a day trip. But that's all I remembered; no detail;s of what we saw or how things looked, just the memory of going there all those years ago. I was curious to see what the place really looked like.

It was 126 kilometres from Auckland to Hamilton which, after we'd left the suburbs of Auckland, didn't take too long to get there. The drive through the countryside was pleasant, with green rolling land punctuated by small towns that we didn't stop at. When we got to Hamilton we drove into the centre of the city. We went for a walk around and had some lunch before continuing on our way to Rotarua, which was about the same distance away from Hamilton as Hamilton was from Auckland.

The landscape became more rugged and hilly as we got closer to Rotarua. Also we couldn't help noticing the odd whiff of sulphur in the air as we got closer to Rotarua and a huge lake which was one of many between rotarua and Whakatane on the coast not far away. The smell wasn't there all the time, but every so often a breeze would bring a whiff of sulphur or methane, which reminded me of rotten eggs, not a nice smell.

We drove into Rotarua and around Lake Rotarua, a huge lake. Wisps of steam or pale gas seemed to drift up off the surface in some places, and again the smell of sulphur drifted in through the car window. The view across the lake was nice and the town itself was very neat and tidy. We found a motel, which we preferred over the many backpacker's accommodations we saw, and booked in there for a couple of nights. It was mid afternoon so we went for a walk to have a look at the town. A lovely town but the ever present smell of sulphur and methane would take some getting used to.

Once we'd settled into the motel, we went for a walk through the town down to the lake. It was late afternoon and the sun was close to setting. The sky was beginning to take on a pinkish hue. The lake was immense, the largest of at least ten almost interconnected lakes between here and the coast. The water looked clear enough but every so often I saw bubbles drift up from the muddy bottom as I stood on the path and

looked into the water. Not far away were bubbling mud pools and geysers that erupted intermittently, so I wasn't surprised to see gas bubbles in the lake.

Taking a thermal bath

Wandering back we had dinner, then decided we would take a thermal bath, since that was a popular reason for people to visit Rotarua and its surrounding areas. In the old days Maori warriors would bathe here after a battle to help heal their wounds, so these volcanic waters gained a reputation of having healing powers. The are full of sulphate and methane so any bacteria in wounds sustained in a battle would be killed by the concentration of these chemicals in the hot water. As for other healing powers, I have my doubts. I suspect benefits gained are more imaginary than actual. If you are convinced the waters will heal something, they probably will, because the power of the mind that believes in the healing powers of the waters will work wonders. Psychosomatic? Who Knows.

It was dark when we walked down to one of the many bath houses and inside the light was yellow and greenish. We had a large bath to ourselves, since there was no one else there. The smell of methane and sulphur was strong and the surface of the bath underwater was covered with a fine layer of green mould that felt slimy as we stepped into very warm water. Every time we moved a bit, tiny bubbles drifted up, like you find in a glass of sparkling water. We didn't stay long in the bath because neither of us liked the feeling of the slimy surface under the water.

"The baths in *Cauquenes*, were better than this," Monica commented after a few moments in the water.

We had gone with Monica's brother to a special place in the foothills of the Andes eleven years ago while on an extended holiday in Chile. *Cauquenes* was famous for its thermal baths. They were much better than this one. Much cleaner, no mould, no smell of sulphur or methane, with barely a tingle in the nose as the steam rose off the water there.

Here, every time I moved, bubbles came up and the smell made me gag and want to sneeze.

We didn't stay long, going back to the motel not half an hour later.

Whakarewarewa Thermal Reserve

This was the closest area of volcanic activity to Rotarua so we went there. At this reserve there are walking paths for those who just want to wander about, but there are also guided tours of the area starting every hour. There is a traditional Maori village, and visitors are welcomed in a traditional manner before being allowed to enter the hall where a concert of singing and dancing was performed. We saw the concert, then eschewing the guided tour, we simply wandered along the designated walking paths through bubbling mud pools and geysers periodically erupting.

A warrior stepping forward to welcome visitors.

Unfortunately the warrior didn't seem all that threatening, and the business of welcoming visitors, to me, seemed contrived, designed specifically for North American tourists who like that kind of stuff. The singing inside the building behind the welcoming party was first class. Who doesn't like Polynesian harmonies?

We went through a special building where we saw several kiwis foraging in the dark. They were bathed in ultraviolet light which was invisible to the kiwis but enabled us to see them. Taking photos was prohibited.

After that we took out time to wander along the path towards where several geysers were erupting.

On the way we saw a recreation of a Maori village showing how it would have looked prior to the arrival of Europeans.

A village, Te Wairoa, had been established by Christian Missionaries in a peaceful valley above a lake Tarawera in 1848. It was abandoned during the Land Wars in the 1860s, then repopulated several years later as a place to welcome visitors to this volcanic area who wanted to see what was called 'The Pink Terraces'. When Mount Tarawera erupted in June 1886, it was the most recent in 20,000 years in the Rotarua area. It only lasted four hours, but it utterly destroyed the surrounding area, burying it under millions of tons of boiling mud and ash. The eruption had been so violent and loud it could be heard as far away as Auckland.

Everything was destroyed, plants, animals, and whoever lived in the area. Te Wairoa and two other small villages nearby, were gone, buried under the mud and ash. Even the shape of the land changed. The pink Terraces were gone. No one who had been in the immediate area survived the eruption. When rescuers from Auckland arrived they could not believe the utter destruction. For five thousand square miles there was absolutely nothing left.

Gradually plants adapted to the boiling water, the steaming bubbling mud, the heat and the humidity, and over a hundred years a complete new ecology and landscape evolved, with plants adapted to the heat and the boiling temperatures. This ability to adapt shows how nature can be reborn, and in situations which would seem unlikely, how quickly life will find niches in which to survive. It only adds hope to the desire of many biologists to find life off Earth on other planets where extreme conditions may be very different from here, and if life can quickly adapt to these volcanic situations, or can emerge in deep sea chasms under immense pressure, then it is almost certain we will find life of some kind on other planets different from our own. Life is extraordinarily adaptable, and we should not close our minds to the possibility of it existing elsewhere in this vast universe.

Pohutu Geyser; *This one erupts between ten to twenty five times each day and is the largest of many geysers in this valley. What's amazing about this place is how close you can get to the geysers to see them erupting. In places, steam can be seen drifting up through the porous ground which why you stay on clearly defined paths through the valley.*

Geysers are basically springs where the water underground seeps into hollow chambers and is heated by the high temperatures. When the temperature reaches boiling point and pressure builds up, the water is blasted out where it rapidly dissipates. Some geysers are almost continuous, while others erupt periodically, and some only rarely.

— Changing States —

It was difficult to photograph an eruption because the water and steam blasts up with such speed and ferocity any image of it is blurred, but how do you photograph steam anyway? These different views, I hope, give an impression of its size.

Even though we were some distance away, you could feel the heat emanating from it. In fact, even the ground we walked on in places felt hot.

Ngamokalakoko.

This is a huge pool of boiling mud. The Maori word for it means Frog Mud Pool. There are no frogs there, they would have been boiled alive, cooked, but the way the mud slowly bubbles up, then splutters a glob into the air, which then fall back down into the mud pool is reminiscent of flogs leaping across a pond, hence the name. It seemed to bubble in slow motion but could I get a picture of the mud in the air as it burst forth and fell back down? No. It always seemed to happen before the instant I pressed the shutter. So any photos of this that I took seem static. Shooting a video would have been a better idea but then I didn't have a video camera or even a digital camera. I was still using an analogue film camera. Film isn't as sensitive as digital sensors and so the detail tends to be washed out as the mud is highly reflective, still the sheer size of the mud pool was impressive and this shows up on the film.

The temperature of the steaming bursts of mud is from 90 to 95 degrees Celsius, and if it has been raining there is more activity. In dryer periods the surface mud in parts dries out a bit and you can see cracks in parts of it between the bulging uprising mud.

— Changing States —

It wasn't raining while we were there and in some plaxces you can see the mud starting to harden and crack, but that wouldn't last long as upwellings from underneath burst through.

That plants could grow inside parts of the bubbling mud was amazing. They should have been cooked, but they thrive, which shows how adaptable and resilient life can be.

Walking down towards the mud pool.

Standing by Pohutu Geyser.

— Changing States —

Sulfurous mud and clay solidified into stone, cracked and broken as it cooled.

Steam rising out of the ground. The different colours in the ground come from sulphur and other minerals deposited by overflowing hot water.

The view of a lake glimpsed from the car as we drove past several large lakes on our way to the coast.

After spending a couple of days in and around Rotarua, we left and drove past another huge lake that we were told was the largest hot water spring lake in the world. We passed by several large lakes as we headed towards Whakatane on the coast of the Bay of Plenty. A fair distance out into the bay is a small volcanic island with a crater that is still active. Tourists go out there to look at a live volcano. We didn't think about it. We didn't even go as far as Whakatane, but turned onto the main highway at Edgecumbe to travel along the Bay of Plenty coast to Tauranga where we stayed for a couple of days.

Little could we imagine that the volcano on White Island would erupt suddenly with disastrous results in December 2019 while a group of 47 tourists were on the island. 22 people died in the explosion and from injuries sustained. Another twenty two sustained severe burns and needed intensive care. Rain and continuing volcanic activity hampered rescue operations.

The eruption was a Phreatic eruption that released steam and noxious gases creating an explosion that launched rocks and ash into the air. This volcano on Whakaari or White Island is an andesite stratovolcano that has erupted many times over the last twenty or so years. Why tourists were allowed to visit the island to see the dangerous volcanic activity is something I can't understand. Whakaari was far more active than the bubbling mud and geysers at Rotarua but something like that could also happen at Rotarua at any time, although it seems less likely than Whakaari or White Island which is still an active volcano. The whole area sits on a very thin crustal layer and is unstable. Considering what happened in 2019 on White Island, I think it unlikely that I would visit Rotarua again if I went back to New Zealand today.

Driving in Tauranga where the roads in the centre of the town are paved with faux cobblestones of varying colours, creating pleasant patterns no matter where you look.

We didn't plan on taking boat trips out of Tauranga. It is a sea port and cruise boats call here regularly, as well as like most ports there is fishing and other tourist activities. We decided we would simply rest a couple of days before driving further around the Bay of Plenty on our way back to Auckland. It was a pretty town to relax in with its wharfs and jetties, its buildings that maintained a maritime feel, and its roads and footpaths that were paved with coloured brick of varying sizes and shapes. The weather was cool, and cloudy, and this didn't encourage us to take a boat trip around the harbour. We simply wandered along the piers and jetties to see what was happening.

We stayed at the Tauranga Motel which was an elegant place overlooking a park with the harbour beyond. Every room had a lovely curved balcony with a garden bed and lawn separating the property from the street and the park beyond. Monica thought it was very nice.

We walked along quiet streets with hardly anyone around, which seemed odd considering Tauranga was a tourist town. It must have been off season. It was nice to lay around doing nothing, to walk around the town and the harbour and smell clean fresh sea air. I dreaded the thought of heading back into the chaos of Auckland, but we had no choice. We drove back, returned the

car, and spent the next night at a motel near the airport, before taking a shuttle bus to the terminal to catch our flight home.

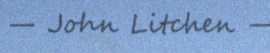

Three years later...
Shinryukan New Zealand Aikikai's 35th anniversary.

This was a big event, a huge event, with Doshu the most important guest. Many senior as well as lower ranked aikidoka from around the world would also be there. I was excited to be attending this week long event and looking forward to catching up with Colin and Billy, my two best friends in New Zealand.

The early morning walk across the tarmac at Coolangatta was a delight with cool crisp air and the warmth of the rising sun beginning to be felt. I was boarding a *Freedomair* flight direct to Auckland.

The flight takes around 3 hours but there was a delay on arrival as the plane waited for a spot to 'plug' into the terminal to allow passengers to disembark. I knew Colin would be waiting for me, but it seemed to take longer than usual. But then I suspect Colin is used to long waits at airports because he is always there to pick up guests. He would be back again the next day to collect Doshu and his entourage, and other guests who might also be arriving.

"We need another driver," he told me once we'd left the terminal and were heading to his parked car, "so I nominated you. You can drive the wife's car. She's away and won't be needing it."

"That's fine by me, but I don't know where anything is."

"I made some maps. Follow me out to the airport tomorrow, and then back to the hotel. We'll be picking up Arai Shihan and his party. Doshu and his group will be collected by Takase Shihan."

"That sounds easy enough."

I paid particular attention as we drove from the airport to Colin's place, but everything looked confusing with traffic backed up and moving at a snail's pace. With Colin deciding to get off the main road and taking side streets and back roads to avoid the traffic, I was hopelessly confused.

Back at the house, as I was unpacking my stuff Colin asked, "Do you want to train tonight?"

"Not really, but I'll come and watch."

I didn't have the energy to even think training after getting up before dawn, around five in the morning, to get to the airport at Coolangatta where it took a couple of hours for the usual tasks needed to board an international flight. I even had my hand luggage searched by security officers, because x-rays had shown something long and sharp like a knife. It was my tube of toothpaste, which they took away and dumped, in case it wasn't really toothpaste. Everyone was so bloody paranoid.

I was feeling a bit jet-lagged, and half the day had vanished as I flew into the sun across the Tasman Sea.

There were only five students at his class that night.

"These are the keen ones," he said. "I guess the rest are resting in preparation for the gasshuku with Doshu."

Suddenly I felt that I should join them, but I had left my Gi at Colin's place.

"Ah, the sign of a true aikidoka," Colin said with a smile when I told him. "No matter how tired, he's got to train. I've got a spare top over here." Rummaging in a drawer he found it and a white belt to tie it with, "but no bottom half," he added.

"That's fine." I was wearing tracksuit pants and they would be loose and flexible enough.

"I've got to warn you," he told the others jovially, "our visitor is a 3rd dan instructor from the Gold Coast."

It was a good class. The warm up exercises were structured differently to what I was used to doing and we concentrated on only three things, since the class only lasted an hour. *Shomen uchi iriminage*, which everyone everywhere in the world practices, *gyaku hanmi katatetori kokyuho*, again a basic application, and my favourite at the time *riotedori tenchinage*. Colin is a good teacher and made some interesting points while explaining and demonstrating what he wanted us to do. I practiced with each of the five in turn and hopefully contributed something towards helping their understanding of what they were doing. I tried to remain soft and fluid, working on my timing and distancing, and gently extending each partner into a position where they had no choice but to take *ukemi* (a controlled fall or roll) to avoid injury. Like most beginners, I found them trying to drag their partner into position and using force or too much strength to impose the technique. This doesn't work, as natural resistance comes into play from the other person, but it would be some years of training before they realize this. I did enjoy the class, because it reminded me of what I might have been like when I first started my training 15 years earlier.

After class Colin and I had dinner at a local Chinese restaurant in Papakura. I had beef with black bean sauce, and it was excellent. The sauce was great. It's hard to get a really good sauce if you want to cook it yourself, and I discovered over the years not too many restaurants have a good black bean sauce, which leads me to assume they probably buy the same sauces as I do at the local supermarket, only in bulk. To find a place that has a genuinely authentic tasting black bean sauce was unexpected.

Confusion reigns

The next morning, we didn't have to go to the airport until mid-afternoon so Colin and I went into Auckland to the Association's bank where he was to organize some of the funds needed for looking after the guests arriving later that day. This was a good opportunity for me to see how to get into and out of the city.

Well, the traffic didn't flow with the freeway gridlocked for more than half the distance into town. There were roadworks with lanes closed, and far too many people trying to force their way into lanes. It certainly increased the stress levels of every driver on that freeway. Apparently, the city of Auckland had grown so rapidly the infrastructure couldn't keep up and the two main freeways into and out of the city suffered gridlock every morning and afternoon during peak hours. But once we got into the city it was easy enough to get around. If I was to be driving later, my problem was not knowing the city and thus not being sure of where I would be going.

Colin kept pointing out various streets and explained where they went and which way I had to go to get people out of the city to the venue where the gasshuku was being held. I had no idea after a while as we seemed to be doubling back or going in circles.

"Don't worry," Colin said. "I made copies of maps of all the places you need to go, so you won't get lost."

That's what you think.

"When we get back, we'll have to go straight to the airport. Just follow me in the other car there and back. We can have lunch at the airport while we wait."

— Changing States —

The car I used was normally used by Colin's wife. It was automatic but gutless. It was slow accelerating and if Colin took off too fast, I couldn't keep up. A couple of times he had to slow down to allow me to catch up. It was midday and the traffic was much less than the earlier peak hour, so the drive to the airport was reasonably good.

We weren't there more than a few minutes when Takase Shihan and a couple of helpers (meaning drivers) turned up, one of whom was Billy. We decided to have a coffee and a sandwich while we waited.

Suddenly Takase Shihan jumped up, "There's Doshu," he said.

I saw Doshu and two others walking along the concourse coming from customs and baggage.

Takase Shihan was over there immediately, and he called us over as well. He introduced each of us to Doshu and his son Mitsuteru, and Fujimaki Sensei.

Moments later Arai Shihan and his group arrived. Colin and I were taken over and introduced to them. I thought we would be on our way then but there was a discussion as to whether we should go straight into town or whether we should go by One Tree Hill so the visitors could get a lovely overview of the whole Auckland area. They were still waiting for one member of Doshu's party to arrive. He was still in customs.

Suddenly plans were changed. Colin was to wait for the last member of Doshu's party while I was to take Arai Shihan and one of the others in my car. The rest of Arai Shihan's group would go in a maxi taxi. Colin told me to follow the taxi. "I'll catch up to you at One Tree Hill."

They waited while I went and retrieved the car. I asked the taxi driver not to drive too fast because I was to follow him and could get lost if I couldn't keep up.

When I got to One Tree Hill almost everyone was there, wandering about taking photos of the views and of each other.

Top: Takase Shihan with Doshu and his son Mitsuteru on One Tree Hill.

Middle: Doshu with Watanabe Shihan.

Bottom: Mitsuteru with Fujimaki Sensei, Doshu's uke for most of the classes as well a teacher of other classes. He missed the boat trip because he was teaching a children's class at the time.

Doshu also took photos...

A few moments later Colin arrived, and it was a nice surprise to discover the missing member of Doshu's group was Watanabe Shihan. He immediately remembered me from two years earlier and started chatting to me in Spanish. As Always, he was all smiles and as jolly as ever. He is a really nice person to talk to as well as to train with.

Colin told me that once we got into town and everyone had organized their rooms, we would all go to lunch. I would ferry Arai Shihan and his senior associates and Colin would take Watanabe Shihan. And later that day we would all go to a Japanese restaurant for dinner. That meant we had to hang around in tow for the rest of the day. It would give me a chance to check out a couple of big bookshops and a record store I remembered seeing on my previous visit to Auckland. It would be my only chance to do any shopping because t once the gasshuku started I would have no spare time having to ferry Arai Shihan and his group back and forth between the venue to the hotel. It would be a very busy week.

It was amusing seeing them taking photos with a variety of digital cameras. Each one in our group took pictures of everyone else in front of whatever there was to see. Each one would give someone else their camera so they could have a picture taken. This way, all had the same picture on each of their individual cameras. They were as excited as a bunch of kids on a school excursion especially when they could see what the photo looked like immediately after it was taken. Digital cameras encourage people to take lots of photos whereas analogue ones using film were limited to how many shots you could get on a roll and then you had to wait for it to be processed and printed. Photography had been revived in the digital age with instant access to the photos just taken, and that was a good thing I thought.

When we got to the hotel the rooms weren't ready, so it was decided to take a short walk to the nearby Sky Tower where we could have some lunch. I left them there and said I would be back at the hotel at 7:30 and Colin and I would be taking them to dinner at a Japanese restaurant. After a beer at lunch, I felt like falling asleep, but I didn't. The car was in the hotel garage, it wasn't worth driving out of town to Colin's place and coming back in a few hours later. I wandered about, looking at shops, sat in a park for a while and watched people going back and forth, finally went back to the hotel where I freshened up in a luxurious bathroom available for guests before sitting down in the foyer to wait for Colin and for the others to come down so we could take them to dinner. I wasn't waiting long before Arai Shihan and his group appeared in the foyer, still taking photos of each other with enthusiasm. Colin arrived. I went down to the garage and got the other car and we all piled into both vehicles. I followed Colin to the restaurant. We both parked in a multi-level car park building, right at the top because it was almost full. Dinner was great. We had a huge variety of Japanese dishes, and they were all first class. Arai Shihan ordered Japanese vodka which I think he called *shocha*. He and his students drank it with enormous enthusiasm.

I drank nothing alcoholic, not only because it would put me to sleep, but because I still had to drive the group back to their hotel and after that return to Colin's place well out of town.

Relaxing at the dinner for Arai Shihan and his group.

Going back after dropping Arai Shihan and his group at the hotel was easy. It was after 11 pm and there was hardly any traffic. But during the day was different when I had to collect them and take them to the gasshuku venue, then return them to the hotel.

It was always during peak hours in the morning and afternoon with all the major motorways and roads gridlocked. We spent an inordinate amount of time sitting or crawling along with miles of cars in front and back. Not a pleasant way to get around, but there was no other way.

Driving in a strange city is often difficult and stressful. Every city has its own idiosyncratic way of driving and the people who live there have no problems, but strangers often find it awkward, with unspoken rules drivers have agreed to not known to them, even though driving is basically common sense.

What made it stressful for me was not knowing where I was going those first couple of days and having to follow close behind Colin so not to get lost. I had to stay close enough to leave no gap or I might lose him. This was hard at traffic lights when he took off quickly and the car I was using hardly accelerated at all. A gap would open up and almost immediately someone would pass me and jump into it. If Colin was to turn he would slow down forcing the driver or drivers in between us to pass him so I could then close the gap and follow him into the turn.

By the third day I knew the way from the hotel to the venue and it was much easier getting around after that because i didn't have to rely on Colin leading the way.

Off to a good start

The Gasshuku began on Thursday and continued until the Sunday. On the Thursday morning we arrived early at the venue so we could assist with the laying of the mats. Colin had a plan mapped out about where to start and which way to go to get the maximum mat space, keeping the different coloured mats from many different dojos in their own groups so as not to mix them which would make if difficult after the even was over trying to find which mats went to which dojos.

The official opening was almost as soon as we'd finished laying the mats. There was just enough time for everyone to go and get changed.

With everyone lined up on the mats, Takase Shihan introduced Doshu, Arai Shihan, Mitsuteru (Doshu's son) and Tony Smibert Sensei from Australia. He and his superb uke Andrew Ross had arrived the day before to be collected by Billy Orr. Sawada Shihan was also introduced as was Fujimaki Shihan who would be Doshu's primary uke for all demonstrations, although he would alternate with Mitsuteru as uke.

The first class was Taken by Doshu, who beckoned everyone to form a circle around him after a brief series of warm up exercises so they could see what he was doing. He explained he would stick to basic techniques fundamental to a deeper understanding of Aikido. Each time he demonstrated something he would get everyone in a circle around him. He used Fujimaki Sensei alternating with Mitsuteru as ukes.

His first technique was *Shihogiri*, a stretching exercise, which was then followed by *Iriminage* from *shomen uchi*. These are two things everyone does at the beginning of any grading test and are considered fundamental worldwide. Doshu pointed out that there are no separate techniques, but that everything flows from one or two simple movements, and that one technique simply becomes another as the dynamics of movement alter.

Every shihan taking later classes also expressed similar variations of the same concept and techniques. It was an eye and mind opener to realize this and to see it put into action so elegantly. No one moves like Doshu. But each shihan had an effortless way of moving, no less beautiful than Doshu, and the power inherent in their movement was incredible.

The best thing of all was that each other shihan trained in Doshu's class as well as the classes taken individually by themselves, which gave many students including me an opportunity to practice and feel what it was like to work with these very high ranked shihan and senior teachers.

Colin was the official photographer, and he nominated me as his assistant so I could wander about at will and take photos. This gave me an opportunity to observe many different people training, and what I saw in many cases from high-ranking senior students was that they were still trying to use strength, still trying to drag uke into position for a technique, still trying to force the technique, rather than allowing it to evolve as an expression of movement created between them. They weren't getting the message from their very senior guests. The power in a technical application comes from within, from your core and it flows out through arms and legs that are relaxed, yet supple and strong. Muscular strength isn't needed if internal energy and movement are used properly while certain principles are applied, such as taking balance away and leading at the moment of contract between the two partners. One can be induced to fall without any use of physical strength; loss of balance and gravity makes it happen. Uke then needs to know how to fall safely.

Watanabe Shihan also took photos, mostly of Doshu's classes in between practicing with whoever was willing to train with him.

— Changing States —

Doshu took us through the whole basic range after *Iriminage*, with *Ikyo, Tenchinage, Shihonage* and *Kaiten nage*. Although we practiced those individually, Doshu demonstrated how one flows into another through the dynamics of movement, and that the expected outcome at the start isn't what necessarily finishes the interaction at the end.

Doshu demonstrating **riotedori shihogiri** *used as a warming and stretching exercise.*

Riotedori Tenchinage *(two had grab, finishing with 'heaven and Earth' throw.)*

Doshu and ***Itiminage*** *with Mitsuteru as uke. I can be seen sitting in the circle watching carefully. Colin took this photo.*

As soon as Doshu's class had finished, Takase Shihan came up to me and said "Quick, go and get changed and meet us out the front. You are going to come on the fishing trip with Doshu. I want you to bring Arai Shihan and his group. Colin knows where the boat is so please follow him."

"Okay." That was a surprise.

I went and got changed and met Colin out front where Doshu and Mitsuteru were discussing with Billy the size of the fish he expected them to catch.

"This Big," Billy said, indicating the size by spreading his arms.

A beautiful afternoon on the water

The sun was shining and there was a soft breeze as we walked along a narrow pier to where the charter boat was moored. Auckland has an incredible marina with what must be a thousand boats moored there. I was the largest marina I'd ever seen.

The moment we'd arrived at the marina Takase Shihan, Colin and one or two others went into a small shop and bought bags of ice to keep the beer cold, bait for the fishing lines, and whatever else they thought would be needed once we were out on the water. I followed taking pictures.

For me, the secret to getting good shots was to be always walking around with a camera and appearing to take shots or getting ready to take a shot. People get used to seeing you with a camera and after a while they ignore you, or simply don't register seeing you anymore. Later they are often surprised when they see the pictures you took exclaiming "I don't remember seeing you there taking pictures."

It was like that on the boat trip. Not only did I have a camera slung around my neck, as did Colin, almost every one of the visitors had a camera and continued taking pictures non-stop. They took no notice of Colin and me. It was the same during the gasshuku, After the first day, no one took an notice of us, which enabled us, and Watanabe Shihan who was taking pictures of Doshu, to wander in amongst those practicing without any of them seeing us.

Doshu with his camera as we boarded the boat. Relaxing while Mitsuteru prepares a fishing rod.

Heading for the boat, getting on board, feeling excited about the trip.

Below:
Mitsuteru with Watanabe Shihan on board.

After half an hour out, the boat stopped and those who wanted to fish baited their hooks or had them baited by someone who knew how to do it, and started fishing. Those not fishing drank a beer or tow and took photos. There was snot much success at first, a few small fish but nothing substantial, the boat was moved to a new location. They kept fishing as the boat moved. Sea birds followed in our wake hoping to catch scraps thrown overboard or to dive in and get something disturbed by the boat's passage through the water.

After about two hours, those fishing had managed to catch 30 or so reasonably sized fish. They would be cooked later at a party at Takase Shihan's house to host all the senior invited guests, and those who hadn't come on the fishing trip who were teaching classes while we were out fishing, would be there.

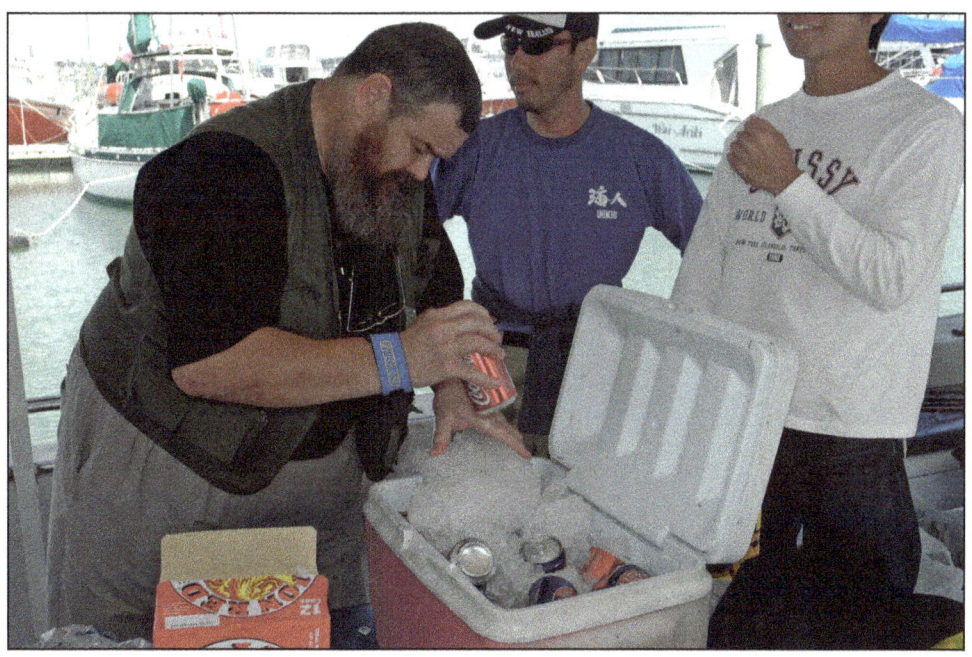

Colin was in charge of the beer and the snacks and he made sure there was no shortage of either.

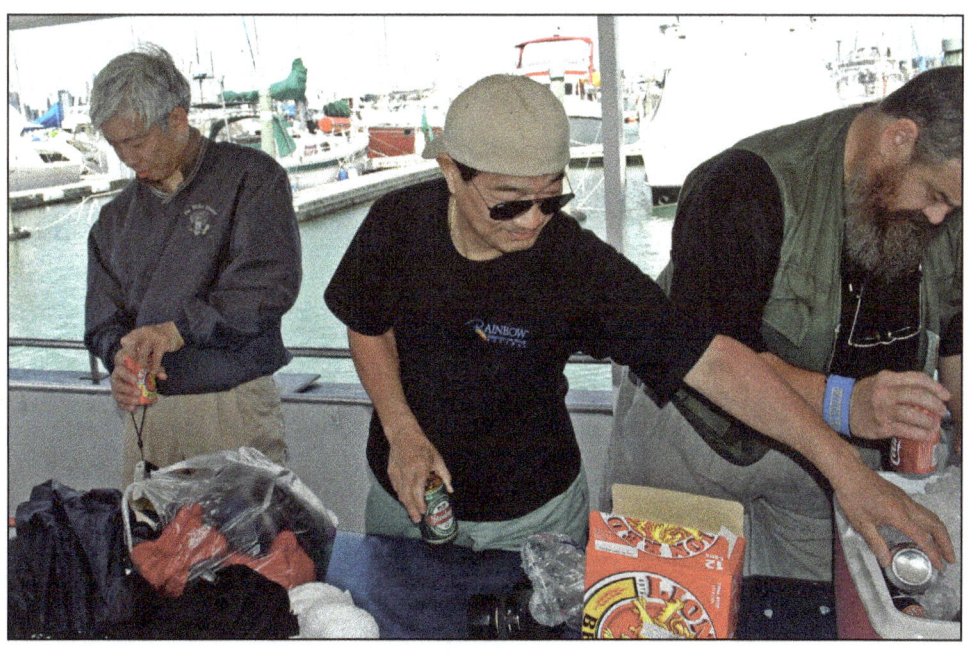

Andrew Williamson Sensei from Christchurch with Doshu and Takase Shihan. Takese Shihan preparing bait. Watanabe Shihan with a fish he caught.

Heading back after a successful two hours of fishing.

Watanabe Shihan, Takase Shihan, Doshu, Mitsuteru,, Sawada Shihan, Arai Shihan.

When all the bait had been used up, Takase Shihan decided we would head back and on the way, take a leisurely cruise around the harbour. Auckland looks fabulous when you look at the city from offshore. As we came closer to the city he got the boat to cruise around the harbour where the liners and commercial ships were as well as the marina and the section where yachts and private boats of all kinds were moored. We also passed several groups of rowers racing, the largest groups I'd seen in one boat. Perhaps it was a 'dragon boat' race? Finally, we got back to where we'd started and it was a very happy group who were looking forward to that evening's party.

The dinner at Takase Shihan's house was a delight, with the senior Shihan mixing and having a jolly good time. Other guests were Tony Smibert Shihan and senior Members of *Shinryukan Aikikai New Zealand* and their wives, creating a most pleasant affair with lots of bonhomie, especially amongst those who had one or two more drinks than they should have.

Colin and I were both tired after a long day of ferrying people back and forth, training and also taking photos, so we decided to leave early in case we were asked to take people back into the city to their hotels.

"They can make other arrangements," Colin said.

Nobody noticed us leave at 11:30 (pm).

One of the things I did was to bring with me a printed proof copy of my Aikido book that I'd been working on for the last couple of years. I had been planning to show it to Smibert Sensei to see what he thought of it, but an opportunity never arose, so the only people who did see it before it was published later that year was Colin and Billy, and they both thought it was great, which was an encouraging indication that I had created something worthwhile.

Back to the gasshuku

Each day, the first class was taken by Doshu, and at the beginning of each class he reviewed what he had explained and demonstrated the day before. This way we got strong continuity and were able to clearly see the relationship between the attack and the response it generated.

Each of Doshu's classes focused on a different attack but the techniques in response were the same. We did *Ikyo, Nikyo, Sankyo, Shihonage, Iriminage, Kotegaeshi, Jujinage,* and *Tenchinage* from varying attacks such as *Katatetori (ai hanmi and gyaku hanmi), Katadori, Morotedori, Ryotedori, Shomen uchi, Yokomen uchi,* and *Ushiro Ryotedori.*

His emphasis on basic and not so basic movements was that it didn't matter what the technical response was, the body movement is the same for all of the *Omote* techniques and similarly the same for all the *Ushiro* and *Ura* techniques.

Doshu: demonstrating Kokyunage.

Doshu: demonstrating Kotegaeshi.

The class following Doshu's was usually taken by Fujimaki Shihan, the youngest of the Shihan guests. He appeared hard and ferocious. He was precise and his movements crisp, his posture, always perfect. He commanded respect because he was Doshu's Uke as well as being an important teacher at Hombu dojo in Japan. Everyone loved his classes.

He came up to us after his first class because Colin and I had been taking photos. The hall was poorly lit with a row of windows along one side high up near the ceiling. We used whatever natural light was available. He told us it was good that we didn't use a flash because he found it distracting when he was trying to teach. Personally, I don't like flash shots because I think it creates too harsh a light. Natural light is always better, and with digital cameras, since there is much more leeway in how the light is processed, I don't think a flash is necessary. Even so, with slow shutter speeds and high ISO, shots are sometimes blurred especially if there is a lot of fast movement. But this can be a good as it adds the sensation of movement and feeling there is much more to the movement before and after the moment that is captured.

Fujimaki Sensei: taking uke's balance

Arai Shihan was completely different. He was a much older person and as he introduced himself he explained that he had been studying and practicing aikido for 50 years and over that time he has taken ukemi for four generations of the Ueshiba family. He began his training taking ukemi for the Founder Morihei Ueshiba O-Sensei, then he took ukemi for the second Doshu, the Founder's son Kisshomaru Ueshiba, and when the second Doshu died he continued training and taking ukemi for the third and present Doshu Moriteru Ueshiba, as well as his son Mitsuteru right here at this gasshuku. Fifty years is an achievement that not many can claim.

Arai Shihan seemed so relaxed and casual with his movement. There was nothing flashy like with the younger shihan. His movement combined small soft circles that completely tangled up his ukes in the process of unbalancing them. I thought he demonstrated superb *kuzushi* (balance taking), taking instant and subtle control of his uke's stability the moment he touched him. Those trying to emulate him were often confused. They didn't seem to get what he was doing. His emphasis on soft movement and suppleness was alien to those who always used brute strength and muscle power to force their way inti a technique. If you were his uke, you wouldn't feel a thing until a sudden explosive *irimi* (entering) movement would slam you down onto the mat. Then you would feel his power.

Watching him as I took photos, he seemed so relaxed he almost appeared asleep as he turned and entered under uke's arm, then turned back in to uke's centre to take him or her completely off balance; then wham! Uke was on the mat without knowing what had happened.

His direct entry into an attack was stunning and devastating. Who would expect a person so relaxed to be able to move so fast. The instant uke moved to attack, Arai Shihan had already entered and was slamming uke down onto the mat. It was like he could read their mind, their intention to attack and act the instant before they commenced. After 50 years of training, I guess this is how it is done. O-Sensei was like that. He could sense an attacker's intention and move in before it commenced so that when it did commence, he was already taking uke down. To an outside observer it seemed relaxed and not necessarily fast, but to the attacker it seemed instantaneous, and you were already heading down to the mat.

Arai Shihan emphasized the same point Doshu had made earlier, that all techniques and movements were interconnected and interchangeable, and should be thought of as one.

I heard people say they were terrified of him and hoped that he wouldn't choose them as uke as he moved about during his class. They had no idea what he would do and weren't too sure they wanted to find out.

His apparent casualness belied the power and dynamism of his technique, with subtle almost unseen movement that always had a devastating effect. It looked as if uke smashed himself into the mat! You had to have him as a partner to feel how helpless you could be, and how much power emanated from his 'oh so casual' body movement

I can attest to that because I practiced with Arai Shihan who also took ukemi for me as we practiced together in Watanabe Sensei's later class.

He also was the first one I'd seen demonstrate the power of a body dropping vertically. He would lead uke into an unbalanced position, a rising position to make uke float momentarily, then suddenly he would drop to his knees onto the mat and uke would come crashing down so fast it was a blur. There was nothing uke could do to resist it. You simply felt this enormous crushing weight bearing down crushing you underneath it. I thought it would be the same as if you were beneath a collapsing building. This was demonstrated with *kokyunage*, and *Shihonage*, but he also did it with *Iriminage*.

He also demonstrated several applications using a bokken, notably *iriminage*. Uke was always cut down in an instant.

Arai Shihan raising uke up so he is almost floating, then suddenly dropping to his knees to take uke down in an instant. There was no stopping the downwards fall.

I am practicing Riotedori Kokuyunage with Arai Shihan during the only class taken by Watanabe Shihan. Arai Shihan showed me how he does this after which he became Uke for me so I could practice the application. On the next page it is my turn to be Nage while Arai Shihan became Uke.

What I loved about this gasshuku was the opportunity to practice with the most senior students and teachers of Aikido who were there.
They happily mixed in and became students to practice under the direction of their contemporaries or of Doshu when he took classes.

The photos on these two pages were taken by Colin.

— Changing States —

Above: Arai Shihan enters with explosive force the instant uke raises his hand to do a shomen uchi cut.
Below: two views of the finish with Watanabe Shihan teaching Riotedori Tenchinage during his only class.

— Changing States —

Arai Shihan using a bokken to do Kokyunage.

With slow shutter speeds and using available light, any fast movement becomes blurred, but this I think adds feeling to the images and clearly demonstrates that there is constant movement and adjustments being made as any aikido application unfolds.

Watanabe Shihan is another of those older gentlemen who can deal with the toughest opponents in such a casual way that you can't see what it is they do. I have practiced with him on a number of occasions, and he was always gentle and soft, but when he projects me into a fall there is plenty of power to make me go down. No question about it.

He was all over the place with his Nikon D100 digital SLR taking pictures by the hundreds. I thought he was Doshu's official photographer. He mingled on the mat while people were training so he could get close-ups, he went around the edges of the mat to take long shots, and as he wandered about, he would sometimes put his camera down beside the mat, jump in and join someone training, taking a couple of turns as uke then nage, before returning to his camera to move around looking for more shots. He was one of Takase Shihan's teachers while he was at university and was often invited to New Zealand to teach at seminars and gasshuku.

He gave the impression he was merely here on a holiday. He wasn't scheduled to teach any classes, however there was a change of plans and on the Saturday afternoon he took the first of the afternoon classes. Throughout the class he never stopped grinning and smiling. He was having such a good time. As soon as he would demonstrate a technique, he wouldn't stop to watch what people were doing but would immediately run into a group and start practicing with them, getting them to throw him so he could feel if they were doing it right. If not, he would correct them then move onto to someone else and do the same again.

I noticed the older aikidoka teachers did this. The younger ones didn't. They might join in, but never took ukemi, they always took the role of nage. In the old days the master teachers taught and corrected their students by taking ukemi for them. (Especially with weapons training) This way he could feel the student's movement and correct it while moving, giving students an opportunity to feel with their own bodies the result of doing a movement properly. Students practicing with a master this way would learn very quickly. Watanabe Shihan exemplified this older method of teaching.

It was amusing to watch a few of the bigger guys trying to force a technique on him that obviously wasn't working. The more they strained the less movable he became. He would let them play a bit and then with a huge grin he would slam them down onto the mat. His grin was so infections that everyone finished his glass with a smile on their faces and commenting to each other about what a great time they'd had.

Watanabe Shihan with his camera, by the edge of the mat during one of Doshu's classes.

The banquet

This took place on Saturday night, and was held at the hotel where Doshu, his son Mitsuteru, Fujimaki Shihan and Watanabe Shihan were staying.

Colin and I went early so Colin could check that everything had been arranged and was ready in the banquet room. David Wong who organized the banquet was already there suitably concerned. He needn't have been, everything was fine.

The foyer of the hotel was a grand spacious place and quite cool. We sat upstairs and had a few drinks with some other early arrivals naturally discussing our various experiences of the last four days of training. It was a happy relaxed group. Someone arrived with a handful of small white flowers. A few important people were given a flower to wear in the lapel of their jacket. Colin got one. Shortly after that we were asked to enter the banquet room.

The official party lined up near the entrance to this grand dining room to welcome guests. Most arrivals congratulated Takase Shihan and his wife for the work they'd put in and the time sacrificed to in establishing and maintaining Shinryukan Aikido and the Aikikai New Zealand Federation.

Inside, the food was superbly arranged as both a hot and cold buffets. There were only eighty-five or ninety people here, out of the couple of hundred that had been training, and they quickly found the tables allocated to them. When Doshu arrived there was a welcoming speech and once again Takase Shihan introduced Doshu and his son Mitsuteru, the Japanese ambassador, and several other senior Shihan who occupied the official table. The ambassador made a speech. Doshu made a speech. One of the politicians, perhaps the deputy mayor of Auckland, made a speech to the group, after which the dinner could commence. Everyone waited until Doshu, and his party had made their selections from the buffet before each table in turn had their turn. The food was as fantastic tasting as it looked.

Once dinner was over, people mingled, finding out who came from where, how many years they'd been training, and all kinds things related to aikido. The highlight for me was the opportunity to have a chat with Doshu and when Watanabe Shihan joined us Colin just had to snap a picture of us together. Doshu asked me how Watanabe Shihan's class was. I told him it was fabulous, a lot of fun, and that Watanabe Shihan had more fun than anyone else. It was true. It was the only class Watanabe Shihan took because most of the time he was taking photos, but he made this class special with his infectious enthusiasm and good nature. Watanabe l just laughed and Doshu chuckled in a more reserved way. His English, I discovered, was quite good and we had no trouble understanding each other.

Watanabe Shihan, Doshu, and me at the banquet.

— Changing States —

Colin at the banquet with his small unobtrusive digital camera.

Although we were told not to approach Doshu, many did and asked if they could have their photo taken with him. This started because a member of Arai Shihan's group approached first. They didn't often see him in Japan since they are a long way from Tokyo, but they have enormous respect for him and what he represents. They travelled at their own expense from Japan to Auckland so they could train in his classes as well as all the other senior Shihan's classes. They did every class on offer. They were that keen. They couldn't resist asking to have their photos taken with Doshu.

Doshu seemed relaxed about it, even resigned to it. I imagine it must drive him crazy getting so much attention, but he was always polite, always acquiesced and was almost always ready with slight smile.

As for taking pictures during training, it was not permitted; except for Watanabe Shihan whom I assumed was the official Hombu photographer and Colin Pearson who was Shinryukan's official photographer, and thanks to Colin, myself as his assistant.

At the end of the first day Colin had some trouble downloading some of the photos he took so he copied mine onto his computer, and right now it's hard to remember which are his and which are mine since we both took many from the same positions.

The dinner was a great success.

Sunday was the last day of the Gasshuku and in the afternoon after the classes were done, each of the visiting Shihan starting with Doshu first, gave a two-minute demonstration. When the most senior Shihan had done their demos, the different clubs withing *Shinryukan Aikido* each gave a brief demonstration of a particular technique they had been studying. The had arranged beforehand that each would present something different from the other so there was no repetition.

There was a demonstration of a traditional Japanese dance and lots of speeches from politicians as well as senior Aikidoka and Doshu. Then when they left it was time to start packing up the mats and for them to be returned to the various dojo from where they had come.

A bit of a shock...

My book, **Aikido— Basic and Intermediate Studies**, was published mid-year (2005) by Trafford Publishers in Canada. 30 copies arrived, but I had to pay customs and import duties totaling almost $300 before the package was delivered. The 30 copies were allocated to me as part of the publishing deal. As happy as I was to see the book in print, I realized that any additional copies I required would have to be paid for at a discount which wasn't much being slightly less than the discounted retail price, but on top of that, if I had a bulk order shipped to me it would again incur customs and import fees as well as expensive postage. It wasn't practical.

I let it go for a while to see how the book would sell and it went very well with a couple of hundred copies being sold over the first 12 months. Unfortunately, the royalty I received was somewhere between $1 to slightly less than $2 per copy sold (depending on the ever-changing exchange rate between the US, Canadian, and Australian dollars), after Trafford took its printing and delivery costs among other fees.

I wasn't getting much out of it at all. For all the work done creating and preparing the book, it was a disappointment.

Being the newsletter editor of *Aikido Australia*, later changed to *Aikido in Australia*, I was accustomed to sending Sugano Shihan copies of each issue printed so I had his mailing address in New York. (*He had asked me to do this, a few years earlier since no one had been sending him copies*). As soon as I'd received the books, I posted a copy and an explanatory letter about how the book was conceived to him. I didn't expect a reply, but it was the right thing to do. I would talk to him later about it at our 40th anniversary summer school (in January 2006).

Aiki Kai Australia flew me down to Tasmania for a weekend, to Deloraine where Smibert Sensei lived and had his art studio and gallery, to help work on a special 16-page booklet for the upcoming 40th anniversary event. I took care of the design and layout; Smibert Sensei wrote most of the featured content. We worked on it in his studio with the help of a couple of other people as well as in consultation by phone with Sugano Shihan who was in New York.

But before we started on it, after Smibert Sensei and a friend collected me at the airport, we went for a light lunch and over that I showed Smibert Sensei a copy of the book I'd just had published.

He had no idea that I had done this, and of course no idea that Graham Morris Sensei was also featured prominently throughout the book as well as being credited as Technical Adviser. He was taken aback.

I explained how it started and evolved over a two-and-a-half-year period, and that I had sent Sensei (Sugano Shihan) a copy and a letter regarding it, so he knew, and had known for a couple of months about it.

He was upset because I had not specifically asked him, or the Technical Teaching Committee, if I could do such a book.

"You should have asked," he said.

"And would you have given permission for me to do it?"

He remained silent for a moment.

Before he could answer I told him I shouldn't need to ask permission to produce a book that reflected my personal understanding of what I had learnt over the years. I didn't have the intention or even the thought of writing an aikido book at first, but it had evolved, I explained, from a series of courses and short classes designed to be taught at a school in Queensland. But when that didn't eventuate, I didn't want to waste the work done, so I continued until there was enough material to complete a reasonably comprehensive book.

"A book that I am proud of," I added emphatically.

A book that was more comprehensive than many other books at that time on the same subject. I know, because I had seen most of the books published on aikido and have copies in my library. I made sure my book covered everything from the most basic movements to all the requirements needed for grading tests in general, up to Shodan (1st black belt) level. It was 280 pages with over 1200 photo drawings and several hundred small sketches to explain movement. An undertaking that took two and a half years of work.

"Can I take this and look at it later?"

"That copy is for you," I said.

"Okay, thanks, we can now concentrate on the 40th anniversary."

And that's what we did. He put the copy of my book on his desk in his studio where several other people there had a look at it before putting it aside.

The rest of the day was spent working on the 40th anniversary booklet's content and design.

At dinner later in his dining room, he told me he would look through the book before going to bed. We watched an episode from a Steven Spielberg series on TV about people abducted by UFOs called **Taken**, (Spielberg was executive producer) and talked about that for a while before going to bed. I had a room in his studio/gallery where I slept.

Surprisingly, in the morning he never said a word about the book.

In his studio a visitor that morning who was a high-ranking karateka and a good friend, picked up the book which was on a desk in the studio and flipped through it. "That's a pretty good book," he said but no one made any comment other than that. He later drove me back to the airport so I could catch my return flight to the Gold Coast, and we did talk about the book. He had written several books as well as contributed to martial arts magazines in Australia and overseas, so I thought if he considered the book to be good, then it was an opinion I valued.

I took the 40th anniversary booklet files home and did the layout for the Booklet, created the print ready PDF file and emailed this to Smibert Sensei who had it printed in Tasmania. The first time I saw the finished booklet was when I turned up to register at the 40th anniversary summer school in Melbourne in January 2006.

Smibert Sensei never mentioned my aikido book again. The TTC never mentioned it. But they didn't stop me from selling copies to individuals attending the various national schools when I was there. I think if it had been bad, they would not have allowed me to sell copies at any function. On the other hand, they never recommended it or mentioned it at all, even though quite a lot of local aikidoka have a copy. Some had bought their copies online through Amazon or Book Depository, which I found encouraging, as well as, I must admit, satisfying. One instructor from Victoria called me and asked for permission to photocopy various pages for his students to use as a reference. We had trained together in Melbourne while I was still living there.

Once I canceled my Canadian contract and became the book's publisher, having it printed in Australia (instead of overseas) enabled me to recover finally what it had cost to be produced in Canada.

Another instructor outside of Aiki Kai Australia contacted me and bought 40 copies which he wanted signed and dated to sell to his students when they started training. He did this a couple of times, which made him my very best customer.

In 2013 I revised the book's layout and added extra material and re-published it through *Lightning Source* and *Amazon* as POD book available worldwide. 10 years on it still sells several copies, here and there, annually, so it has become by bestselling book, and something I will always be proud of.

40th Anniversary January 2006

The booklet features a photo I took at winter school on the Gold Coast in 1999. Low light, slow shutter created a blurred image that shows the circular movement inherent in a technique called Kaiten Nage (circular throw). This same image was used on the posters produced to advertise the event sent to Aikido dojos around Australia.

Melbourne's weather was atrociously hot, in the 40s Celsius, with super-hot dry winds sucking the moisture out of you. I couldn't help feeling sorry for the overseas visitors coming from North America, England

and Europe. It was winter over there, and for them to fly into an extreme Australian summer must have been horrific. There was, however, a cool southerly breeze which tempered the heat for the first couple of days.

It was a longer summer school than normal with the first three days devoted to the usual training concluding with Sugano Sensei taking the Dan gradings on the Wednesday, leaving the next three days open for the most important international visitors, Sensei's special guests, Doshu Moriteru Ueshiba, (head of *AikiKai* worldwide) and Yoshimitsu Yamada Shihan (of New York Aiki Kai and Chairman of the United States Aikido Federation) a long-time friend of Sugano Shihan. These two and those accompanying them would find the heat of a Melbourne summer very difficult.

On the first two days, the local students from around Australia settled in and got themselves used to the heat. There were huge fans all around the training space to keep the air moving since the building wasn't air conditioned. They were told to drink plenty of water and to take it easy because of the heat and still many showed the effects of dehydration, and heat stress.

On Tuesday evening there was a sudden change around 6pm. We were at a restaurant in Lygon Street Carlton, a short walk from our accommodation at Melbourne University. When we went into the restaurant it was 42 Celsius, and humid, almost unbearable. An hour later when we emerged from the restaurant the temperature had dropped to 28 Celsius and a blustery cool southerly wind was blowing dust and detritus along the street. It was such a relief to feel that cooler air. Everyone would get a pleasant sleep that night and would be feeling refreshed when it came for grading tests on Wednesday afternoon.

On Thursday there was an influx of students from other aikido organizations who registered for training in Doshu's and Yamada Shihan's classes. Our special guests had arrived that morning and were on their way to the dojo. There was a feeling of excitement as people lined up in seiza waiting for Doshu to arrive.

Before we started, everyone was asked to line up for an official photo with our main guests, Yamada Shihan, Doshu, and on Sensei's other side, Takase Shihan sitting in front. Once the photos were taken, everyone lined as normal and waited for Doshu to begin the first class for the day.

The temperature had crept back up to near 40 Celsius so a warning was again issued to everyone to remember to hydrate and be aware of how the heat can affect them. The heat was extremely dry. You didn't seem to sweat, and the dry heat sucked it up instantly without you being aware. It was far too easy to become dehydrated and disorientated. There were doctors and nurses on hand to treat those afflicted by the heat. On Friday and Saturday, it was 40 and 41 Celsius. And the mats were full. Over these two days other senior visitors from overseas also took classes in the afternoons. Takase Shihan from New Zealand, Ken Cottier Shihan from Hong Kong, and Louis Van Thiegham Sensei from Belgium all taught interesting sessions and when they weren't teaching, they joined in with the training. Again, I had the opportunity to train with Takase Shihan as a partner.

The mat space was always crowded and often practice had to be in groups rather than pairs, but it was probably the best summer school Aiki Kai Australia had held up to that time, certainly in terms of numbers as well as the variety of masterful instruction from the best in the world.

The celebratory dinner Saturday night was a great success with those in attendance having a chance to mingle and chat with the invited guests and have their photos taken with them. During that dinner I had the chance to talk to Sugano Sensei and asked him what he thought of the book I had produced. I asked if he had been upset that I had done it and he said, not at all. He thought the book was good. He didn't have the chance to say much else because others interrupted and wanted to talk to him as well, but that okay as far as I was concerned.

If anyone later commented to me about the book no matter how senior they might be, I would simply tell them that Sugano Sensei said he thought it was good. And that was that!

At the dinner party with Sugano Shihan

On the last day, Sunday, the temperature hit 44 Celsius. A phenomenal temperature with hot blustery winds blowing dust and rubbish about. At the end of his class, Doshu seemed exhausted. The heat had got to him. When some students wanted to have a photo taken with him, he seemed reluctant, although a few were taken, (one with me).

He disappeared soon after to get changed and find somewhere cool to escape to. Photos of other senior teachers and students were taken in the entrance to the dojo some of which later appeared in subsequent newsletters. But it was too hot to feel anything more than wilted.

I felt sorry for the guys who had to transport the mats back to their various dojos that afternoon with the temperature staying at 44 Celsius all afternoon.

— Changing States —

A moment to rest in between classes. Sugano Shihan with Doshu and Yamada Shihan sitting near a side-door where a large fan blew fresh air towards them.

Doshu.

I played around with some of the images afterwards, extracting parts of the background to see if I could get something different to use in the newsletter for the reports of the summer school and these were some of the results. Above with Doshu doing nikyo ura, and left, entering into iriminage. I did this with Doshu, Sugano Shihan, and Yamada Shihan, for the newsletter report.

I wanted to give the images a slight three dimensional appearance, by having part of the participants emerging out of the photo and extending into the surrounding space. And with other images, I wanted the background to be clear of any distraction so only the subjects and what they were doing was there to see.

— John Litchen —

Yamada Shihan

Sugano Shihan

Doshu kindly agreed to have a photo taken with me outside the dojo entrance after the demos and formalities on the final day had been concluded. It was about 11 am and it was already 44 Celsius.

Going home

I was packed and ready to leave by 1 pm.

My flight home wasn't supposed to leave until 6 pm so I thought I would go into town and visit a bookshop or two, but it was too bloody hot.

The street outside the entrance to the accommodation building was devoid of people. They were all hiding from the extreme heat. There were a couple of people who had stepped outside, and were waiting by the entrance for taxis to take them to the airport or other places.

I found Graham Morris here. He had called a taxi to take him to the airport. He was on an earlier flight than me. Feeling how hot it was I decided instantly that it would be better to go the airport where the terminal was air-conditioned and wait there instead of hanging around in the city all afternoon. Graham was okay with sharing his taxi.

Exiting the taxi in front of the terminal building was like stepping into a blast furnace. The heat and the dry wind slammed into us hard enough to knock us over. I staggered to the back of the taxi to get my bag and almost fell over as the boiling wind buffeted us ferociously. With our bags anchoring us, we made it into the terminal where there was no relief to be found. It was jam-packed with people milling about because their flights had been delayed or even canceled, and it was stiflingly hot and humid. The air-conditioning couldn't cope with so many people inside at once.

Many country flights had been canceled because the tyres of the planes had melted into the tarmac, while all interstate flights were delayed. My return flight to the Gold Coast was supposed to depart at 6 pm but was delayed for two hours. I didn't get home until 11 pm that night.

During the week of training, I was one of a very few who were allowed to mingle on the mat with a camera to take photos and I took shots of all the invited guests as well as our regular teachers during their classes. I was able to get quite close to shoot photos in the middle the action, and took well over 1500 photos, some of which were used in the subsequent newsletters reporting on the event, but the majority remain in my personal collection and have not been seen. I produced my own personal report using the photos of the event for reference purposes, but hardly anyone else has seen that report apart from Smibert Sensei to whom I sent a printed copy (220 pages of text and photos of Doshu and other senior teachers and guests taken during their respective classes), and presumably the TTC if he has shown it to them.

— Changing States —

> Part Five
>
> Becoming a downhill stroll

A cliché

"*It's all downhill now,*" people used to tell you when you reached the age of forty.

How many times have I heard that cliché at a birthday party?

How many times have you seen a reference to it on a birthday card?

Of course, it was said as a joke, but underlying the joke was the serious thought that given the average human lifespan of between 70 to 80 years and you'd reached forty, you were halfway to the end of your life. Everything was downhill from then on.

I don't know how many times I heard this during my thirties and forties, but as far as I was concerned it was nothing more than bullshit.

With improvements in medical science and better healthy lifestyles, people at forty, (including myself), were more active and younger looking than those who often stated that worn out cliché.

Fifty was now the benchmark, the halfway point.

I was more active and healthier at fifty than I ever was at thirty, so my own belief was that sixty was the point where you started to slow down. It was past the hallway mark since very few people lived much beyond one hundred years, but I did think sixty was a point from which you could start to slow down a bit. It might be downhill from then on, but there was no need to rush. Just take it easy and make it a slow downhill stroll, instead of a race.

After all, no one wants to get to the end.

During the year 2003 when Monica and I were both 63 years old we were reminded of the mortality of living creatures, and that all of us have finite lifespans with much variation regarding length and conditions during those remaining years. In another two years Monica would be eligible for the Age pension which once was a sign of the end of times, but these days with better health and better living conditions, it signaled a time to slow down and appreciate the life you've had. I wouldn't be eligible until I turned 67, two years later, but as a spouse I could apply for spousal support which was the same as the Age pension. It would be converted to the Age pension once I'd reached the appropriate male age.

Many animals don't live anywhere near the lifespan humans enjoy, or endure depending on conditions and where they live, which is sad to contemplate, especially if you have pets that you love.

Two sad losses

None of us are prepared to lose a dear pet. But inevitably it must happen since we outlive our pets by many years, that is unless you have a pet elephant. I guess if you have lots of pets then losing one isn't so hard, but when like us you only have two cats, and these are the only ones we've had, it is hard. Somewhere around 2002 I heard the ruckus and ran out into the yard to see what was happening, but it was all over when I got there. Shady was being attacked by a feral cat that came into our back yard. She made a futile attempt to defend her territory, but against a large feral cat she didn't stand a chance. It was almost twice her size. It took off and raced up and over the back fence the moment I appeared. I was surprised that she hadn't run away when that big cat came into the yard. She was a timid cat and would often run away from raucous birds that came into the yard and chased her along the side path.

Shady slinked past me and went inside. She was obviously hurt, and I followed her. She went into the garage and tried to hide in there. She wouldn't let me touch her, snarling and scratching as I tried to see where she was injured. She had a tear in her side towards her belly and it was bleeding. After a struggle and lots of scratches which she really didn't mean to inflict on me, I managed to get her into her cat box so I could take her to the local vet nearby at the Robina Village shops.

At the clinic she calmed down and let the vet take her out of her box. The vet cleaned her wound and used several stitches to hold it together. She put a small tube in to drain excess fluid as the wound healed, and she gave Shady an antibiotic injection, and told us to come back in a week to have the stitches removed.

As soon as we got home, Shady headed straight for our bedroom and hid herself under out bed, where she stayed for several hours before tentatively emerging later in the evening.

The wound healed quickly but she absolutely refused to let me put her back into her cat box to take her to the vet. She planted her feet on either side of the opening, and I simply couldn't force her into it. She snapped at me and tried to bite me. I gave up and she took off, straight into our bedroom and under our bed again. I rang the vet and explained I couldn't get Shady into her cat box to take here there.

"Don't worry, I'll come there and do it. It'll only take a few minutes." And ten minutes later she was here, which was nice of her. Shady recognized her as someone who had helped her, (she was very good at calming stressed animals) and she came out from under the bed. The vet quickly took out the stitches and the tube she'd inserted to drain excess fluid, gave her another antibiotic injection, and said "she seems fine."

She was fine for around six months, after which she began to seem lethargic and listless. She hardly seemed interested in eating anything. She wasn't herself. I thought she may have got an infection from the attack that still lingered. I took her to the vet again and she recommended that we take Shady to the veterinary hospital in Mudgeeraba for some tests.

It was a fifteen-minute drive to the hospital and once there, they confirmed after blood tests that she did indeed have an infection. She had Feline Enteritis, what they loosely termed, Feline Aids.

They gave her an injection and said it might help, but, if she did have Feline Enteritis, there was no cure. A regular injection every couple of weeks would help. So we started doing that and for a couple of months she seemed good, but then slowly she started going downhill again, become listless, not eating, hiding under a bush in the backyard where I think she'd decided she would lie down there and die. She would lie there all day and wouldn't come out. She didn't object if I picked her up and sat her on my lap, but she didn't purr either.

At the hospital they said it was a waste of money giving her more injections because they were no longer helping. She was very sick, and she was dying. She was 13 years old and that was a good age for a cat. We should consider having her put out of her misery.

It was a shock hearing this. We went home and talked about it, but the main thing was Shady was obviously unhappy. She was dying, and again she would sip a little water from the swimming pool, and then retreat to her hiding spot under the bush by the pool where she waited for the end. It was upsetting to see her like this. A few days later we rang the hospital and told them we would bring her in as they had suggested.

She didn't object to me putting her in her cat box. She was by then used to it since we'd been taking her to the hospital for injections every two weeks for several months.

Monica and Brian came with me. Together we went into the surgery where Shady was lying on a metal examination table. Her front leg had been shaved to expose the veins where the vet would insert the needle for the injection. Shady looked up at us and I thought I saw in her eyes an understanding of what was about to happen. I thought for a moment that she was trying to thank us. Brian was petting her softly. I touched her and she seemed shivery, a bit nervous, but she didn't move. The vet depressed the plunger and the needle emptied.

'I'll just take a minute," he said. "She'll just fade away."

Brian stood right in front of her, and I couldn't see into her eyes. I wanted her to see me one last time before she died, but it wasn't to be. I moved closer, but she was already dead. The spark had left her eyes for ever. In those last few seconds, I had missed that moment.

"She's gone," the vet said almost in a whisper.

Less than a minute was all it took. So quick!

I reached out to touch her, and it was like touching a heavy stuffed toy. There was no life there at all.

We left her for the hospital to dispose. I didn't want to know how they did it.

We paid the bill and went home where I sat feeling such a loss it was impossible to explain.

I never thought I would be so upset. But I was… Over a cat!

She had been a part of our lives for thirteen years. She had chosen me to be the one she loved unequivocally, and she was as much a part of me as was Monica. I felt like a piece of my heart had been torn out. I would miss her sitting on my lap purring loudly, miss having her follow me around the house in the morning as I opened the curtains and looked out of the windows to see what kind of day we would have, she would look out of the windows as well, and Monica too would miss her as Shady often sat next to her when she practiced yoga in the back yard and tried to copy some of the stretches she did. She was a clever and empathetic cat. We had learnt to communicate with each other over the years. For me, there would never be another cat like her.

These were two of the last photos taken of Shady before she became obviously sick. Even then, she seemed listless and only wanted to sit or lay down quietly while she waited for the end…

Sunny missed her too. For a couple of months, he wandered all over the house, looking in every room, every nook and cranny, searching for her. They had been together with us all their lives. He looked sad. He didn't know what had happened to her. One day she was there, and the next she was gone. I don't think he got over it, but eventually he did stop looking for her. He too became listless and spent more time lying down and sleeping than he once did. He was obviously grieving for her and looked sad all the time.

A few months later at the beginning of October 2003 he started scratching his right forehead above his eye. Something there annoyed him, and we saw that it appeared swollen. Within days the swelling had increased and the skin broke where he scratched it and started seeping blood. By the end of the month (31st October 2003) the lump had increased noticeably and his scratching of it caused constant bleeding which he tried continuously to wipe away with his paw. We took him to the vet nearby and she said he was developing a tumor, but because of its location it would be difficult to operate to remove it.

It got worse. By the end of the month and the start of November the swelling increased until an enormous lump made his head misshapen with his right eye partly closed. We put a collar around his neck so he wouldn't scratch it. We hoped that with the collar preventing him from getting at the tumor it might begin to heal. It didn't. It was weeping blood and pus-like matter.

It was the 17th of November, and the tiny lump that had appeared just over a month earlier was now a huge mess half the size of his head.

"We should take him to the animal hospital and have him put down," I said.

But Brian wouldn't hear of it. He insisted that we get more antibiotics to treat him.

"He really is suffering…"

"You spent a lot of time and money on trying to save Shady, why can't you do the same for Sunny?"

"Because this is different. If they operate, they will have to remove part of his skull and that would expose his brain. It can't be done."

He continued to insist that we don't have him put down, but that we should try more antibiotics or whatever other treatment was possible.

But after a few more days, Sunny was worse than ever, and it was obvious to Brian the poor animal was suffering terribly. We couldn't let this go on any longer. We took him to the animal hospital in Mudgeeraba and they euthanized him in much the same way as they had Shady the year before.

Sunny missed Shady and spent a lot of time laying down and staring into the distance.

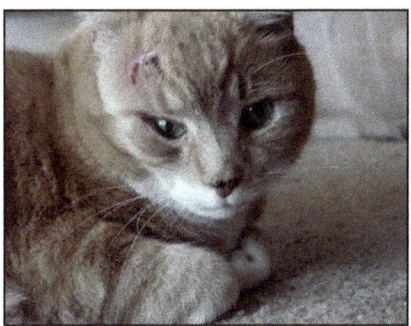
18-10-2003, the first appearance of what was to become a massive tumor

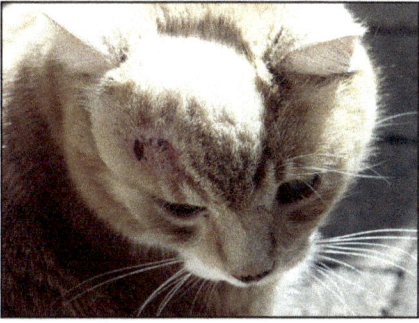
20-10-2003, two days later it was already showing signs of forcing his right eye shut.

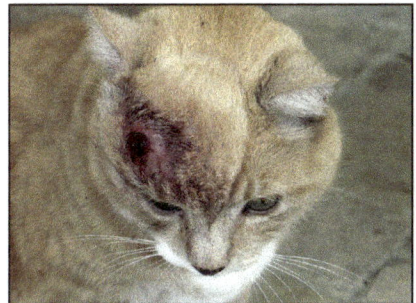
31-10-2003 the tumor had broken open and started bleeding..

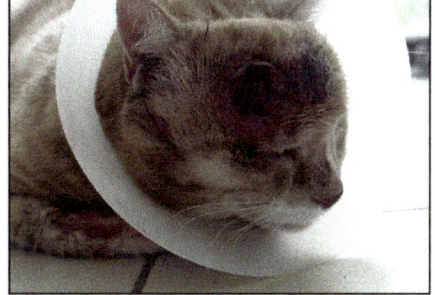
17-11-2003, the collar was to try to stop him from scratching it or trying to clean it.

I thought Sunny looked thankful as he looked at us while the hospital nurses prepared him for the injection.

This time I saw the spark leave his eyes as he faded away.

We never got any pets again after we lost Shady and Sunny. I wouldn't have been able to bear the loss when they died as they inevitably would.

Accidents happen

We are subject to massive amounts of rain up here during the wet season. Sudden storms with ferocious winds, hailstones, and rain that pounds down so you feel like you are standing under a waterfall if you are caught out in it can occur unexpectedly. Monica always went for a walk in the late afternoon and one day she got caught in a storm and came home drenched, looking like a drowned rat.

— Changing States —

It was the same day I noticed water bubbling through a drainpipe on one side of the house. Either there was so much water going down from off the roof that it could not get away through the storm water drainpipe quick enough because the gutters in the street it drained into were full and overflowing, or somewhere underground the storm water pipe was broken or blocked. The water had nowhere to go so it bubbled back up through the joint at ground level.

The next day, as things dried out, I found the ground near that storm water pipe was boggy so I suspected the pipe underground was broken or blocked and that's why the water couldn't get away.

A couple of years earlier I dug a one and a half metre hole where the sewer pipes coming from the house had been broken and tree roots had grown into the pipe and blocked it. I dug the hole to save paying someone a few hundred dollars to something I could easily do. I paid a plumber to come and fix the exposed broken sewer pipe, which took him less than half an hour, then I filled the hole afterwards. I didn't mind digging holes and trenches even if the ground was hard. It took two full days to dig that hole deep enough to expose the sewer pipe, and half a day to refill it once it was fixed.

I bought several lengths of storm water drainpipes not knowing how much had to be replaced, glue to join the pipes and some sleeves to help join the lengths together. I started digging after removing the paving bricks. The ground was soggy and sticky and more difficult to dig than if it had been dry and hard. There was a lot of clay in it, and this made it hard to get it off the shovel after scooping it out of the trench. When I got down to where the down pipe joined the actual storm water drainpipe, I discovered it had broken and shifted. Beyond the break it appeared that the storm water pipe leading from the back of the house towards the front and down under the lawn to the street gutter, was crushed flat after years of ground subsidence. Generally, these pipes are flexible and will break at either end where there are connections to the house rather than in the middle, but this pipe was crushed flat as well as broken off from the joint.

I would have to dig a trench under the side pathway to see how far along the pipe was crushed. I pulled up the brick pavers and stacked them against the wall of the house. The mud, sticky and heavy with clay, I shoveled it out on the other side of the path where a narrow garden bed was located. Fortunately, the pipe was only 30 centimetres under the ground and not a metre or more like the sewer pipes. Facing towards the front of the house, with the house on my right side, I dug forward and shoveled the mud and clay out and dumped it on my left. I had gone several metres along before coming to a good section of pipe. I assumed that from there on it would be intact.

Attempting to dig around the crushed pipe I managed to get a substantial amount of sticky mud on the shovel and swinging left to dump it I overextended and started to fall onto my side. This would not have been a problem if my feet could turn, but they were in a narrow trench, and almost stuck because of the clay and soft mud, so they didn't move, couldn't move. My upper body continued to twist and the weight of the mud on the shovel pulled me over. There was a sudden excruciating pain at the back of my right leg, and I felt something snap.

I crawled out of the trench and sat there for a while, but when I tried to stand up, my leg right leg wouldn't work. Every time I tried to walk it collapsed under me. I managed to hop and drag myself around the back of the house to the other side and went into our bedroom. By the time I got there I could walk gingerly, but it was horribly painful behind my right knee. I must have torn the cartilage.

That was confirmed after I went to the doctor and he sent me to have an MRI scan which revealed that I had torn the cartilage almost all the way through, and it could only be fixed by having an operation. I was booked in for an immediate operation, but that meant a 12 week wait. Normally it was something like two years. These kinds of cartilage tears are common amongst football players so the operation itself is routine. Arthroscopic surgery that takes little more than half an hour and the damaged cartilage is either stitched back together, or the damaged part is cut away, so the tear doesn't get worse. You go in early in the morning, and half an hour after the operation you can go home.

Feeling a lot better after a couple of days, I went back to the trench I'd dug and which had dried a bit since it was exposed to the air. I removed the crushed pipe, replacing it with a new segment glued into place. I tested it by running water though it to see if it emptied out into the street and it did, so I filled the hole and left it for a while. The dirt needed to settle before I could replace the brick pavers.

This little accident happened in November 2007. I was scheduled to fly down to Melbourne for summer school training in January 2008. There was no way I would be training with a torn cartilage in my right leg, but with the use of a walking stick, I could get around to a degree. I couldn't cancel the flights without losing the money, so I went to Melbourne and wandered about the dojo taking photos of the event.

In April I went to the Robina Hospital for the scheduled surgery, and it was done at 10 in the morning. The doctors assured me that I would have 95 percent usage of my knee and would have no problem walking or doing anything normal, but it would take at least three months to recover fully after the surgery.

Once the operation was done, I was allowed to walk into a small lounge room and wait for Monica to come and get me. I had a cup of tea while I waited. Monica was late because she'd missed the turnoff to the hospital and had to follow the damned road for several kilometres before a big roundabout allowed her to turn around and come back to the hospital.

No one told me anything about what to do while recovering. When Monica came, the doctors had returned to tell me that the knee would be swollen for a few weeks but that would come down and after that it would be fine. They never mentioned anything about a walking stick or using crutches. I found I had to use a walking stick because I couldn't put any weight on my right leg as you do when you walk normally. I had to support my weight by leaning on a walking stick in order to step with the right leg.

I walked out of the hospital without a problem. My knee was numb, and I didn't feel anything. I got into the car which was awkward because I couldn't bend my right leg much with all the bandaging and because it was swollen. But as soon as we got home, the numbness started to wear off and it became quite painful. I took a painkiller and an anti-inflammatory and sat in my reading chair with my leg extended, supported on a footrest.

That was the second time in my life I'd been to hospital for an operation, and Monica had to come and get me. I certainly hoped there would not be any more.

The first few days were bad, but after a while it started to heal and the swelling went down. It was worse trying to sleep at night than it was during the day. During the day I could distract myself by reading or watching TV, or just sitting in my chair and looking through the French doors out into the yard where birds flitted amongst the trees. Monica fussed over me and we had many conversations over a cup of tea.

It took longer than the three months the doctors told me, closer to six months. After that I went back to training with some trepidation and had to modify the way I took ukemi (controlled falls) so my right knee never touched the mat and no weight was put on the right leg. If I damaged it again, the doctors said, I would need a full knee replacement.

It made me re-evaluate ukemi forcing me to make it softer, and more fluid, which in turn improved my aikido in general.

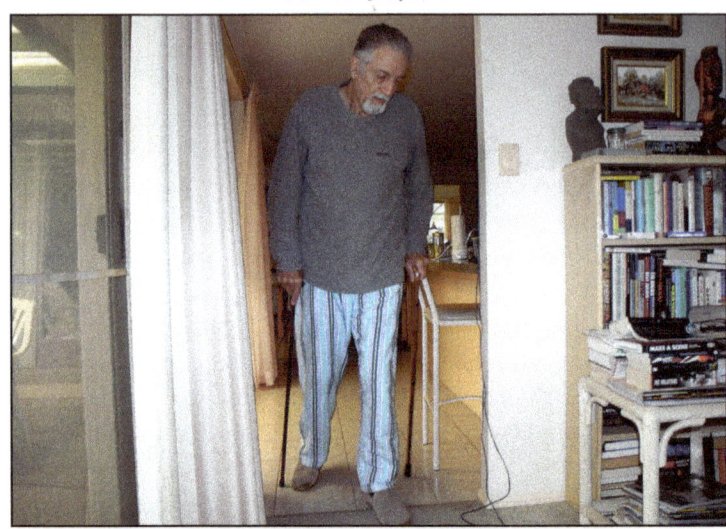
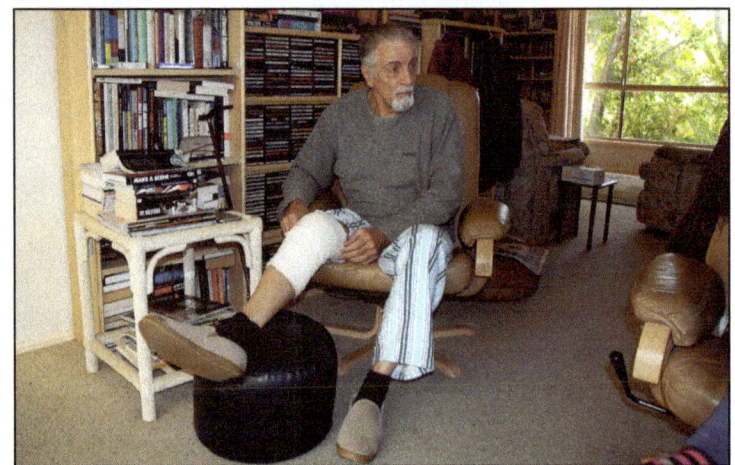

Having removed the bandage to change the dressing for the first time after coming home, it's clear to see how swollen the knee joint was.

The arrow painted on my right leg by the doctor after confirming it with me before the operation took place was to make sure they operated on the correct leg. That arrow was visible for a couple of weeks afterwards.

Some of the swelling was caused by a neutral fluid they pumped into the joint to make it expand, so it was easier for them to access and work on the damaged tissue.

Previous page: walking into the lounge room using two walking sticks for support, and sitting in my chair to take off the bandage so I could change the dressing.

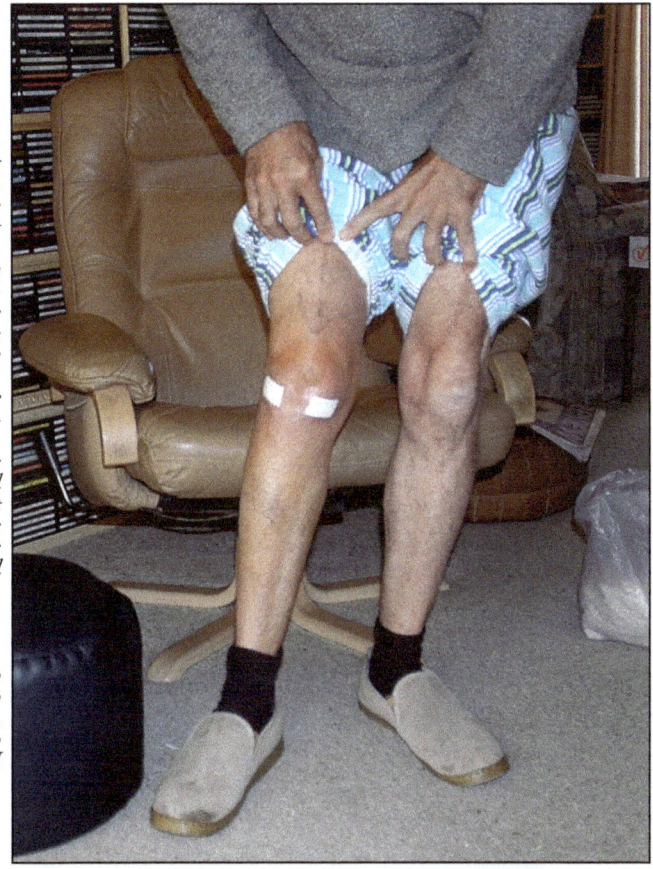

Evolution of a story

Every story I have written so far has had a long period of gestation and evolution. One example is **The Great Flood**, first written as a 3500 word story published in *Tirra Lirra Literary Quarterly* in volume 4, #3, in 1994.

The idea came to me as I was driving the pickup and delivery van for Williamstown Dry cleaners. I used to pass a house in Korroroit Creek Road on my way to North Altona from Williamstown. In the front yard of this house a man was building a yacht out of concrete. I found that astonishing, building a boat out of concrete. But then I thought, if you can make a boat out of steel, then why not concrete?

He first made the shape of the hull and the deck out of what looked like chicken wire mesh, like you would put around a chicken coop to keep the birds in. This was the foundation and the reinforcing for the concrete. It was super fine concrete that was sprayed on and troweled smooth, then sanded and polished until it glistened like mirror. It was then sealed to make it waterproof.

The boat sat like this for months as no doubt the builder was working on fitting it out inside. Then one day it wasn't there. Someone told me a crane had lifted it onto a flat bed and it was taken down to the waterfront in Nelson Place where it was moored at one of the piers.

I thought there's got to be a story in that...

But that's as far as it went. A few years later I was doing Aikido at a new dojo initiated by one of my instructors. After training one day he invited us to his place in East Keilor for a party and I discovered a yacht being built in his front yard. He lived in a house half way up a hill with a view across towards the Maribyrnong River. This boat, my instructor was building out of steel. When it was finished and when he retired in another year he would have it shipped to Lakes Entrance where he intended to retire.

During that summer, we had one of Melbourne's infamous thunderstorms and massive amounts of rain with flooded streets in most low lying areas. It made me remember a massive summer storm when I was still a student at University High School. Walking out to catch a tram down into the city to go home, all the trams had stopped. Elizabeth street was two feet underwater with shops along where it crossed Bourke Street and Collins Street flooded. It was one of the worst floods ever. There was water in all the shops along what is now the Bourke Street

Mall and along Elizabeth Street. Elizabeth Street was once the site of a a creek running down towards the Yarra River, so it was natural that the water flowed this way from higher areas of the city.

Remembering that I thought what if an old guy was building a boat on his front lawn believing that a great flood would one day occur and the only way to be safe was to have a boat ready when needed. Neighbours laughed at him, thought he was silly, even his wife had her doubts regarding his obsession with building a boat, but one day the once in a 1000 years storm hit and massive floods surged through the city. He got his wife and together they climbed on board the yacht he had built on his front lawn, and the flood waters carried it away through the city and the storms that pounded everything with sheets and waves of rain. The currents of the storm water rushing through the city carried the yacht with the old man and his wife through the city and out into vast sea of waves and rain.

It was all too much and the old man suffers a heart attack while enduring the storm in his boat, and the next day when it was over, the wife found herself in the yacht floating in a lake in the city with a crowd of people wondering how a yacht got to be in the lake in the middle of the city's gardens.

A slightly expanded version with a more detailed section regarding the floods in the city centre was later published in 1998 by a West Australian publisher and was part of a collection of stories for summer reading, called *Readers' Paradise*. The same publisher six months later included another of my short stories **A Beach too Far**, in a collection called *Winter Warmers*.

After moving to the Gold Coast I decided to collect the few stories I'd written and had published into one book, but the problem was the stories were not long enough. I sat down and thought about **The Great Flood** and decided to expand it into a novella, by creating more interaction between the old man, and his curious neighbour and how he went about building his boat, and what his wife thought about it. I also included snippets of newsflashes regarding floods and other matters relating to climate change, things that could be relevant to the creation of wilder weather and more intense floods. I kept the same style, with the characters being generic rather than particular. I now had a story of around 15,000 words. I also wrote another novella about a hunt for a mysterious catlike creature preying on sheep and farm animals in Western Victoria called **Rockbones**. With these two novellas and two other short stories that referenced each other briefly I had the material for a book which was published by *Zeus Publications* in 2003. The book was

Convergence — Aspects of the Change. Copies went on sale in Dymmocks book shop at Pacific Fair and a few were sold. I had a book launch at the Gold Coast Writers Group but only sold one copy there. (*Typical*)

A few months later one of my friends who practiced aikido came up to me and told me she'd bought a copy at the book shop and loved the Great Flood story. She wanted to know if I was going to write a sequel.

I sat down and thought about it and decided I would write a sequel. It took around three months to write a story of about 80,000 words. It was written in the present tense rather than the past tense, because the present tense gives it more immediacy. I sent it off to a publisher but it was not accepted. In the meantime I decided to revise and rewrite the original *Great Flood* as a novel and this time I gave the characters names and delved into their motivations and relationships (*also in the present tense to match the sequel*) more than I had before. I also introduced some new characters and added incidents that were in the other two short stories in the original collection. Finally I put the two new novels together as one book in two parts ending up with a book of 480 pages called ***And the Waters Prevailed***. (*A quote from Genesis.*) The second half of the book which was the sequel to the original novella was called ***A floating World***. The complete book was 160,000 words long.

A limited number of copies were printed but I did do it as an eBook using *Smashwords* where it is still listed. Having discovered a number of typos, I revised and corrected those as well as altered the ending and set the book up through *Lightning Source* for distribution and sales. This was a few years later. I retitled the story calling it ***A floating World***. The two halves inside are still called *And the Waters Prevailed*, and *A floating World*. The cover art on both editions is the same only the title is different.

At the Burleigh Library function room for the book launch of ***Convergence - Aspects of the Change*** *before it eventually became* ***A floating World***.

— Changing States —

*At Borders Bookshop in Robina (2011) for my book launch of the first edition **And the Waters Prevailed.** Monica was as proud of it as I was, and she was there for the launch.*

My good friend Travers was the first person to buy a copy of it from the bookshop.

Standing beside the shelf in the shop displaying books by local authors.

A few days later Christine came down to see us and we went to the Town Centre for lunch and of course visited Borders' Bookshop so she could see my book sitting on the shelves. She used her mobile to take a couple of photos: me beside the bookshelf displaying my book, and one

of Monica and me together in one of the restaurants beside the lake near the new front entrance to the centre. By this time Monica had recovered from her allergic reaction to the drug administered for atrial fibrillation but had yet to regain some of the weight she'd lost during that episode.

Monica with Christine. This was not long after her fright and the severe loss of weight. Still, she was happy to be out and about, and feeling good.

A flashback to the beginning of a slow change

Over time we stopped attending the Gold Coast writers' meetings although I kept in touch with some of the members. It was after one of these last meetings we attended at the Burleigh Heads Library when we were leaving and heading to the car in the library car park, Monica suddenly started to fall over. It was like a slow-motion movement. She was about to step off the footpath to walk across the car park, our car wasn't far away, when she started to collapse downwards. She didn't say anything. She looked bemused. It was as if the ground beneath her had become soft and she was sinking into it.

I grabbed her arm and stopped her from falling any further.

She looked at me and said, "I feel dizzy."

She had gone completely white.

We stood there, unmoving, with me holding her so she wouldn't fall. A moment later the colour returned to her face.

"What happened?"

"I don't know. I suddenly felt nauseous, and everything started to swirl around. I'm okay now."

"Can you walk?"

"Yes."

Holding on to her arm in case she started to feel dizzy again, we walked over to the car.

We sat in the car for a while with the windows open so the cool sea breeze could clear the stuffiness out.

"Are you still feeling dizzy?"

"I'm okay."

She seemed fine, as if nothing had happened. But it did worry me. An unexpected sudden fall can be quite dangerous no matter where it happens. Even worse if it happens on the hard bitumen surface of a car park.

A couple of weeks later we were together in the kitchen. Monica was waiting for the jug to boil. I was standing a couple of feet away. We were about to have a cup of tea together.

Suddenly she started to collapse. She hung onto the bench as her legs gave way beneath her. Again, it seemed like she did it in slow motion. Almost like she lowered herself down until her bottom touched the floor and she let go of the bench and rolled back. Luckily, she didn't hit the back of her head on the tiles. She was on her back on the floor before I could move.

I helped her to stand up and led her into the lounge room where she sat in her reading chair beside the window.

"It was an attack of vertigo," she said as she sat down.

She seemed fine. I made the tea and she took a tablet she'd got on prescription to counteract vertigo.

Monica in the kitchen about to prepare a cup of tea

She fell a couple of times again, in the kitchen, or in the lounge room over the next few weeks. The falls were almost slow-motion falls, like her legs would slowly give way and she would sink down to the floor, landing on her bottom and rolling back to finish laying on her back. She couldn't get up without me helping. We saw her doctor and were given tablets to counteract the vertigo and the nausea, and after a while she seemed okay.

This was towards the end of 2008, but for the next year or so she seemed fine.

Like all of us as we age, Monica also had deteriorating eyesight with cataracts slowly developing. Her optometrist sent her to a specialist for examination and over two years when there was little change in the development of the cataracts, he made an appointment for her to visit the specialists at the hospital. "There is a two year or longer waiting list, so I wouldn't worry too much," he reassured her, "but it's better to get in early in case the cataracts become worse over the next couple of years. The Hospital will notify you when your appointment is due, but Like I said, you won't hear anything from them for at least a couple of years."

We soon forgot about that future appointment.

In November 2009 Monica had heart palpitations, a shortness of breath, and appeared quite ill. She had pain radiating down her left arm. I got her into the car, and we raced around to the emergency department of the Robina Hospital, where they admitted her immediately suspecting a heart attack.

"Why didn't you call an ambulance," They asked me when I brought her in.

"It was quicker for me to bring her here myself, rather than wait for an ambulance. Who knows how long that would have taken."

Ambulance wait times and ramping was not as big a problem in 2009 as it is today in 2023, but since the hospital is only five minutes' drive from where we live it was quicker for me to take her there instead of wasting time making a phone call and waiting for an ambulance to arrive. Time was of the essence. She was rushed into the emergency ward and connected to the usual machines for monitoring heart, pulse, breathing, oxygen levels, etc.

They kept her there for five hours and finally concluded that she had an uneven heartbeat and that she had suffered from heart palpitations. (Atrial Fibrillation) They suspected a blockage in one of the arteries, but that seemed to clear up. She was also feeling dizzy, but not nauseous.

They gave her medicine to regulate the heartbeat. They didn't say she'd had a heart attack, which is what I suspected, but it was bad enough. Her mother had also suffered from Atrial Fibrillation later in her life, and I wondered if that was something Monica had inherited from her. They took X-rays and discovered she had scoliosis of the spine, which we already knew from her visit to Chile in 1994. They also said her blood pressure was too high and needed to be regulated. They prescribed the usual drugs to control the uneven heartbeat and recommended that she take a low-dose aspirin once a day to keep the blood slightly thinner so clots wouldn't develop in the heart to cause further problems. They wanted to see her in a week's time and an appointment was made. She was then discharged, and we went home.

What we didn't know was that she was allergic to the drug they normally give people for heart palpitations. (*Digoxin*) It caused her oesophagus to swell up and she couldn't swallow food; could barely even get liquids down. This didn't occur immediately but over several days. It also made her constipated. We went back to see them at the hospital, and they couldn't figure out why she started losing weight. It never occurred to them that she might be allergic to the drug prescribed.

After tests, which included a bladder test, the insertion of a camera down into her stomach to see what could be wrong (*endoscopy or gastros-*

copy) and even a *colonoscopy*, they couldn't figure out why her oesophagus had swollen to prevent her from eating properly, except to suggest it could be the result of food or drug allergies. That seemed logical since Monica had previously had allergy problems when we first moved to Hoppers Crossing, but they had dissipated after we moved to Williamstown. Her weight dropped dramatically over the two weeks while she was undergoing these tests, going from around 60 kilos down 45. She looked so scrawny.

Finally, they realized it could be a side effect of the drug prescribed so they changed it to a different one, (*Cordilox*), after which she began to normalize. Gradually she gained a good colour and although she gained a couple of kilos, she remained thin, but she seemed happy enough.

Before the Atrial Fibrillation problem

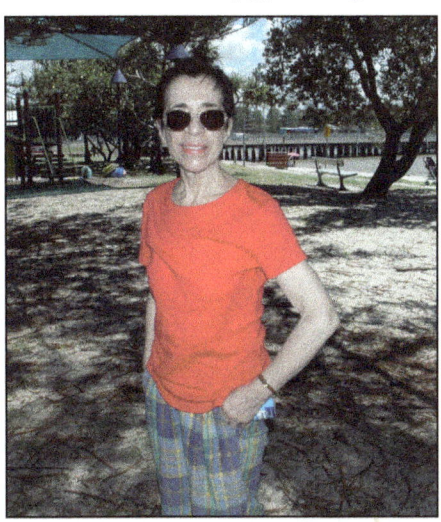

After her stint in the hospital and her allergic reaction to the initial medication.

— John Litchen —

Before: while on a walk on the path around Burleigh Heads.

After: resting at a table at Tallebudgera.

— Changing States —

At home after she started to recover.

But then the occasional bouts of vertigo with its dizziness came back. We went to see her GP and she was stunned to see how frail Monica appeared compared to how she'd been six months earlier. She immediately wrote a letter for an appointment to see a specialist at the Robina Hospital and told us they would contact us for an appointment soon. She also sent Monica for a bone density scan which we did the following day. She was worried about osteoporosis and that if Monica was losing bone density, any fall would be much more serious if she broke a bone in her hip or leg or arm.

When the results of that test came back, she prescribed vitamin D tablets to be taken twice a day to help rebuild density and strength in the bones.

Another visit to the hospital

Six months later a letter came from the Robina Hospital. Monica thought it was about her eye examination. She remembered the specialist had made that appointment two years earlier.

We went to the Robina Hospital and when the specialist doctor saw her, he made all kinds of examinations to test her nerves, and responses to specific stimuli, her balance and how she walked, but he never once looked at her eyes.

"Aren't you going to examine my eyes?" She asked.

"I suppose I can," he said, somewhat perplexed.

He did look at her eyes briefly and then said, "I'm a neurologist. The examination we've done has nothing to do with your eyes."

And when Monica looked confused, he added, "I'd like to book you in for a scan of your brain, to see if we can find out what is causing the vertigo and the dizziness leading to the falls you've been having."

He prescribed tablets for her to help control the vertigo but explained that the tablets wouldn't make it go away. They needed to see inside her brain to find out exactly what was causing the vertigo and the unexpected falls.

Two weeks later, we were back at the Robina Hospital for the scan of her brain. She was very nervous about the scan, feeling claustrophobic the moment she discovered that she would be inserted inside this massive machine so her brain could be scanned. The doctors and nurses were very kind and good at calming down nervous patients. I had to wait outside while the scan took place. Once the scan was done, we were given an appointment to see the neurologist the week after for the results.

Bad, and not so good news

The neurologist had the pictures of Monica's brain on his computer screen. He sat us down so we could see it clearly and then went on to explain what was there.

"You've had a number of minor strokes," he said, pointing to certain areas of the image. "But these are not a concern. See this dark area here," (he magnified the image slightly) "It's fluid that is pressing on the part of the brain that controls your balance. This is what is causing the vertigo, the nausea, and the loss of balance leading to a fall.

"It's what we call Normal Pressure Hydrocephalus. For want of a better term, it's fluid on the brain. Under normal circumstances, fluid that builds up in the brain is dispersed via the spinal column into the lymphatic system and eventually leaves your body. In the case of *NPH* it doesn't get dispersed and slowly builds up with increasing pressure that in turn damages different parts of the brain. As you get older, your brain shrinks a bit, and the fluid inside it generally fills the space, but if the pressure builds because it can't escape via the spinal column then you have a problem.

"It can affect memory as pressure against that part of the brain increases. It caused increasing incontinence. Loss of control of hands, and ability to walk and balance. It's all very slow and insidious. Not noticeable at first, but in time it gets worse.

"What can be done about it?" I asked.

Monica remained silent while she thought about what she'd been told.

"There are two options. The first is to do nothing, and learn to manage as you slowly decline, and the other is to put a shunt in the brain to release the excess fluid. If this works, then the problems NPH causes will be diminished, and a degree of normality can be restored."

"It appears there is only the one option then."

"But she may not be suitable."

Neither of us said anything. We waited for him to explain.

"We'll have to send her to the University Hospital for examination by the neurosurgery department. They will extract fluid from the base of the spine to see if that reduces the pressure in the brain. And if that works, then they will consider surgery to put a shunt in. This is basically a one-way valve inserted into the brain that releases excess pressure allowing the fluid to flow down a tube towards your stomach where it will be dispersed.

"It's a complex operation that requires brain surgery, and they may not consider it because," and he looked directly at Monica when he said this, "you are seventy years old, and you have atrial fibrillation which creates a problem when administering anesthetics during this operation, or any operation for that matter. The success rate is only fifty percent. It doesn't work half the time it's done, and of those that do work, there are often problems with infections which require removing and re-inserting the tube that drains from the shunt. But let's not dwell on that now. Let's set up the lumbar spinal test and see what happens then. I will recommend that you have the surgery, but ultimately it is up to the neurosurgeon in charge whether they go ahead and do it or not."

Outside, back in the car on the way home, Monica said, "*Estoy asustado. No me gusta nada el idea de la operacion.*"
"Let's just wait and see what the spinal tap results are first. No one can decide anything until after that."

Two months later we were in the neurosurgery ward at the University Hospital and Monica was being prepped for the lumbar puncture. Before that a physio therapist came in and took her though a series of exercises that involved balance, walking, nerve function and coordination. The exact same tests would be done immediately after the lumbar puncture to see if removing 30 ml of fluid from her spine made a difference.
They had trouble inserting the needle into her spine because of the scoliosis, the twist in her spine. They took her down to the scanning room where a cat scan was used so they could see which direction to insert the needle to extract the spinal fluid. Monica looked distraught when she came back. The physio came in and made her do the exact same exercises as before. We were allowed to go home after that.
The next day the neurologist called and said that the result showed a slight improvement, but they wanted to do another lumbar puncture to verify the results, so we went back to the hospital for a repeat of the lumbar puncture and the physio to determine the results. This time she had to stay there a couple of days for further assessment. While we were there, we saw a number of patients who had already undergone the insertion of a shunt. They were there because of problems with infections. Seeing these patients and knowing of the problems they were having was off-putting for both of us.
"I don't want to be like that," Monica said.
It was almost a relief when we got the news that she was not suitable for the operation because the lumbar puncture showed no improvement,

which meant a shunt inserted into her brain wouldn't make much difference. On that basis, and because of her age, and ongoing atrial fibrillation, they decided against the operation.

It was a relief because Monica wouldn't suffer the problems those people in the neurosurgery ward were having after the operation to insert a shunt, but it filled us with trepidation considering the possible slow decline *NPH* would cause over time with her ability to walk and manage everyday activities without suddenly falling over, possible loss of memory, incontinence, shakiness and other similar symptoms like Parkinson's.

It was not something to look forward to. But then it wouldn't be something sudden, it would develop over a long period of time. Monica preferred that than having an operation which at best had only a 50 percent chance of success, but most likely would have serious side effects.

We were given a regular 6-month appointment regime, so the neurology department could monitor her. They also sent her to a small medical health precinct close to the Robina Hospital for cognitive tests and physiotherapy. She joined a group that exercised early in the morning once a week. It was a 12-week course. The cognitive tests were scheduled for a test every six months to monitor cognitive ability and possible decline. Monica found these tests utterly boring and at times silly. She liked the physio although she found it hard. One of the things they tried to teach her was how to get into and out of bed. I think the exercises and the training was geared towards people recovering from a major trauma to help them get better. In Monica's case she wasn't getting better, but over time would get worse. Our hope was that the physio would at least help maintain her present ability and slow the decline.

I didn't think much of the cognitive tests either, but they did show after a year and half that there was a decline in her ability to write and draw simple things like a clock face showing the time. I noticed her signature got more ragged, les controlled, over time as well. Her memory seemed reasonably intact over this time.

We managed to get the physio regime extended for another 12 weeks after a visit to the Gold Coast University Hospital where we had to go every six months for the neurologist to see how she was 'progressing'.

The most notable effect was a decline in her ability to walk. At first, she used a walking stick for support. I rearranged the chairs in the bedroom so they faced the wall and she could use the backs of the two chairs for support as she went to the bathroom. In the bathroom I installed a rail along the windowsill for her to hold onto as she walked to the basin, and in the shower stall another rail for her to hold while showering. She would hold onto my arm as we went to the town centre for lunch, or simply as we walked from the bedroom to the kitchen or somewhere else in the house.

In November 2011 Zara and Fred came up for a visit and Christine came down from Ipswich and we had lunch at the Town Centre. Christine took a few photos on her phone. At this stage Monica was doing okay. And occasionally we would meet Christine at the town centre for lunch.

Above: Monica and me with my sister Zara and her husband Fred.
Bottom: Me with Monica, Zara and Christine.
At this stage, Monica did not need a wheelchair and could walk unaided as long as she was careful.

These shots from Christine's phone were the last pictures taken of us with Zara and Fred. We haven't seen them since then although we regularly speak on the phone.

Six years later, (2017) Christine took this photo when we had lunch at the Town Centre. Monica had regained some of the lost weight, but was unable to walk and had to use a wheelchair. It was a nice lunch and we enjoyed ourselves.

Nearly a disaster

In 2014 Monica's GP prescribed tablets to be taken to control a fungal infection that Monica had in her toes. It seemed that external fungal treatments didn't make a difference, so the doctor suggested this medicine which would work from inside, via the blood stream where it could attack the fungus affecting her toes. I got the prescription filled and Monica took the first tablet that same night.

The very next morning, her skin seemed a bit blotchy around her cheeks and in a couple of spots on her back. She thought nothing of it. "Looks like a bit of eczema," she said. She put some cream on it and thought nothing more about it. She took another tablet before breakfast. She was supposed to take two a day. She took the next tablet at night before going to bed.

The next morning when she got up, she was horrified to see the 'eczema' had spread all over her back and chest, and face. She was covered completely with red splotches, that were incredibly itchy. We called her GP and told her what was happening. She said not to take any more tablets. She asked us to come there so she could see Monica. When we got there in the afternoon, her GP took one look at her and said, "I'm sending you up to the Robina Hospital, right away."

Monica was distraught as much as the doctor was stunned at the reaction from the tablets she'd prescribed. She wrote a letter and handed it to me. "Give this to the triage nurse at the emergency ward when you get there. I want you to take Monica to the hospital right now, right away."

I had taken some photos of the rash and printed them so I could show the doctors at the hospital.

At the hospital, after reading the GP's letter and seeing the photos I'd taken before we went to the GP, they admitted her and sent her to a ward where two other patients were located. A gaggle of training doctors and nurses as well as one resident doctor came to examine Monica, who was getting more upset by the minute. The rash was worse by then than it had before we got there. Her whole body was covered with this horrible red rash and in places skin was starting to ulcerate and flake off. They had no idea what was wrong other than it must be a severe allergic reaction to the anti-fungal medication she had been prescribed.

On her admission form they described it as *exfoliating dermatitis* and mentioned that she has NP Hydrocephalus which has affected her gait and ability to walk and balance.

— Changing States —

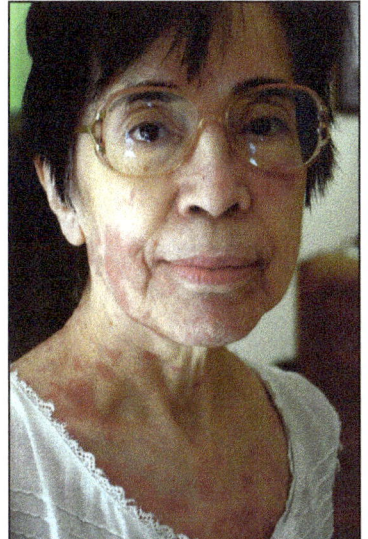
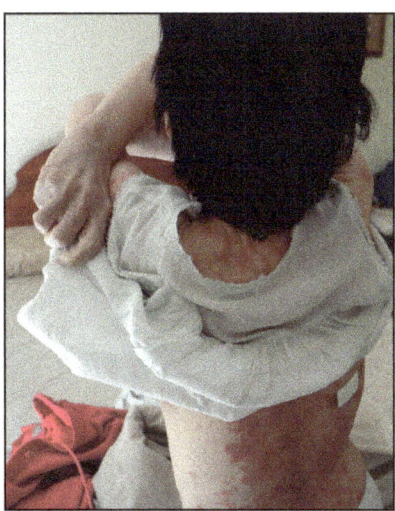
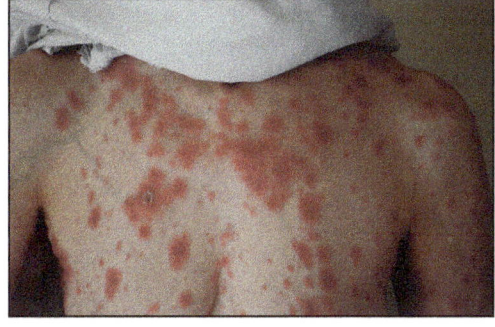
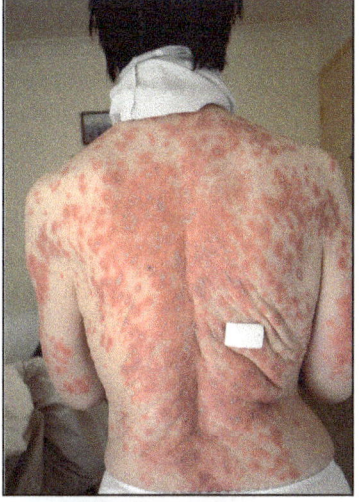

The horrified look on Monica's face when she saw herself in the mirror says it all. This was the morning after the rash first appeared. It was all over her, and it got worse as the day wore on. I took these photos so the hospital doctors could see how rapidly the affliction progressed. It got worse by th afternoon when we went to the hospital. There were other photos, but we don't need to see them.

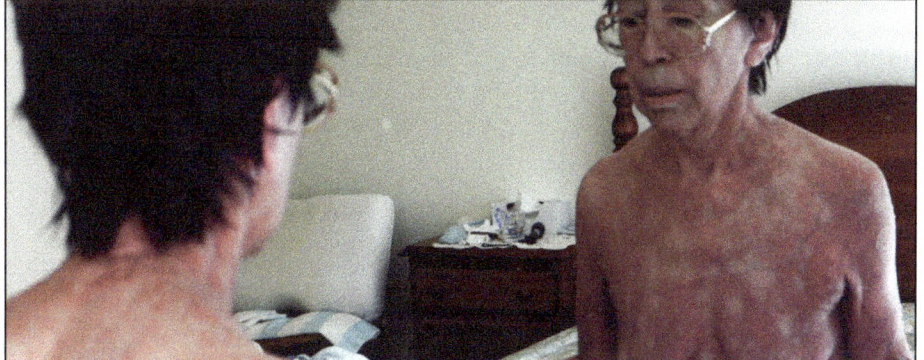

They tried a number of things, none of which made any difference, and after two days with her complete body still affected by this horrible rash they said they would send her to the Southport Hospital to see a skin specialist.

They couldn't get an ambulance so they asked me if I would take her there. I got the car and we drove up to the hospital. I parked right in front by the main entrance and helped her out of the car. She was having trouble walking. Inside they told me at the front desk to take her to the fifth floor where the skin specialist was seeing patients. I got her seated there and it was obvious there would be a wait since Monica was an extra and not one of his scheduled consultations. While she sat there and waited, I went back downstairs and shifted the car to a parking spot on the other side of the road from the hospital, went back and waited for her.

We waited several uncomfortable hours to see this skin specialist and when we got to see him, he was convinced that it was an extreme case of exfoliating dermatitis.

He'd never seen a case this bad.

When we explained how we thought it had come about he told Monica to never take that medicine again.

"It will kill you. You are having a severe reaction, almost an anaphylactic reaction to the anti-fungal medicine."

He called the Robina Hospital and made some recommendations, and then told us to go back there for the treatment.

"What it is doing is killing your skin. I don't know if the treatment I've asked them to give you will work, but there isn't anything else we can try."

And on that cheerful note he sent us back to the Robina Hospital.

I had to get Monica to wait in the foyer while I went and got the car, then we drove back to Robina and she went into the same bed as she had used before. The nurses hooked up a drip and plugged it into her left arm, and after that we could only wait to see what effect it would have.

The next morning, the rash seemed to have diminished somewhat. The red colour was fading and the skin on the surface was drying and flaking off. The nurses changed the bed while Monica sat in an armchair. They also swept up the flakes of dried dead skin that had fallen onto the floor. By late afternoon it was clearly improving with much more dead skin flaking off and falling to the floor. We went for a short walk while the nurses again changed the sheets, and again we left a trail of grey flakes along the passageway. After five days in the hospital, Monica had lost all her skin as new skin (fortunately) regrew underneath. They let us go home after that.

It was another year before the letter came for her to see an ophthalmologist at the University Hospital and when we went for the examination booked three years earlier for her by her eye specialist, they found that her eyes had not changed and that the cataracts that were developing had not got any worse. They didn't see any need for an eye operation at this time or any time in the near future.

That was a relief.

One less thing to worry about.

Adjusting to a changing way of life

Monica's doctor suggested we contact Aged Care services for assistance in managing her health. We did this and they put us onto a home care package, that also included incontinence assistance. One of the first side effects of NP Hydrocephalus was increasing incontinence. Buying and using those special pants was expensive and the assessment nurse who came to see us organized the package so that we would get incontinence assistance. That meant Aged Care would supply the necessary pants as well as deposit a small sum once a year into Monica's account to help with buying new sheets and underlays, all stuff we would need as time went on. The package also included physiotherapy once a week with a physio coming for half an hour to take Monica through exercises to maintain her ability to use her arms and legs, to balance and walk, and whatever was needed to get around the house. An occupational therapist came to recommend changes that would make it easier for Monica.

We had bought one of those wheelie walkers and she started using this to walk with. The problem with this device was that Monica would lean forward as she walked, and this put pressure on the walker, in effect pushing it away from her. Sometimes her legs couldn't keep up with the forward momentum of the walker and it would get away from her making her fall onto her knees. Although the walker had brake handles, if it got ahead of her, Monica wasn't quick enough to let go to grip and apply the brakes to stop the walker from moving too far ahead. It wasn't a problem on the carpeted section of the floor but as soon as she got onto the smooth tiled section, it started to run away from her.

In the period before the package had been approved, we had been going to a community centre in Varsity Lakes, a new suburb adjacent to Robina, where there was a session of exercises run for older people. Monica attended these sessions regularly for about eight months. Normally after each session we would go the Robina Town Centre for lunch.

One day, part of the exercises was to walk from one end of the community hall to the other, using the walkers that several people had with them.

The floor was a polished wood floor and very smooth. Monica's walker got too far ahead of her because instead of standing straight and using it for support as she walked, she tended to lean forward with all her weight on it which pushed it away from her. It was like it was pulling her forward and once it got beyond a certain point, she fell onto her knees and ended up lying on the floor. It wasn't a hard fall, because she hung onto the wheelie walker until her knees actually hit the floor, before letting go. But at her age, and with the medical problem she was enduring, any fall could be disastrous.

There was minor panic as everyone rushed to help her. Once I got them out of the way, I had to lift her and get her seated in a chair where she calmed down and recovered. Her knees were scratched and fortunately no real damage was done. A bit of bruising showed up later in the day. She didn't participate in the rest of the group exercises but watched from the sidelines.

She had trouble walking back to the car when the class finished, so we went home rather than to the Town Centre for lunch.

Monica decided later that afternoon that she wasn't going to do any more of those exercise in case she had another fall, which was a pity because they were a good bunch of people, and everyone got on fine. We'd been going there for almost a year. When she didn't return, they sent her a get-well card a couple of weeks later with everyone having written a message to her.

She was also having difficulties in walking from the bedroom to the living area of the house and had to be supported (by me). It seemed there was no strength in her legs, and after a few steps, she had to stop for a rest. She was wobbly and had to hang onto something just to stand up.

The health precinct told us she could get a wheelchair supplied by the government, but we would need to have an occupational therapist come out and assess her, after which there would probably be a six month wait before getting the wheelchair. I thought about that and decided the six months would be too long, so I went to Pacific Fair where there was a gigantic pharmacy that had wheelchairs, and I bought one for her to use.

Having the wheelchair was both good and bad. Mostly good though. I would park it beside the bed on her side and she would sit up, then stand and turn and sit onto the wheelchair, I could then wheel her into the bathroom to help use the toilet, or down into the kitchen where she could sit in this chair at the table for meals, or further into the lounge room where I would help transfer her from the wheelchair into her reading chair. I could fold the wheelchair in half and lift into the back of the car, after first getting her to stand by the passenger door, turn and sit in the passenger seat. At first this was easy. She would stand with her back against the side of the passenger seat, and once she was sitting half on it, she would lift her legs and swivel into the seat.

Getting out was easy. Swivel so her legs were outside then stand and sit on the wheelchair which I would have positioned close to the door. We often went to the Town Centre for shopping and lunch and having the wheelchair made it easy and practical.

The downside of using the chair was that it accelerated to loss of strength in her legs, so after a while even standing for the few moments needed to transfer from one chair, or the bed, onto the wheelchair became difficult and I had to lift her to do it.

Getting into the car became a real problem because she simply couldn't stand up enough to be able to sit on the passenger seat's edge, and because of the door frame being low, I couldn't lift her to get her into the passenger seat without her head bumping the door frame which prevented her from getting into the car.

One time, before I could even start to lift her or help her sit against the passenger seat she collapsed onto the ground. It was very hard for me to lift her back into the wheelchair after that. This happened when we went to see her GP for her six-monthly check-up. We were going back to the car to go home. It happened again a few days later when we were getting ready to go to the Town Centre for lunch. I couldn't get her into the car as her legs gave way and she collapsed onto the driveway beside the car.

It was a slow-motion collapse and she wasn't hurt, but trying to lift an inert person who hasn't the strength to assist by pushing up with her legs is a problem. It was like trying to lift a dead weight by leaning over and picking it up. It was a huge strain on my back. I had to get her to sit and lean against the side of the car, then by getting under her arms, attempt to lift her high enough to get her bottom onto the wheelchair seat. When I finally managed to get her onto the chair we went back inside the house. Both of us were too exhausted to even think of going anywhere.

After that we decided I would have to do shopping by myself whenever we needed something, while she stayed in her reading chair with a book to read or while watching TV or just looking out of the window to see what went on in the backyard with birds that kept flying about.

There were different birds at different times of the year, but they were always visible from the back and front windows.

Birds in our yard

Different times in the year would see a variety of different birds. Towards spring we would have pigeons and magpies and crows b nesting nearby and then we would see baby birds learning to fly and survive. With different flowers during the year we would attract birds like lorikeets and parrots, Galahs and cockatoos, something that looked like a cross between a magpie and a crow, kookaburras on rare occasions, but crows and magpies were there all year round.

We were never attacked by nesting magpies although they had nests somewhere in our yard or very close by. We weren't stranger to them because we also lived here.

— Changing States —

The kookaburra was sitting on the pool fence outside our bedroom door.

Sometimes we would find two ducks in the pool and they would fly away if I went too close to them, Once I even saw a crane by the pool. But of all the birds that came into the yard, one ferocious little thing on hot afternoons would dive bomb the water, zooming down and hitting it with its chest, splashing furiously and wildly flapping its wings to take off and return to the fence or the trees and bushes around the pool where it would shake itself free of the water that was still stuck to it. I often wondered what would happen if it stayed a fraction too long, or went a bit deeper than it expected when it hit the water. Would it be able to get up and fly away? It never happened though.

It was extremely difficult to catch it in photos, and I took hundreds over many days in order to get the few here that captures it in action.

Hitting the water at speed it would almost be completely submerged, but its forward momentum and furious flapping wings would lift it out of the water so it could fly back up into the trees and palms overhanging the pool.
Some days it would do this several times, other days only once. I don't know if only one bird did this, but I only ever saw one by itself. It was the same bird or one of the same birds that used to chase Shady along the side path. When the Birds of Paradise flowers were in bloom, this bird would fly from flower to flower to extract the nectar.

— 425 —

A duck in the pool

One morning in September 2019, I went into the yard and saw I a small duck swimming in our pool.

This was not unusual in itself because we often had a duck or two spend an hour or so in the pool on many different days over the years. You sometimes see them in pairs foraging on people's front lawns in the winter after a cold night when dew covers the grass making it damp forcing small insects and worms to emerge.

The lake at the Robina Woods golf course where there is an abundance water bird life is not that far away from us, perhaps half a kilometre.

But this time it was unusual because the duck was there every morning when I went into the yard. As soon as I got near the edge of the pool the duck would swim to the furthest part from me.

When I moved away from the edge of the pool the duck jumped up onto the edging and quickly slipped under the overhanging leaves of the Golden Canes planted by the pool's edge. I thought this was unusual because other times, the duck would simply fly away after a short time in the pool.

The next morning, looking through the window I saw the duck again on the edging and it took off and flew up over the house, so I went outside and had a look under the cane fronds and there was a nest.

There were seven eggs in the nest.

About an hour later saw the duck returned. She landed in the middle of the pool, swam to the edge beneath the Golden Canes and hopped up and quickly slipped in under cover and could no longer be seen.

She stayed there all day. If I went out early enough I would see her swimming in the pool for a few moments before taking off and flying away. She would return about an hour later, to the pool, to her nest where she would stay unless I went too close. If I got close she would jump into the pool and swim as far away as she could in order to distract me.

Looking online I discovered it takes about 28 days for ducks to hatch and so we waited, and watched. The weather after the second week started to get very hot and by the end of the third week, we were every day with temperatures in the mid-30s C. It even got to 35 C one day, and all that time the duck sat quietly on the nest.

In fact, 2019 was the hottest year on record up to that time.

After 28 days I figured the eggs must have been affected by the extreme heat. It was unusually hot for late Spring. As we edged into December and the beginning of summer, the hot weather continued without relief. Too bloody hot. I thought for sure the eggs had been killed by the heat, and the poor duck would be sitting there starving while she waited for them to hatch.

When five and a half weeks had gone since I first saw the eggs in the nest I was positive the ducks were not going to hatch. I didn't know how long the eggs had been in the nest before I actually saw them, so five and half weeks at the least seemed too long.

A couple of days later (*December 13th*) I opened the bedroom curtains. The sun had been up for at least an hour and a half even though it was just past 6-30 am and immediately looking at the pool I saw the duck standing on the pool edge and unbelievably there were the 7 ducklings in the water directly beneath her struggling to get out.

They couldn't flap their tiny wings and jump up like she could. She jumped back into the water and swam around with the little balls of fluff trailing along behind. She jumped out again and they struggled to do the same but the height from the water to the pool edging was just too high.

They had probably followed her into the water at dawn just after they had hatched. They looked as if they were exhausted. I tried to catch them and take them out of the water but they kept swimming away so I couldn't get near them from the edge.

The mother got back into the water and swam as far away as she could get, with the little ones following close behind.

The ducklings were getting exhausted trying to get out of the pool but the edge was too high for them to jump up like their mother did. They kept as close as possible to her while she walked around lookio9ng for a way to get them out.

— Changing States —

The mother duck was getting agitated so I had to figure something out. They needed some kind of ramp to walk up to get out of the water. A wooden plank was no good because it floated and kept moving as the water rippled. Suddenly I thought of a rock bank. Make a ramp out of rocks in the water so they could walk up them. I grabbed three large sandstone rocks from the garden and placed them in the shallow end to create a rough ramp. The rocks were half submerged with just the tops sloping up towards the rim of the pool.

While I was doing this the duck and her 7 ducklings were swimming back and forth as far away from me as possible. Walking around the pool towards them I managed to make them swim towards the rock ramp. The mother jumped out a metre before it and the little ones bunched up underneath but couldn't get up. As I walked nearer, she edged along away from me and stopped just beyond the rock ramp.

The little ducklings swimming along trying to keep up with her bumped into the rocks and immediately started climbing up them and out of the water. As soon as they were out of the water, they followed their mother back to the safety of the nest under the Golden Canes. There they stayed for about two hours.

Once they had calmed down and recovered from their ordeal in the pool, they emerged. The seven little ducklings followed in a line behind their mother as she led them away while searching for a way out of our back yard. I followed them as they went around one side but couldn't get out. They went right down the back but there was no way out there either.

Eventually they returned to the pool and after staying in there for a few minutes, climbed back out over the rock pile and went back to their hidden nest. I opened both side gates, hoping that they would find their way out and down to the nearby lake in the golf course where there are plenty of ducks, other water birds, turtles, fish, frogs, and many other native creatures.

 I had to go and do some shopping, and when I came back at four-thirty I checked the nest and it was empty. There were several crows flying or hanging around the Golden Canes, and I thought something awful could have happened. Those crows would hurtle down out of the sky to latch onto the ducklings and eat them without compunction.

 There were no ducklings in the nest and the mother was nowhere to be seen. There was no way she would desert them. She would fight the crows to protect her young.

 I couldn't see them anywhere in the yard so I assumed they must have found their way out and were heading down towards the lake in the park beside the golf course. I was disappointed in not being there to see them leave. I would certainly have followed them at a discrete distance to make sure they got to the lake safely. Unfortunately, there was no way I could know which way they went.

I went down to the nearby lake to see if I could find them but had no luck. The lake is large and extends into the Robina Woods golf course, where it makes a wide circle to the other side of the course and beyond. The ducks could be anywhere in that lake. There were lots of ducks in amongst water hens, Ibis, and other birds. There was no sign of a duck closely followed by a small gaggle of ducklings in this part of the lake that had public access. I hoped they were okay. But then this happens in this area often enough for traffic to stop while a duck and her ducklings cross a street on their way to the lake, and there are always plenty of ducks in there so I guess they would have made it and will survive.

Monica adored the little ducklings.

"They are just beautiful," she exclaimed when she saw them following behind the mother.

It was something special, because it was the first time since we'd been living here (almost 25 years) that we'd had a duck nesting in the garden beside the pool.

We'd often seen ducks in the pool, but never had anything like that happen before.

It happened again the following year and this time we had nine instead of seven ducklings.

And the year after that, the crows that had started nesting in the trees near the back of the house attacked the nest one day and destroyed the eggs as they ate their contents.

That was a bit sad, but nature is what it is, and there's not much you can do about it.

The ducks have not been back to nest since then.

Noises in the night

Every time we heard a possum at night it gave Monica a fright. She was nervous and was startled at every unexpected sound.

When we heard the sudden flutter of tiny footsteps followed by a loud thump, I knew a possum had jump from the higher part of the roof to the lower edge where a short leap across to a tree or a golden cane would give it access to developing fruit, a clump of berries, or new leaf shoots that it could devour with relish.

Every time I tried to grow tomatoes, the plant never got more than a few centimetres tall before a possum stripped off the leaves and the plant withered and died within days.

The cherry tomatoes, which would be better for it to eat, never had a chance to develop. It didn't touch the tarragon, basil, or parsley: too aromatic perhaps?

We used to hear the possums raucously serenading each other in the mango tree at the back of the house. Always in the middle of the night they would wake us up with their hissing and coughing, sounding like some monster from a horror film. If you didn't know that awful noise came from a possum you would be frightened.

I took a photo one night as it sat on the pool fence outside our bedroom's sliding glass door.

For several years we were invaded at night by fruit bats as well. They were attracted to the ever-growing mango tree which after twenty years was enormously large. The bats would hang upside down in the tree, too many to count, and they would squabble and squawk, and drop shit everywhere. Eventually we had the tree removed, cut down and taken away, both because it was far too large to be growing in a suburban backyard and would begin causing damage to the house's foundations, and also because it attracted fruit bats which kept us and no doubt our neighbours awake for half the night.

Once the tree was gone, the bats stopped coming. You can still hear an odd one flapping past at night as it searches for something to eat, but we no longer have hundreds coming in at night like we did before.

A turtle in the pool

On another occasion in June I saw something dark in the bottom of the pool. I thought it was probably a large leaf from the Philodendron that grew in the far corner by the back of the pool. But as I got closer to have a look, it moved. It looked like a turtle.

How the hell could we get a turtle in the swimming pool?

And why our pool?

We were a long way away from the lake for a little turtle to have walked, And it would have done this during the night. It would have to had walked up a steep slope to get into our yard as well. Maybe it had been taken from the lake by a crow or other large bird that was unable to hang onto a slippery heavy weight and it dropped it, so it fell into our pool. I'll never know. But there it was, hiding at the bottom in the deepest part.

I grabbed a mask and snorkel and jumped in. The water was freezing.

I chased it around for a bit, surprised at how fast it could swim, but eventually I got hold of it and put it on the pavement beside the pool. Climbing out of that freezing water, I put it into a bucket so it would not end up hiding somewhere in the garden where I couldn't find it.

Once I got dressed again, Monica and I went down to the lake near the golf course and let it out of the bucket on the bank of the lake. It lifted its tiny head and looked around, then suddenly took off heading straight into the lake.

We couldn't believe how fast it could run. I always thought turtles would move ponderously slow like tortoises. This one ran across the water covered with lily pads making tiny splashing noises as it went. After a couple of metres as the lily pads thinned out it disappeared beneath the surface, no doubt delighted to be back home.

— Changing States —

The strange shape at the bottom of the pool.

The water dragon

One of only three photos of it running along the pool coping. It always took off unexpectedly and was too fast to capture an image. This one is blurred because of its speed.

— Changing States —

One day I noticed a tiny lizard that was different from the usual ones that ran about. This one perched itself on rocks in the garden beside the pool, and spent a lot of time running around and hunting insects by the poolside. I tried to get shots of it running but it was too fast. From completely m immobile, it would take off in an instant and be several metres away before I could react fast enough to press the shutter button. It would stop as suddenly as it had taken off, and remain immobile again for long moments. Over a period of a year it grew from a couple of centimetres to about fifteen centimetres long,

Then it was no longer there. It had vanished. I suspected done of the kookaburras that sometimes appeared in the yard or on the fence by the pool had snatched it and eaten it.

Content at home

Having to be at home all the time, I started taking more notice of what happened in out garden, the birds that came in at different times, the lizards, the animals like possums that came into the yard from the nearby reserve. I enjoyed taking photos where I could as a way of recording the events that occurred in the yard.

Fruit bats would start appearing at dusk. They made a lot of noise as they flew overhead into the trees. The house on our pool side had several Cocos palm trees that had started to bear fruit which looked like clumps of dates. The bats initially came for the Cocos palm fruit. The Council ruled that Cocos palms were an invasive species and proceeded to remove them across the coast. Homeowners were encouraged to cut them down, and our neighbour did that.

That stopped the fruit bats and nocturnal visits from possums. Although when our mango tree started getting bigger with much more fruit ripening, the possums could be heard squabbling in the tree behind our bedroom. the bats came back again. They are pestiferous at the best of times, but when they are just outside your bedroom window it becomes unbearable. The tree seemed to grow a metre higher every six months. I could no longer get anywhere near the fruit at the tree's apex and that's what attracted the bats. The tree towered above the back of our house and the roots spreading out started lifting the pavement. It got too big too quickly. Once we had it removed, we stopped getting nocturnal visits from possums and bats.

With all this in our own back yard, what need was there to travel anywhere?

Our last trip together had been to Auckland in New Zealand, but since then we'd not gone anywhere. With Monica's slowly deteriorating health, taking a trip somewhere was not practical or even advisable.

We were quite content at home, so much so that when the Covid pandemic hit and everyone went into lock-down, it didn't bother us at all because we'd basically been doing that for several years already.

Becoming more noticeable

Monica's problems with walking and balance were a result of the *NP Hydrocephalus* putting pressure on certain areas of her brain which controlled those activities.

It was also beginning to affect her memory a little, as she started to ask me from time to time, "*¿Donde está mi mamá?*" Where is my mum? "*Quiero ver me mamá.*" I want to see my mum. "*¿Cuando va venir mi mamá?*" When is mum coming?

Not all at once, but one or the other from time to time, and I would have to tell her, and explain that her mother had passed away in 1983. I would then have to give the vague details that I remembered from the letter her brother Hugo had written to her, and she would get upset. It was like she was hearing it for the first time, and it was a shock.

It made me sad as well to see how it affected her.

She had been very close to her mother, being the only daughter and youngest child.

Home Care package

The first couple of times after the Home Car Package began, one of the ladies that visited to keep her company, would take her for a walk around the neighborhood in her wheelchair, but she had trouble pushing the chair up the steep driveway coming back. If I was home, I would have to do it for her, but once when I was out shopping, I came back to find them waiting on the grass by the bottom of the driveway, waiting for me to push the wheelchair with Monica back up the driveway and into the house. She stopped taking her for a walk after that. Then they changed the lady who came to keep Monica company and a walk with the wheelchair simply wasn't considered.

From my point of view, apart from the physio who helped her with exercises to maintain strength and control with her arms and legs, the only reason for the other visitor was to allow me some respite from looking after Monica, to give a break in which I could get some time alone or go and do essential shopping without having to think of rushing back to see if she was okay by herself.

I must say at this point that Brian was no help at all. He'd had several problems which I won't go into here, but one night when I had gone to aikido class, I came back to find Monica on the floor. She was sitting against the armchair he used waiting for me to get home. She didn't seem hurt but was simply waiting. When I asked him why he hadn't helped her to get back into her armchair, he said he wasn't strong enough to lift her, all he could do was to drag her up against the chair, so she was sitting rather than lying on the floor. He did have an injured shoulder and was undergoing treatment for it, and that was the reason he hadn't tried to lift her. She'd been sitting like that for half an hour.

I quickly got her into the wheelchair and then transferred her back to her own armchair. But I feel if he'd really cared he would have tried, and somehow managed, but instead he chose to leave her there for me to help when I got back.

I realized then I would no longer be able to attend aikido classes anymore, certainly not the Monday or Wednesday night classes. I couldn't leave her for two hours even if she was sitting in her chair. She could lean over for something and topple out. Previously we'd managed by having me prepare the evening meal before I left, and when I got back I would re-heat it and we would eat then. I could still attend the early Saturday class. Monica would be in bed when I left and when I got back around 10 am I would then get her up, take her into the bathroom for a wash, dress her and have breakfast together.

This was okay for a couple more months, but I had started to lose interest in continuing. Perhaps I was trying to do too much, and was getting too tired. There was no way I could keep up my training and be there for Monica. Even if I cut the time in the class short to come back earlier, it was pointless. Once a week is virtually the same as not at all. Useless. So I stopped going to that morning aikido class as well.

I did miss the training at first, but I quickly became reconciled to the fact I wouldn't be doing it anymore. I was too old anyway and had been thinking about slowing down or giving it up. With Monica needing to be looked after full time, it was time to do that. Although I told myself I would go back to it one day, I knew at 78 years old, the longer I stayed away from it, the harder it would be to get back into it.

A horrible moment

We had been receiving the care package which was level two for around three months when I got a phone call from the nurse who had assessed Monica for the program, wanting to know how she was doing. That was nice, and timely too, because the night before something horrible had happened.

It was around ten pm. We'd been sitting in our respective armchairs and reading when Monica looked towards me and said "I can't see anything."

I stood up immediately.

"Everything is blurred."

I swung her chair around, so she faced the TV on the other side of the room. Brian had been watching something and had left it on when he went to the toilet.

"Can you see the TV?"

"It's a bright blob, that's all I see."

I went close to her and held up my hand in font of her face. "Can you see this?" I asked as I moved my hand back and forth.

"Just a moving shadow."

She couldn't see anything. She couldn't see the large print on the cover of the book she was previously reading. She couldn't see me as more than a dark blur in front of her. I looked into her eyes, and they were blank, unfocused.

"I feel really strange," she said.

"Maybe we should get you into the bedroom and you could lie down."

"Okay."

She had no control of her body and couldn't stand up. I had to get her arms around my shoulders and neck so she could hold hands at the back of my neck and this way I managed to lift her up enough to be able to swing her around into the wheelchair. I did the same to get her out of the wheelchair and onto the bed. She'd wet herself so I had to change her clothes and wash her before getting her into her nightie. Her pulse seemed strong; her breathing was strong. I thought if she was going to be like this from now on, I would not be able to manage, I would need some help. I didn't know what to do.

"I feel a lot better now," she said. And as she said this, she looked at me.

"Can you see me?"

"Yes, a bit blurred though."

That was a relief.

In the morning she seemed as normal as she had been before the late-night incident. She had no trouble standing up and turning to sit on the wheelchair. We had no trouble with her in the toilet and washing afterwards. She enjoyed her breakfast in the kitchen and was still sitting at the table when the phone rang. It was the nurse who had made her original assessment.

When I told the nurse what had happened the night before, she immediately said she would place Monica on a level four package. She suspected that she'd had a mini stroke. She came around a couple of hours later to have look at Monica after which she conformed the level four package. This was communicated to our care supplier, and they arranged for increased days of physio and an increase in the number of visits by someone (especially someone who could speak Spanish) to assist Monica with washing and going to the toilet as well as keeping her company by having someone to talk to. It was also arranged for a nurse to call once a month to check on her.

They could also send someone around to clean the house and do domestic chores, but I said that wasn't necessary as I would do that. Any excess that accrued by not having a domestic worker come in twice a week went towards buying equipment that Monica could need. Arranged by them, we got a bidet installed on our toilet which greatly assisted in washing Monica after she'd been to the toilet. They supplied an extension to the shower and a special rubber base that sat on the floor in which I could sit Monica on a special waterproof wheelchair (also supplied by them) to shower without trying to get her into the shower recess. Fortunately, our en-suite bathroom was big enough for that.

Who are you?

She never had another mini stroke, but her slow deterioration continued.

At times her memory failed her, and she would look at me as if I was a stranger and ask "*¿Quien eres tu?*" Who are you?

Or sometimes she would look at me oddly and ask, "Are you my brother, Hernán?"

I would tell her that I was her husband, John. That we had been married for 47 years (or whatever number it was when she asked the question), and then wait for it to sink in. A moment later she would smile and exclaim, "*Ah mi marido, Eres mi Marido John.*" Then she would relax and everything would be normal again.

Something like that usually happened when she woke up in the morning. And after she'd remembered we would have a light breakfast on the small table beside the French doors so she could look outside to see the swimming pool and the birds that might fly around in the garden. The rest of the day would be better.

Sometimes she would look at me and state, "*Estoy muriendo John.*"

I would try to reassure her that she wasn't dying, but deep down inside, both of us knew it was the truth. I would say something inane like, "everyone dies sooner or later. You shouldn't think things like that. It only makes you upset."

What can you say when someone makes a statement like that?

I didn't know. I could only reassure her that it wasn't going to happen anytime soon. But having said it, she would cheer up and talk about something else.

She also started losing the ability to use her hands, at first, with difficulty in writing her name and making the entries she used to make in diaries where she kept records of medications taken and stuff like that. There was a stack of notebooks in which she kept a record of all the meals cooked by her and me and whether they were good or not so good. These entries also included the recipes for what was cooked, but that stopped around 2017 when she started having trouble with controlling her writing. She could no longer pick up and hold a pen in a way that could be used.

We were sent an occupational therapist who examined Monica's ability to use eating utensils and she made suggestions as to what we could do. They purchased special plates and forks with large handles easier to hold and this worked okay for a while, but as her ability to use her hands became worse, from nerve damage caused by the pressure put on areas of her brain by the *NPH* even using these became problematical.

Seeing someone gradually lose the ability to do things everyone takes for granted is heart-wrenching.

What's worse, is knowing there is nothing you can do to prevent it.

Another problem emerges

Because she spent so much time sitting, being unable to walk, or resting in bed, she began to develop ulcers (bedsores) on the right side of her buttocks. At first they didn't seem too bad and the nurse who came once a month showed me how to treat them.

Unfortunately, they rapidly go worse, and the nurse started coming every day to change the dressing and treat the ulcer. Having to ability to raise the bed was a bonus for treating the problem. Once we'd stopped them from getting too bad, the nurse stated to come once a week and then later once a fortnight, before returning to the monthly visiting schedule. I changed the dressing and treated the ulcers daily and made sure she changed positions regularly as well as spending a few moments standing a couple of times a day. It took months for the ulcers to disappear.

A new wheelchair was supplied to her with a special pressure release cushion to sit on as we moved around the house. This was a weird rubber cushion with fifty air filled protuberances inside an absorbent cloth cover designed to spread pressure, so no single spot took all the weight.

Sometimes in the 2020s she would be really pleased when I wheeled her into the bedroom, and she would see her bed made up. We had been supplied with a special bed for her which we could lower to enable her to get in and out of it or raise it so I could make the bed without having to bend over. We could also raise the bedhead, so she didn't have to be propped up with pillows and cushions if she remained in bed, or raise the foot area to prevent swelling in the feet. This bed was part of the care package and was on loan to us for as long as we needed it.

Monica in her wheelchair arriving in the bedroom.

She would see the bed made and exclaim that it was her favourite room, but the moment I turned the wheelchair to take her into the bathroom, she would exclaim, "*no me gusta ese cuarto, No quiero ir alli.*" I don't like that room. I don't want to go in there.

It was like she was a little girl. Having herself washed and cleaned (after going to the toilet) and her teeth brushed before going to bed, was something she decided she no longer liked. Nevertheless, I would tell her it had to be done. Once in the bathroom she relaxed and didn't say anything else. Her incontinence had become worse, so we often had to go to the bathroom for her to be cleaned and washed and then changed into fresh clothes.

Generally, her condition was never as bad as we were told it could be. The worst part of it was during the last few months when she lost the ability to use her arms to feed herself. She could pick up a fork or a spoon but would sometimes drop the food before getting it into her mouth. I had by that time started to feed her when on the bad days she couldn't manage. I'm sure she was frustrated when that occurred, but she kept trying.

The thing is when you are looking after someone full time, 24 hours a day, you don't notice how they are deteriorating, because it is by tiny increments every day or every week, but because you are with the person 24 hours a day, you tend not to notice. You automatically adjust to it, and you help as needed without thinking about it.

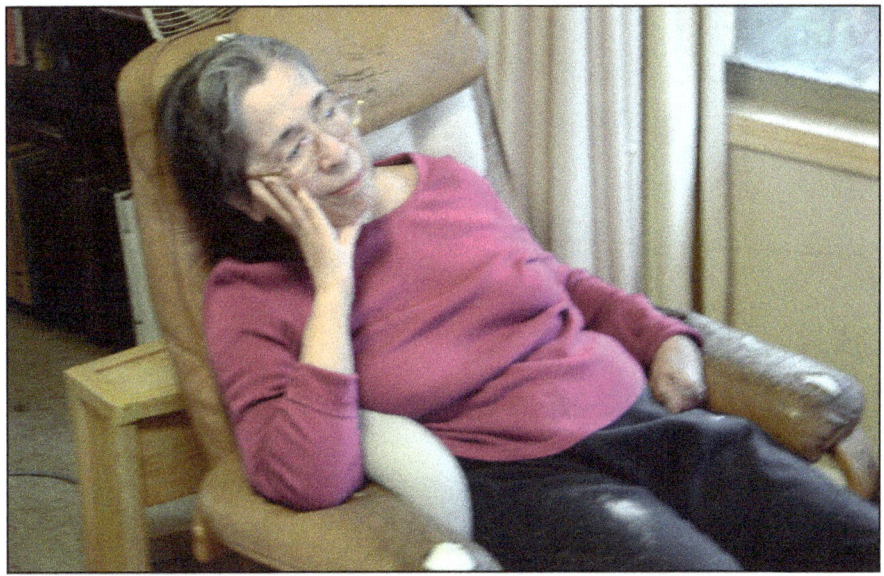

Sitting in her favourite armchair beside the window and facing the large glass doors allowing her to see what goes on outside. By this time she'd lost interest in reading and was content to look out the windows.

Having been unable to walk, and having to spend most of the time sitting down, over the last couple of years she put back on the weight she'd lost when she had that bad reaction to the tablets given to her for her heart fibrillation. There was no strength in her legs though. She couldn't stand an balance anymore and had to be assisted by me to get out of the chair into her wheelchair to go anywhere in the house or outside. She had arthritis in her left hand and the bandage visible was to hold in place a small tube to prevent her fingers from digging into the palm of her hand.

She didn't want me to take photos of her, but I insisted and took some. She said the photos showed up her wrinkles. Wrinkles or not, at 81 years old when I took these photos, I thought she looked pretty good.

She looked content, happy,, and that's all that mattered.

The pictures on this page were taken in February 2020 during a very hot summer.

The photo on the next page was taken at the end of May 2021.

Her tendency to lean over to the right was more pronounced and I had to hold her up straighter whenever she had a cup of tea or something to eat.

— Changing States —

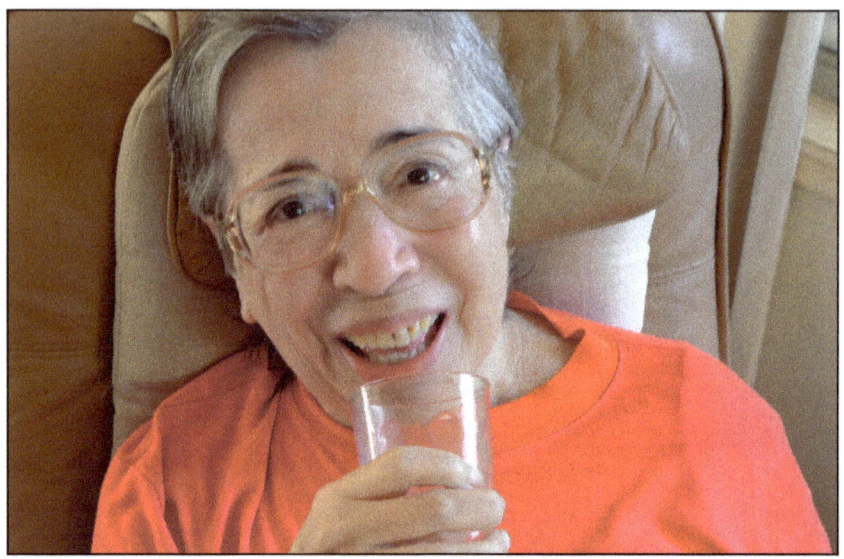

Enjoying a glass of cool water in April 2021.

Over the next few months, although I hardly noticed, she deteriorated at faster pace. We celebrated our 81st birthdays together, as we always did because they are only 8 days apart, on April 4 and April 12.

Naturally it was a subdued celebration with the two of us sharing a sip of wine and a cup of tea with a slice of cake afterwards. It was enough to realize it was our fiftieth year together. Coming up in a few months, the last week of September would mark exactly fifty years since we met. And we'd been married for forty eight and a half of them, so it was something to look forward to.

There had been a phone call from Gladys who now lived in Melbourne, to wish her a happy birthday, and from Christine in Brisbane.

"Sonia didn't call?"

"Sweetheart, Sonia passed away a few years back. Don't you remember? She called to say good bye to you when she knew she didn't have much time left. She rang all her friends."

"I don't remember."

And she was upset to be told about it. I had answered the call from Sonia and I passed the phone to Monica who was sitting in her chair by the window, but I don't think she understood what Sonia was trying to tell her. Sonia had been in a nursing home for several years and when she felt that her time had come, she called all her friends one by one to say goodbye to them. I thought it sad, but very sweet. I've never known anyone else who did that. Sonia was a lovely person.

> The worst days of my life
>
> Monica's last two weeks.

I blame Brian for accelerating her demise. Not directly, but indirectly.

It was a Saturday afternoon. The end of the first week in September 2021. He and I were having an argument in the laundry which got out of hand. He started throwing punches at me, and as we struggled, he spun me around and I fell over onto my back on the tiled floor. I went down with my leg twisted and my right side hip hit the ground and the back of my head smashed against the floor. I was numb for a moment, then I felt a throbbing in my head. There was blood on the floor and when I sat up and ran my fingers through my hair it was full of blood. I stood up, but my hip was so painful I had trouble standing up. I grabbed a hand towel and used it to stop the flow of blood. I started hobbling towards the office where I sat in the chair there, hoping I would feel better in a few minutes.

Monica was sitting in her lounge chair by the window and was unaware of what had happened.

I tried to stand up once the pain had diminished but found I couldn't move properly or stand up. The pain in my hip was excruciating. I called an ambulance, because I thought maybe my hipbone had broken or fractured when I hit the floor. It was a hard floor. The bleeding from where my skull had split when I hit the floor, had stopped, but what worried me was it felt like there was severe damage to my hip.

When the ambulance came, they gave me a pain killer tablet, checked to see that the bleeding had stopped. My hair was matted with blood. They asked several specific questions to determine whether I might have a concussion from the fall, then the two paramedics held onto me as I stood and helped me to sit on the stretcher. Once I was lying on it, they wheeled me out of the house. On the way out I told Brian to call the care agency so they could send someone to help Monica. She would need to be changed or taken to the toilet and later put into bed.

Suddenly he was all contrite and called the care agency. I've no doubt he made himself look good to them as he contrived a story as to why I was suddenly in the hospital, and he needed someone to come and look after Monica.

Our last two weeks

The last two weeks have been the worst in my life. After injuring my pelvis in a fall necessitating a night and a full day in hospital since I couldn't walk, with the doctors thinking I'd fractured a bone, it turned out all the damage was soft tissue damage, with no fractures. Which was confirmed after both X-rays and Cat Scans. On pain killers and anti-inflammatory, I gradually became able to walk after about 7 or 8 hours, although I had to use walking sticks. The pain in the hip persisted and I couldn't put any weight on the right leg. To move it I had to lean on the walking stick so no weight would go down onto the right leg, then I could move the leg forward, where I would lean on the walking stick again to take the weight while moving the left leg. It took several hours of lying on the bed and only standing up or sitting on the edge of the bed from time to time, before I could attempt to walk. And then it was only small tentative steps using two walking sticks for support.

But the big problem was there was no one at home to look after Monica, and she needed care full time since she was basically unable to do anything unassisted. She couldn't get out of bed, she couldn't stand up without me supporting her, she couldn't go to the toilet etc. Brian called the organization that was looking after her care package, and they came to see what they could do.

The only solution was to send Monica to the local hospital (where I was) so she could be looked after because her full-time carer (me) was in the hospital. All they could do that afternoon was to make her a meal in the evening and take her to the bedroom and the en-suite where they cleaned and changed her before getting her into bed. Our case manager arranged for an ambulance to come the next morning, (Sunday) and they brought her to the Robina Hospital.

When they brought her in the day after I had been admitted, the nurse came with a wheelchair to get me so I could see her. They were processing her at the emergency entrance. They later moved her into the same temporary short stay ward in the bed right next to me. That was great because I could manage the few steps between the two beds and could stand beside her.

When the evening meal arrived, I helped feed her because there was no one else to do it. All the nurses were busy since we were in the emergency ward. Monica looked bewildered and had no idea of where she was. She didn't even know who I was at first when they took me to see her at the processing entrance. There was so much confusion and noise as emergency cases were being brought in with ambulances ramped up outside. There were nurses and medics and paramedics and paramedic trainees everywhere you looked, as well as half a dozen stretchers with patients strapped to them. A nurse wheeled me over to her side, and with her was one of the same paramedics who had taken me to hospital the day before. She greeted me and asked if Monica was my wife.

"Your husband is here," the nurse who guided my wheelchair told her.

Monica looked at me, but she didn't really see me. There was no recognition in her eyes.

"*¿Quien eres tu?*" She asked. "Who are you?"

"*Hola querida, Soy tu marido John. ¿No te acuerdas?*" "Hello sweetheart, I'm your husband John. Don't you remember?"

Her eyes lit up and she smiled.

"*Ah mi amor,*" she said.

Then the nurse took me back to the short stay ward where I had been staying overnight. I kept practicing standing, which I could manage, but couldn't walk because the pain in the right hip was excruciating. Over an hour or so it began to diminish, with the help of painkillers, and I could actually put weight on that leg. With the help of a wheelie-walker I managed to take a few steps. It was about this time they moved someone into the bed next to mine. The curtain had been drawn but I recognized Monica's socks, so I knew it was her. I immediately stood up and crossed the short distance between the beds, opened the curtain separating us, and sat on the wheelie-walker next to her bed.

For the next hour we talked and kept each other company. She wanted to know why she was in the hospital, and I had to explain that it was because I wasn't at home or able to look after her. They brought her into the hospital so she could be looked after while I was temporarily incapacitated. Dinner arrived, not for me, but for her. I didn't get one because I was waiting for the doctor to write me an official discharge letter. They were going to send me home. I helped to feed her, and she enjoyed the dinner because it was the first meal she'd had all day.

About an hour after the dinner, a couple of orderlies came and took her to another ward. We were in the emergency ward, and they needed the space for another short-term patient. It was around 8pm.

Suddenly the short-term ward was half empty. Some patients had been sent home, but I couldn't go until the doctor had written my discharge letter. It seemed particularly empty because they had taken Monica to another ward where she could be looked after for a couple of days until I recovered.

They sent me home later that night, around 9 pm. The head nurse called a taxi, and she wheeled me out in a wheelchair and left me on the footpath beside the entrance to the emergency section.

"The taxi should be here in about five minutes," she said, and left me there.

It was freezing, waiting outside, but the taxi came quick enough. I stood and hobbled over to it.

It was the 9th of September 2021.

Monica stayed in the hospital for another two days. I went there each of those two days to be with her, and it was obvious that she was deteriorating quite noticeably. They really didn't do much for her in there. They had given her a bath because she had soiled herself with no one at home to help her. They had to do that with two nurses taking her clothes off, fitting her into a sling with which they moved her into the adjoining bathroom. When I came in next to see her, I was limping and using one walking stick for support, she was half sitting up in a hospital gown in the bed. The TV was on but without sound. She was just staring at the blank wall. I gave her some water to drink, but she seemed hardly able to swallow it. Her mind had wandered, and she wasn't really aware of her surroundings. *This is not good,* I thought.

I tried to engage her in conversation, but she wasn't taking much notice of me. When the evening meal arrived, there was no one there to help feed her.

"*No tengo hambre,*" "I'm not hungry," she said.

But when I started to feed her what looked like a vegetarian Shepard's pie with some other steamed vegetables beside it, she ate readily enough. She was quite hungry. She'd had hardly anything to eat all day, or to drink, so she was dehydrated. I don't think anybody came to help her eat the breakfast or lunch they would have given her. She was incapable of feeding herself at that point. It seemed worse because of the hospital environment. At home, although I often helped her, she usually managed to eat a little by herself. It was awkward and she often spilt or dropped things, but she made the effort. She always tried. But here in the hospital, she seemed unable to do that.

Cold dry hospital rooms don't help if you are slightly dehydrated. They only make it worse. The next day was the same. Sometimes she would know who I was and at other moments she seemed to drift off while staring into 'space' or at the blank wall opposite the bed. I stayed with her all afternoon and again helped her with the evening meal. It was the 11th of September 2021.

The nurse in charge said they were going to send her home later that day, but the doctor hadn't signed the discharge letter (which we never got a copy of anyway), and it was too late to book an ambulance. She would have to wait until the next morning. That meant she was 3 days in the hospital.

Finally, they sent her home, in an ambulance around 11 am the following morning. They called from the hospital to say she was on her way. The ambulance arrived and two orderlies brought her in. She was still wearing her hospital gown. They gave me a bag with her belongings and then transferred her with some help from me from the stretcher into her wheelchair. One of the ambulance orderlies was from Spain and he spoke to her in Spanish, which helped. Her eyes lit up when she heard her own language and she responded to him. Then they left.

She was happy to be home and her mood immediately brightened. Unfortunately, she had gone so far downhill with that short stay in the hospital that it was much harder to transfer her from the chair to the toilet and the en-suite where I could remove the hospital gown, wash her and get her dressed in her own clothes. I was still recovering from my recent fall which made it really difficult to help her. She had no strength in her legs and arms after three days in a hospital bed. I had to hold her up with one hand while trying to dress her or wash her with the other. Once I got her cleaned and changed, we headed back to the lounge room, and she stayed in her chair by the window looking out over the back yard. We had a cup of tea together and a small sandwich for lunch. She seemed really happy to be home. She was smiling and we chatted a little.

She picked up after a couple of days and things were much better. But she was still suffering pain in her legs, sometimes her groin or stomach, as well as being highly sensitive to a touch on her arm or shoulder.

A couple of times she vomited for no obvious reason, and went all clammy and white, but this would quickly pass. She kept insisting that she was okay.

She started to feel much better, much more like she had a few weeks earlier. She'd been home almost two weeks when my sister Christine, rang on the Thursday and said she would like to come for a visit. She had no idea that both of us had been in hospital for different reasons.

"Yeah, come down. I've got a copy of my latest book for you."

"That's great."

She rang back a few minutes later and asked if Tony could come with her since he hadn't seen either of us for far too many years. Tony was the younger of her two boys. The last time we'd seen him had been at Christmas in 1996, the year after we'd moved to the Gold Coast.

"Bring him along. It'll be good to see him again."

"We'll come down tomorrow for afternoon tea. I'll bring some cakes."

Friday, and Monica had been home for just on two weeks since the hospital stay. She was happy to see Christine and Tony. She didn't recognize him at first, but when Tony said who he was she remembered. It had been 25 years since either of us had seen Tony, and he had grown a lot bigger than he was the last time we saw him. We had a lovely afternoon. Tony took a couple of photos of us together, which was nice, even though the photos aren't that flattering. They were the very last ones I will ever have of her. But I didn't know that at the time. Christine gave me her old phone since I didn't have a mobile, and I experimented briefly with it by taking a couple of pictures of Monica sitting in her favourite chair.

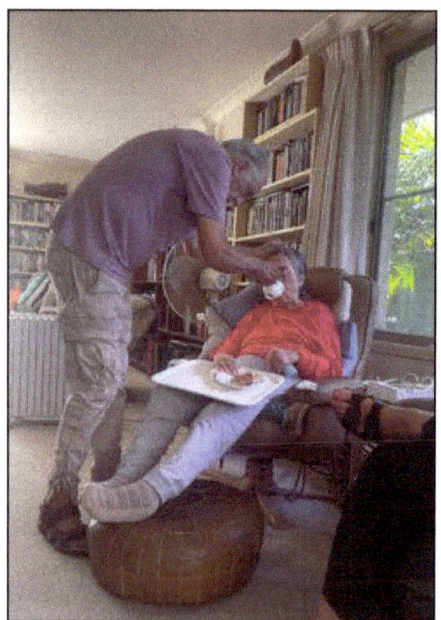 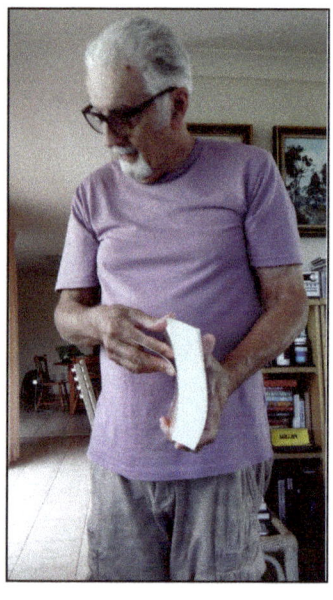

Tony took these two photos on his phone, of me helping to hold Monica's head straight while she sipped her tea.
Me with the book I was to give to Christine.

After they had gone, I asked if she remembered who had visited us and she said immediately "Cristine and Tony. It was a long time since I saw Tony."

"Yes, it was." I was happy she remembered so clearly.

"It was a lovely visit."

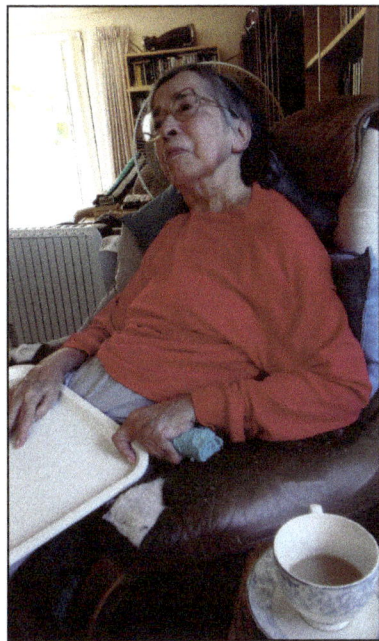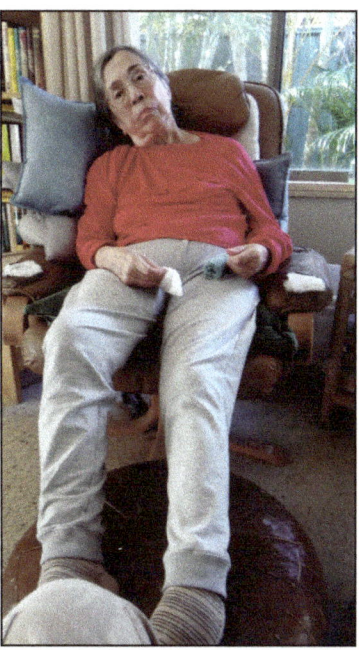

The two photos I took with the phone given to me by Christine. My first attempt at using a mobile phone since I had never owned one before. Sadly, it is clear from these images how far Monica had deteriorated and how sad she looked at that moment. But still, I treasure these two photos because they were the last pictures I ever took of her.

Sometimes her memory was a bit vague, a result of her *NP Hydrocephalus* which puts pressure in certain areas of the brain, causing damage.

Balance and the ability to control muscles in the legs and arms are one of the side effects. Memory loss or fragmented memories are another awful effect. Incontinence is a major effect, all caused by the ever-increasing pressure of fluid in the brain affecting areas that control motor function and nerves.

It also affected her speech making it difficult for her to pronounce words in English. Sometimes it was a real battle to get the words out, in which case she would get frustrated and switch to Spanish.

For me, it was so painful to see her deteriorate like that, there were times I just wanted to sit down and cry, but I had to put on a brave face and try to cheer her up as much as I could. It was not fair that someone so beautiful and loving could be put through that. But even when she was at her worst, she often asked how I was, if I was okay. She cared so much; it was unbelievable.

Sometimes, after I had taken her to the toilet, washed and changed her, she would tell me, "*Siento tan desgraciada.*" "I feel so undignified."

She was embarrassed that she was incapable of doing these things for herself, and even though we had been married for 48 years, she still felt uncomfortable with needing me to do these things for her. But there was no other way. If I wasn't there to help her, then who would?

I now realized how rapidly she had deteriorated, and that with helping her every day, I didn't see it so much, because it was only a little each day, and some days she would be better than others. But the last few months were not that good. Sometimes she would tell me how lucky she was to have me by her side, but the truth is, I was the one who was lucky to have her. She filled our life with joy. She filled me with joy.

Over the last few months, she often said to me in Spanish, "*Siento mal,*" I don't feel good, and quite often, "*Estoy Muriendo,*" I'm dying.

What can you say when the person you love, with whom you've spent two thirds of your life, tells you that? And she would say it with conviction. She believed it. It wasn't just a throw-away remark. I would try to reassure her that she would be fine, but she knew better. I knew it too, or at the very least, suspected it to be true, but I refused to admit it to myself.

Her English (a second language she learnt in her late 20s) started to disappear, or she would have trouble getting her tongue around the English words, so she reverted to her native Spanish. Which was fine because I had no trouble speaking with her in Spanish, even though my ability to speak it had diminished. More than 50 years had passed since I learnt rudimentary Spanish while living in Mexico for 11 months in 1968.

On the Sunday morning (26th Sept 2021) around 6 am I woke up to find her struggling to breathe.

She was gasping, her chest heaving and the sound she was making was frightening.

I leaned over and tried to comfort her, but she was barely aware that I was there. Her eyes were open but unfocused. I felt her shoulder and it was clammy. Her face was as white as porcelain, not her usual colour. I jumped out of bed and ran around to the other side of her bed to lift her up so she could breathe a bit better. A few months earlier we had gotten rid of out queen size bed and replaced it with a hospital-type bed for her, and a regular one for me. With her bed I could raise or lower it, could lift the feet the centre or the head, whatever was needed to make it more comfortable for her.

She calmed down a bit as her breathing eased and she realized I was beside her.

She managed to say, "*me duele, me duele el pecho.*" It hurts, my chest hurts.

She was very pale, and her back was clammy and sweaty. After a few moments her breathing eased and she seemed more relaxed. The chest pain had gone but she still had breathing problems. It would become very quiet, as if she was holding her breath, and then her abdomen would start pumping as she tried to suck more air into her lungs.

"I'll call an ambulance," I told her, but she insisted she didn't want to go to the hospital.

"*No quiero ir al hospitál, llama un doctor.*"

"I can't call a doctor on Sunday. I can call 000 and get an ambulance. They will take you to the hospital."

She shook her head, and I could see she didn't like the idea of going back to the hospital, but what else could I do?

Then that frightening ragged breathing would start again., and the same breathing cycle would repeat.

After half an hour she settled a bit. Some colour came back into her face, and the clamminess disappeared. She seemed a lot better, but she kept repeating that she was dying.

There was nothing I could do, and in fact had no idea of what to do. But we waited to see if she would improve and for a while, she seemed quite relaxed. But then the ragged breathing started again.

It was becoming far too erratic.

"I have to call an ambulance."

She looked at me but didn't say anything.

I called 000 and explained what had happened and the lady kept me on the phone while the ambulance was on its way. She kept asking how Monica's breathing was and was relieved when I told her she was still breathing, though it was uneven and at times very labored. She stayed on the phone with me until the paramedics walked in the front door which thankfully was only about ten minutes after I'd called. They were really quick.

The ambulance arrived at 11 am, with two paramedics and another extra person who had equipment to deal with a heart attack. They immediately connected a portable ECG monitor to check her heartbeat, connected an oxygen bottle with a tube put into her nose so she could get enough oxygen into her lungs, then they transferred her to a stretcher and off she went in the ambulance to the hospital. She was not happy to be going to the hospital. She looked scared but resigned.

I followed them down the driveway and told Monica I would follow the ambulance up to the hospital, but she either didn't understand or simply didn't see or hear me. Her eyes were open, but I don't think she saw anything.

"You did the right thing to call us," one of the paramedics told me.

Half an hour after they left, I went to the hospital and they told me they'd put her in an isolation ward and I couldn't see her. The reason they put her there was because of her very labored breathing. All patients with breathing problems went in there. That included patients with Covid. Fortunately, there were none of those there at that time.

I insisted that I should be with her, and eventually, because she was only speaking in Spanish and they couldn't understand her, they allowed me to come into that ward so I could translate and they could get a rundown on her medical condition from me which would help them understand what her situation was.

They knew she'd had a heart attack so they took an X-ray which showed she had a blocked artery leading into the heart and would need to have a stent inserted to open the artery. They notified the Gold Coast University hospital where the cardiac ward was located and said they would transfer her up there as soon as they could get an ambulance. Meanwhile they'd put a cannula in each of her arms to take blood for testing and so they could administer medications, and that was very painful. She had a blood pressure sleeve on her arm to monitor her pressure, and an oxygen tube into her nostrils to make sure she got enough oxygen. They had continuous readings coming from the ECG which was connected to her through various leads on her back and chest. They also gave her a diuretic to help get rid of the fluid in her lungs, which they told me was a result of the heart attack, and that necessitated inserting a catheter into her bladder to drain the urine. They wouldn't let me see them do that. They closed the curtains to hide the bed and told me to wait over by the reception desk. I heard her scream and call out loudly *"me duele tanto, me duele tanto."* It hurts so much. She kept saying it over and over until they'd completed the insertion of the catheter.

It was a horrible thing for her suffer so much, in pain while all this was being done, but she settled down after a while. But all she would say while I was there with her was to repeat *"me duele tanto,"* adding *"estoy muriendo."* It hurts so much, I'm dying.

The attending chief nurse told me the doctors in the cardiac ward would assess her and probably do the operation early the next morning. They had called for an ambulance to transfer her but there would be a long wait because they were all busy.

We waited and waited. I comforted her as best I could, talking softly to her and she answered me a few times. She even corrected my grammar when I said something in Spanish that was incorrect. They'd given her a pain killer via a tablet crushed in a teaspoon of jam, which she ate with relish because she'd had nothing to eat since waking up with chest pains. She was too sick for them to even think of giving her anything other than a little water.

As the day wore on, the bouts of breathing became worse. It was like she was trying to breathe through a bucket of water. It was gurgled and raspy. Her abdomen pumped hard to get air in.

Yet her oxygen levels were very high since she was still connected to the oxygen supply through the tube in her nose. Breathing like this would last five minutes or so then she would calm down and breathe more shallowly.

It was heartbreaking to see her like that, to be there, to feel so useless. I could do nothing other than keep her company. She didn't have to tell me anymore that she was dying. But I had hopes that when they transferred her to the other hospital where they would put a stent in to open the blocked artery, she would be much better. The attending doctor kept reassuring me that getting her to the cardiac ward in the other hospital and inserting a stent was the best option and she would be okay after that.

Finally, at 7pm, about 8 hours after she'd been admitted, the ambulance people arrived to transfer her to the Gold Coast University Hospital. They disconnected her from all the stuff she was connected to in the ward, transferred her to the stretcher, and reconnected her to portable equipment. I followed them down to where the ambulance was parked at the emergency entrance.

She looked lost. She had no idea of what was going on other than it was painful and awful. They told me if I followed them to the other hospital, I wouldn't be able to be with her until they'd settled her into the cardiac ward, so I went home. I told her I would ring the hospital in a couple of hours to see how she was going and would come and see her in the morning. I don't think she was aware of anything I said. I waved to her just as they were closing the ambulance door. Whether she saw me do that or acknowledged it I have no idea.

I was feeling horrible myself, and concerned about what was happening to her. The ambulance hadn't left as I walked across the street to the car park, but as I drove out of the car park it turned into the road behind me. I don't remember the drive home, only that I was walking in the front door. Brian was in the kitchen and wanted to know what had happened and how she was. By the time I'd finished telling him it was 8.25 and I said, "I'm going to ring the hospital and see how she is."

I was looking for the number to call them when the phone rang. It was the doctor from the cardiac ward at Gold Coast University Hospital and he said straight up "There's been an incident."

"What kind of incident? What does that mean?"

They had assessed her condition and were going to do the operation to insert the stent that same night. They didn't want to wait until the morning.

"Her heart has stopped, and we can't get it started again," he said to me. "The nurses are still doing CPR. She's had no heartbeat for the last ten minutes. What do you want us to do?"

"Well, you should know better than me what to do, you're the doctor."

"The thing is," he explained, "if we can revive her, she will have considerable brain damage, and we have no idea what she would be like. Has she told you what she would like in a situation like this?"

Actually, she had, and we had a signed Medical Power of Attorney. We'd done this with our GP about 10 years ago. If her condition was bad, or in a vegetative state, she didn't want invasive surgery or to be revived if there was no chance that her condition would improve.

I told the doctor, "If you think she would have irreparable brain damage which would make what was left of her life an absolute misery, then you can stop trying to revive her."

He acknowledged what I said.

She'd already been dead for ten minutes when he rang.

I told him I would come there right away. I wanted to see her, and of course, talk to them.

It was 9pm when I got the University Hospital, and it was closed. Everything was shut. I managed to get in through the emergency entrance and someone took me up to the fourth floor where she was in the cardiac ward.

A nurse asked me to wait in a quiet room while she went and got the doctor. He turned up a few minutes later with head of the cardiac department, and they explained what they had been doing. They had examined her and decided it was an emergency and they would do the operation immediately rather than waiting until the next day.

While they were trying to explain to her what they were going to do, she was speaking in Spanish to them which they could not understand. They said she didn't appear to be in any pain at that point and was relaxed, then she went quiet, and her heart just stopped.

They immediately commenced CPR but could not find a heartbeat and could not get it started again, that's when the doctor rang me. They also said that her blood tests showed a massive build-up of acids in her muscles which were killing muscle tissue, which explained the loss of use of her legs and partially her arms over the last two weeks. It would also explain her very erratic heartbeat while she was in hospital. They said she'd had a massive heart attack; but I think she'd had a series of small heart attacks over the last few weeks with nausea and slight vomiting a side effect. I think those small attacks had built up enough damage so that when she had another one on the Sunday morning around 6 am it was cumulative and overall looked massive.

She knew she was dying, which is why she kept telling me that over the last three or four weeks. But that is an assumption on my part because it's hard to know if that was something she really meant or knew, or simply was an expression that people say when they don't feel good.

In any case, I do think she'd decided after all the indignity of being in a hospital and connected to various machines and monitors, that it was all too much to bear. She didn't want to suffer it anymore and she let herself go.

They told me she stopped talking, went very quiet, and died. The nurses immediately commenced CPR, but it didn't work and after ten minutes of that the doctor rang me to explain what had happened.

My regret is that I didn't follow the ambulance from the Robina Hospital up to the Gold Coast University Hospital, to be with her. I would have been there at the end, and perhaps it would have been some comfort for her... And to me as well. I also regret not thinking to ask the doctor what she had said just before she died. I was so upset I never thought of it. He may not have understood her, but he could perhaps have been able to repeat something of what she had said. It probably would have made sense to me.

After I had finished speaking with the doctor and the head of the cardiac department, a nurse came in and asked if I would like to see her, to sit with her for a while.

She took me into private room and there was my beautiful Monica lying on a bed with a sheet covering her up to her neck. Her colour was good, her face was relaxed exactly as if she was asleep. I kissed on the forehead, and she was still warm, exactly as she would have been if she was asleep in bed at home. I told her how much I loved her, and that I would miss her so much for the rest of my life no matter how long or short it was to be. And then I started crying and held her delicate hand in mine. Her fingertips were just starting to get cool.

When I had calmed down, I wiped the tears from my eyes and went back outside the room to the nurse's station and one of them explained what would happen. She would be taken down to the hospital mortuary where she would stay until whatever funeral home I get to arrange the funeral would come and collect her. They would also take care of the death certificate and notify the registrar of births and deaths so I wouldn't have to be concerned with that. They gave me an information booklet about what to do when someone dies which was of some help over the following days.

We were inseparable, we'd been together exactly 50 years on the day she died, the 26th of September, and married for 48 of them.

She was the best thing that ever happened to me. She was my whole life.

I'm not sure yet how I will manage without her, but I guess I will.

Even though the house is empty and lonely, in the back of my mind, I keep expecting that she will come home from the hospital, just like the few other times she'd been in the hospital.

But this time it's different, and she won't be coming home.

It will sink in next Tuesday (4th October 2021) when we will have a quiet funeral service. Oddly enough, I am looking forward to the service because it will give me some certainty and 'closure' as they say.

Note: the last part of this book 'Our last two weeks' was written two days after Monica passed away, and before the funeral service. It was one of the hardest things I have ever written. I sent it to my friend Bruce Gillespie and he published it in his SF Commentary magazines. I have used it again as the final part of this memoir without changing any of it except for a comma here and there.

— Changing States —

I Got booked for speeding on the way home from the hospital, even though I'd been going a bit slower than when I had rushed to the hospital after that awful phone call. There were no cars on the road that late at night so I obviously went faster than I normally would have.

But I didn't know about it until four weeks after the funeral service.

No excuse accepted. It cost me $183, for doing 112 kph in a 100 kph zone.

The problem with the M1 is parts of it are 110 kph while other sections are 100 kph. They always seem to put the mobile speed cameras a few hundred metres past where the speed limit changes and catch everyone coming out of the higher speed zone into the lower one. Even if they are slowing down, the camera gets them before they can finish dropping to the lower speed.

A couple of days later I posted a few photos of Monica on my Facebook page so people I know would be aware that she had passed away. These were photos taken during our the first few years together, and are favorites.

Taken on the beach at Altona , summer 1972

Two of the photos from the Facebook page.

— John Litchen —

*A moment together at the Melbourne Botanical Gardens 1972.
At the house in Williamstown 1986*

I did a bit of research into *funeral parlours* and found one in Mudgeeraba, not far from us, which offered a selection of services and contacted them regarding a funeral. They were quick to respond and sent someone around to see me. A simple service was arranged with them taking care of everything. All I had to do was supply them with some examples of Monica's favourite music which they would play during the service. I found it difficult to select music because her tastes had changed over the years but settled on things she had been listening to over her last twelve months. Her interest in Chilean music had revived after years of not wanting to listen to it, so the first selection I thought appropriate was a song by a Chilean group detailing what you would find if you come to Chile. I guess she had been feeling nostalgic for her home country after half a century in Australia because she kept listening to this old CD her mother had sent to her 40 years ago. We hadn't listened to it for such a long time, but in the last 12 months she listened to it at least once a week if not more often. The other songs were two by Buika, sad, romantic, nostalgic songs sung with her raw flamenco voice accompanied by Chucho Valdez on piano. They are all songs now that would make me burst into tears if I heard them again, so I haven't played them since the funeral service.

Unfortunately, Covid lockdowns were in place in every state in Australia during 2021 and no one could travel interstate, not even for a funeral. The maximum number of attendees was set at 20 in Queensland, but that didn't worry me because there would only be my sister Christine who came with her younger son Tony, and me attending. Brian didn't want to come, and he used the excuse that his mother had told him she didn't want him to see her dead in a coffin. We weren't going to have a viewing so that didn't matter. If he didn't want to come, that was it, his choice. Tony set up his phone to record the service and broadcast it via Zoom to my brothers and sisters and their families in Melbourne, so in effect, they attended remotely. Only one of my friends from aikido turned up. Travers Hughes, who had seen the Facebook page and rang me to ask about it. I did get a response from 40 or more Facebook friends who had also seen the notice I posted, but that was only on Facebook.

But Monica was pretty much a private person and she wouldn't have been bothered if not too many people attended.

The brief service was held in a lovely chapel with a beautiful image displayed on a big screen of mountains towering above a lake that reminded me of a place we'd seen in southern Chile when we were there. The coffin was draped with white shroud and there were heaps of beautiful flowers, and a lovely picture of Monica that I'd taken on a picnic we went on around 1990 in Ferntree Gully. Tony and Christine and Travers all had lovely things to say about Monica, and I had trouble trying not to cry as I spoke about how lucky I was to have met her and been married to her for half a century.

Then it was over, and we left. Christine, Tony and I went to the Town Centre for a late lunch, and some reminiscing.

I had decided to have Monica cremated. My intention had been to one day return to Chile and to take her ashes (or a portion of them) to be scattered across the land that was part of her father's property where she had been born. I absolutely hated the idea of having her buried in the ground in a cluttered cemetery the traditional way. With her being cremated, I could keep her ashes in an urn. One day I will scatter them into the ocean so they can be carried out to see towards Chile, since it now seems unlikely that I will make a return trip there.

I know she would have wanted a traditional burial, but then funerals are for those still living who are left behind, not for those who have departed. I'm sure she would have agreed with my choice. It was a lovely heart-warming service, and I feel a lot more content now that it is over.

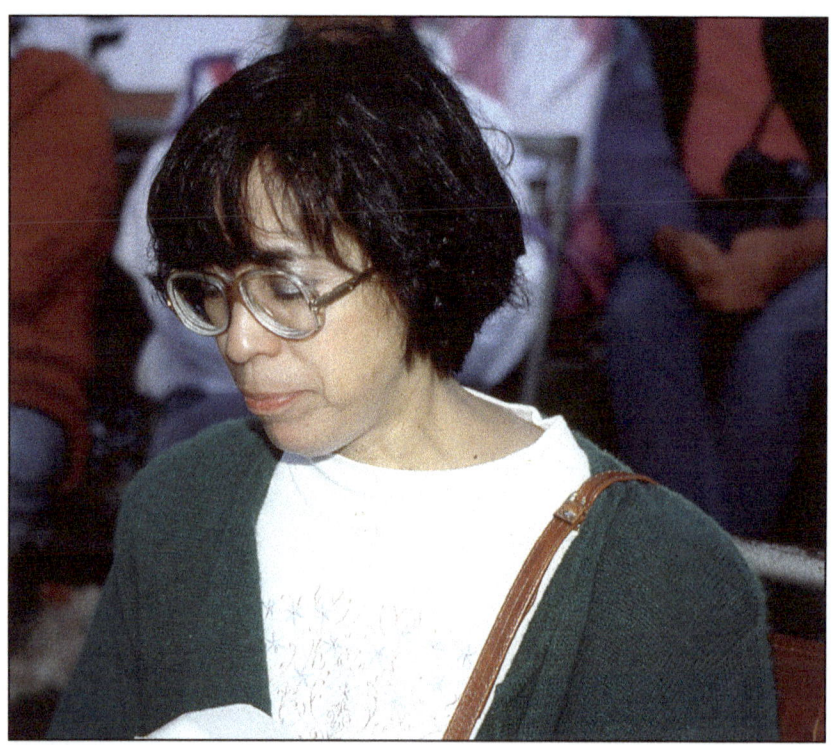

A brief summary

Monica Marina Correa Marquez was born on the 12th of April in Curepto, a small town in Chile, a few hours' drive south of the capitol Santiago. Her father owned a small farm and produced wine.

Correa was her family name, (after her father) and Marquez was her mother's family name. In Chile, the mother's family name is always a part of a person's full name. When we married, technically in Chile she would have been known as Monica Marina Correa Marquez de Litchen, but in Australia she dropped her two family names and took mine to become Monica Marina Litchen. (Marina was also her mother's Christian or given name.) Oddly enough, our wedding was not registered in Chile, since we didn't know we had to do that, so she is regarded there as a *soltera*, an unmarried woman, and is recognized only by her maiden names.

Monica never actually spoke much about why she left Chile in 1970, only referring to the reasons in passing a few times. She was 30 years old, a single woman, who saw no prospects of having a good life in Chile at that time. It must have taken a lot of courage at her age to give up her life in Chile, to go somewhere foreign where a different language was spoken, to try and start a new life. She was very close to her mother and missed her immensely, as she did her three brothers and their extended families. But she took the chance, and left in search of a better life.

At the time when she left, the government of Chile had elected a communist leader who almost immediately started nationalizing business, industry, and land ownership. She, like many others, disagreed with what the government was doing, but being single, not tied down with a husband or children, she could leave in search of somewhere better. She also told me, as a joke, that there were no interesting men in Chile, and she would have to look elsewhere. There must have been some truth in that because she was still single, in a country where generally women were married in their early twenties.

Monica was one of many (thousands) who took the opportunity to migrate to Australia. I have a vague recollection that in the 1970s Australia was promoting the immigration of single women to the country because there was a perceived shortage of women and too many men. South American women had no trouble getting visas for permanent residency in 1970.

There was a wave of immigrants from Chile in the 1970s, people escaping the harsh regime imposed by Allende. The same thing happened years later when Allende was removed by Pinochet and the chiefs of the armed forces, creating another wave of people fleeing what they saw as another, quite different, oppressive dictatorship. And so it goes.

She arrived in Sydney in October 1970 with two other women and joined a small community of people, mostly single women around her age (30 to 35) who had all migrated from various South American countries for similar reasons; escaping political repression, in search of an opportunity for a better life.

It just so happened that Monica who had secretarial qualifications as well as a degree in Humanities from the *Universidad Catolica de Chile*, and could speak rudimentary English, found herself a job as a receptionist in the radiology department of a hospital in Sydney. Here, she met my cousin Mary, who also worked in that department.

When the girls decided to move to Melbourne 10 months later, Mary was also visiting her brother who lived in St Kilda. She caught up with Monica and her two friends who had rented a small apartment in Elwood. She rang Mum, her auntie, and explained why she was in Melbourne, and Mum immediately asked her to bring her two friends from Chile with her, "so John can practice his Spanish." It was September 1971.

I had recently come back from Mexico where I'd spent 11 months, but not speaking any Spanish at home since returning in 1969 it was quickly disappearing. I was looking forward to talking to someone in Spanish again.

When the girls arrived with Mary and she introduced them to us, I knew right at that instant the Monica was the one for me. I was 31 years old (8 days older than Monica), and well past the time most men settle down. Until I saw her, I had been unaware of how lonely I had been feeling.

There was a song, a Cuban rumba I used to play with the band in Acapulco, called *Que Linda Va*. Literally: How beautiful she goes. The very first line says *When I saw her for the first time, I fell in love.* (*Cuando yo la vi por primera vez, yo me enamoré.*) It then goes on to say how beautiful she walks, how beautiful is her smile, how wonderful is her soul and so on.

Monica was like that. There was something that emanated from her, that filled the room with a feeling of love and caring generosity, and her smile lit up the room. I fell in love with her the moment I saw her, the moment she looked into my eyes when we were introduced and I shook her hand. Her smile just filled me with joy.

As I found out a few days later when helping her and her friends sort out a problem with the St Kilda police regarding a robbery of all their clothes from the flat while they were at work, she felt the same way about me.

From that moment on near the end of September 1971 we were inseparable. We were together for 50 years, and married for 48 of them. Sadly, she passed away on September 26, 2021, 50 years from the day when we first met.

— John Litchen —

**Monica Marina Litchen
April 4, 1940 - September 26, 2021.**

This is the last of a series of memoirs covering my life from 1958 until the year 2023. There are six volumes five of which include my beautiful wife, Monica, my very best friend, and the joy we found in being together for fifty years.

I have no idea, and can't even imagine what my life would have been like without her by my side, all I know is that I consider myself lucky to have met her when I did, lucky to have fallen in love with her, and even more lucky that she reciprocated in kind.

I miss her terribly, but she lives on in my mind and in the pages of these volumes of memoirs.

There is much that hasn't been included for obvious reasons, but also, to include everything would require fifty volumes and that would be an impossible task. The five volumes that include my life with Monica I hope, highlight what a wonderful and caring person she was. In total there are 2412 pages over the five volumes with somewhere around 3500 photographs documenting our life together. They were written over the last two years of Monica's life, and the time since she passed away.

Three and a half years of remembering, writing and collating material, cleaning old photos of which there are literally thousands. The ones that appear in these volumes are less than ten percent of them.

I do hope readers enjoy my recollections over these volumes, and thank you all from the bottom of my heart for caring enough to read them.

John Litchen - February 2023.

www.ingramcontent.com/pod-product-compliance
Lightning Source LLC
Chambersburg PA
CBHW042116300426
44117CB00020B/2966